SECOND
WORLD WAR
CARRIER CAMPAIGNS

Second World War Carrier Campaigns

by

DAVID WRAGG

Pen & Sword

MARITIME

First published in Great Britain in 2004 by
Pen & Sword Maritime
an imprint of
Pen & Sword Books Ltd
47 Church Street
Barnsley
South Yorkshire
S70 2AS

ISBN 1 84415 052 6

A CIP catalogue record for this book is
available from the British Library

Typeset in 11/13 Meridien by
Phoenix Typesetting, Auldgirth, Dumfriesshire

Printed and bound in England by
CPI UK

For a complete list of Pen & Sword titles please contact
PEN & SWORD BOOKS LIMITED
47 Church Street, Barnsley, South Yorkshire, S70 2AS, England
E-mail: enquiries@pen-and-sword.co.uk
Website: www.pen-and-sword.co.uk

CONTENTS

ACKNOWLEDGEMENTS

In writing any book such as this, the author is indebted to those who make his life so much easier. I am very grateful to Jerry Shore and his enthusiastic team at the Fleet Air Arm Museum at RNAS Yeovilton, and for the help always so willingly provided by Ian Carter and his team at the Photographic Archive, and John Stopford-Pickering at the Sound Archive, of the Imperial War Museum in London. It is only fair as well also to remember those naval aviators who committed their own experiences to print; people such as Norman Hanson, author of the brilliantly-written *Carrier Pilot* that so manages to cover the joys of naval flying and of young men away from home for the first time on a big adventure, and the sadness and tragedy of warfare when one's comrades, close friends in the confines of carrier life, disappear, often in terrible circumstances. Other writers in this vein are Charles Lamb, with his classic *War in a Stringbag*, and Lord Kilbracken with *Bring back my Stringbag*; recommended reading, all of them.

David Wragg
Edinburgh
November 2003

INTRODUCTION

In 1939, it was a very perceptive or foolish naval officer who welcomed command of an aircraft carrier rather than, for example, a cruiser. Many given such posts must have felt that they were being sidelined. Aircraft carriers acquired their designation 'CV' because the United States Navy originally assessed them as being equivalent to cruisers, providing a support role for the battleships. Only the American *Saratoga* and *Lexington* and the Japanese *Kaga* and *Akaga* matched battleships in their displacement tonnage. Between the two world wars, only the Americans really showed due enthusiasm for naval air power, the potential of which began to be increasingly understood and appreciated after exercises close to the Panama Canal Zone by *Saratoga* and *Lexington* in 1929. Even the Imperial Japanese Navy had senior officers who felt that it was their duty, and a kindness as well, to discourage bright young officers from transferring to naval aviation. As for the British, they had lost control of their naval air power, along with the aviators and aircraft, on 1 April 1918. Yet, little more than twenty years after the first true aircraft carriers, that is ships designed to operate and retrieve landplanes, appeared in 1918, roles were increasingly reversed so that the aircraft carrier became the new capital ship, displacing the battleship into a support role, providing intensive anti-aircraft fire for the nearby carriers and also undertaking heavy coastal bombardment. During the Second World War, the only major operations conducted without the benefit of carrier-borne aircraft were the Battle of the River Plate and the Anzio and Normandy landings.

The aircraft carrier was born out of frustration with the performance of the seaplane, because this couldn't carry a decent bomb load, nor could it fly fast enough and climb quickly enough to counter the menace of the German Zeppelin. So desperate had matters become, that the Royal Navy even tried launching fighter aircraft from lighters towed at speed behind destroyers, a ruse that

1

worked, but involved the loss of an aeroplane each time it was used as the pilot had to ditch in the sea. At first, navies were reluctant to commit themselves to carriers, but for the Royal Navy, it was an opportunity to use a battlecruiser that had become an embarrassment, designed for a dare-devil operation that had been scrapped and so heavily armed that whenever its 18-inch calibre gun was fired, the hull rippled and rivets flew across cabins. Equally sceptical, the United States Navy converted a collier.

Despite some early operations with the first aircraft carrier, HMS *Furious*, it was in the Second World War that the aircraft carrier came into its own, with the battleship rendered obsolete overnight with the Fleet Air Arm's attack on the Italian fleet at Taranto, and this message was reinforced by the Japanese attack on the US Pacific Fleet at Pearl Harbor a little more than a year later.

The success of the carrier was surprising in that the Second World War started badly for the carrier. Britain's *Courageous* was sunk by a submarine at the end of the first fortnight; *Glorious* was lost to battlecruiser shellfire during the withdrawal from Norway. It was not until the new *Illustrious* crippled the Italian fleet at Taranto, using just twenty-one obsolescent biplanes that the significance of the aircraft carrier was finally realized. Yet, an indication of just how things might have turned out came when two British carriers were sent on a costly and unsuccessful attack against Petsamo and Kirkenes. The Japanese attempted the same at Pearl Harbor, using six carriers and more than 350 aircraft, but in pulling the US into the war, sowed the seeds of defeat. Within six months, the Japanese carrier force was devastated in the Battle of Midway, losing four ships. Without the carrier, Pearl Harbor would have been impossible, and without it, the defeat of Japan would have been difficult in the extreme, as US forces battled their way across the Pacific where distance and the shortage of suitable airfields meant that carrier-borne aircraft spearheaded the assault on island after island, until they finally got within reach of Japan itself.

These were the high points of carrier operations during the Second World War, in the course of which the aircraft effectively displaced the battleship and battlecruiser as THE capital ship for the war years and for the uneasy peace, interrupted all too frequently by regional wars, that was to follow. It was also the war in which aircraft carrier tactics, developed under the pressures of wartime, improved, and in this book, these have been explained, augmented by eyewitness accounts. The role of the carrier in convoy protection and the way in which carrier aircraft were used to provide cover for invading ground forces in the Mediterranean and Pacific campaigns complete this story of a warship that came of age on the eve of war in Europe, and then matured fully in seven years of warfare, culminating in the massive battles that occurred as the United States Navy fought its way across the vast reaches of the Pacific Ocean to take the war home to Japan.

The book begins with the early wartime experience, including the problems faced by the Royal Navy in launching the right ships, but failing to find the right aircraft at first. The different theatres of war are then covered, showing how each contributed to the development of the carrier and naval strategy.

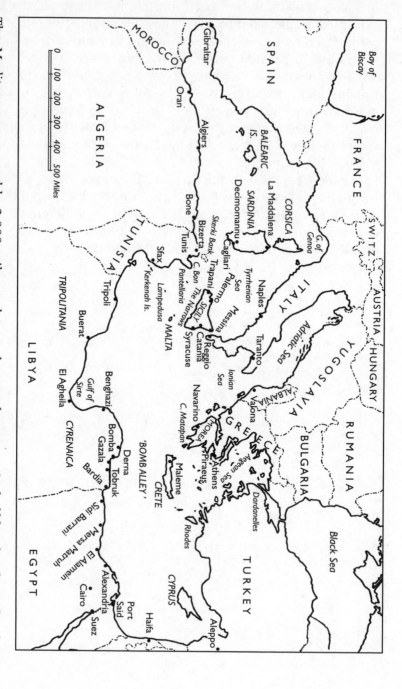

The Mediterranean, roughly 2,000 miles end to end, was almost cut in half by the 'leg' of Italy. Heavy Axis aerial attack made this an extremely difficult zone for aircraft carriers.

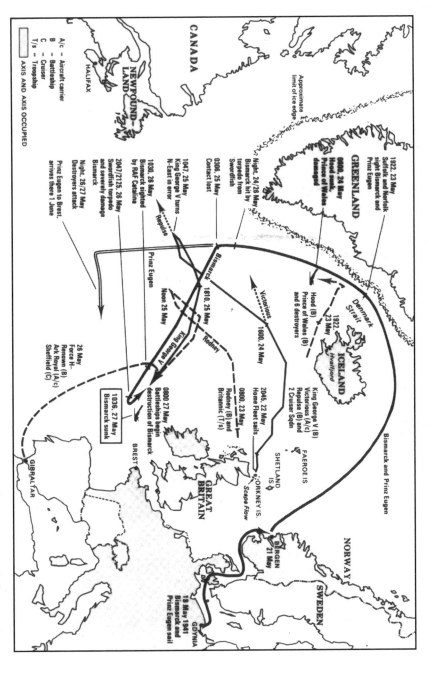

The hunt for the *Bismarck* involved both the Home Fleet and Gibraltar-based Force H, and the carriers *Victorious* and *Ark Royal*. (FAAM Cars B/81)

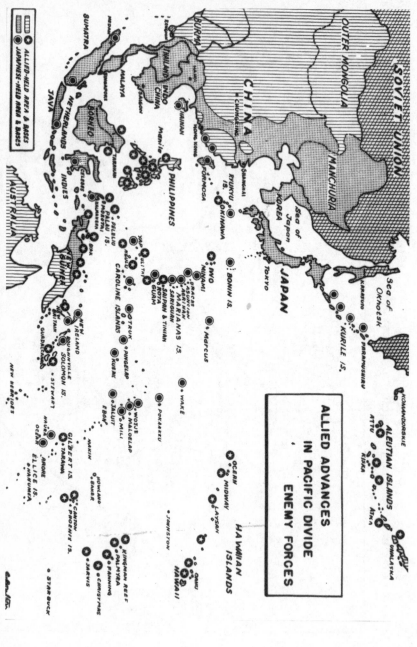

The vast distances of the Pacific, with the island groups used as stepping stones on the way to Japan, while the Japanese for their part wanted to cut Australia off from the United States. (IWM NYF73462)

I

NO PHONEY WAR AT SEA

'. . . at that moment there were two explosions, a split second apart, the like of which I had never imagined possible,' recalled Charles Lamb. 'If the core of the earth exploded, and the universe split from pole to pole, it could have been no worse. Every light went out immediately and the deck reared upwards . . . In the sudden deathly silence which followed I knew the ship had died.'

The Second World War had started badly for the aircraft carrier and for the Royal Navy.

Lamb was in the wardroom aboard the British aircraft carrier HMS *Courageous* on 17 September 1939, exactly two weeks after the outbreak of the Second World War in Europe, when she was torpedoed by *U-29* in the Western Approaches and sank within twenty minutes, taking with her 500 men, almost half her ship's company of 1,200. The carrier had been 'trailing her cloak', conducting an anti-submarine sweep with just two destroyers as escorts, but it was the submarine that had found her, firing three torpedoes, of which two struck the ship.

Even with the benefit of hindsight, no one can say for certain that *Courageous* might not have been lost anyway. Nevertheless, it is certainly true that not only was her escort well below the minimum for such an important ship, but also that anti-submarine sweeps were akin to searching for a needle in a haystack, leaving the hunters exposed so that often it was they that became the prey. Had she been doing something useful, escorting a convoy, the submarines would have been attracted while she was ready for them and with adequate escorts available.

The irony was that Lamb himself had trained as an officer in the British Merchant Navy, but had joined the Royal Air Force during the years of the depression, seeing aviation as offering a more secure future. He was one of around 1,500 RAF personnel who opted to stay with the Royal Navy and switch services when the British Admiralty finally regained control of its own naval aviation between 1937 and 1939.

Courageous had also changed careers! Lamb and the ship had that much in common. Originally laid down as a battlecruiser during the First World War, *Courageous* had been one of a class of just three ships that were known in British naval circles as the 'Outrageous-class', having a shallow draught and heavy armament, 15-inch guns on *Courageous* and *Glorious*, 18-inch on *Furious*, for a planned, but abandoned, attempt to force an invasion of Germany through the Baltic in the First World War. The penalty of the shallow draught was that on one occasion, during the night of 8 January 1917, in the undemanding weather conditions of a sea state 4, barely choppy water, *Courageous* broke her back, her stem lifting by three feet! This meant that the three ships were absolutely useless, and it must have been with some relief that the Royal Navy was able to cover its embarrassment by starting the step-by-step conversion of the third ship into the first true aircraft carrier, HMS *Furious*. Happily, the Washington Naval Treaty of 1922 also placed upper limits on overall fleet sizes and on the total tonnage for each category of warship, leaving the Royal Navy with too much battlecruiser tonnage, but a considerable allowance for aircraft carriers, and in common with the Americans and the Japanese set out to convert two battlecruisers into aircraft carriers. In her new guise, *Courageous* rejoined the fleet in 1928.

That those negotiating and drafting the Washington Naval Treaty had put so much emphasis on the aircraft carrier seems strange, as between the two world wars, there was little to suggest that senior naval officers had wholeheartedly adopted the cause of aviation. Nevertheless, the United States Navy converted the battlecruisers USS *Lexington* and *Saratoga*, and the Japanese started to convert *Akagi* and *Amagi*, but the latter was wrecked beyond salvage on the slipway during conversion, when an earthquake struck the Yokosuka area and the Imperial Japanese Navy replaced her with a converted battleship, the *Kaga*. Battlecruisers were ideal for conversion, since they were faster than battleships, always useful when launching and recovering aircraft, and before conversion their lightly armoured decks had left them vulnerable to bombs, and indeed even falling shells.

This 'battlecruiser generation' of aircraft carriers were quickly rated as being the best of the early designs, and especially in the case of the Royal Navy. In the United States Navy, *Lexington* and *Saratoga* were its first significant aircraft carriers as the converted collier *Langley* could scarcely be regarded as anything more than an experimental vessel. That the United States Navy could, in 1920-21, lay down a class of six large battlecruisers seems strange today, but these were by far the largest aircraft carriers of their day when they commissioned as such in November and December 1927. Both had large hangars, more than 450 feet end to end, 70 feet wide and 21 feet deep, built on top of their hulls which were to remain the largest hangars on any carrier until well after the end of the Second World War. There were separate maintenance shops on both ships, and a 120 feet long hold beneath the hangar deck was meant to accommodate aircraft either waiting assembly as spares, or dismantled so that they could be sent for major overhauls or repairs ashore.

The loss of one of the Royal Navy's seven aircraft carriers so early in the war was even worse than the simple statistics might suggest. Four of the remaining aircraft carriers were already regarded as obsolete, too small or too slow and too old for modern aircraft, and had not war intervened, they would have been scrapped. In effect, the Royal Navy had lost one of its three best ships.

While the Royal Navy can take the credit for the invention of the aircraft carrier with the step-by-step conversion of the unwanted battlecruiser HMS *Furious*, even before the ship saw her first operation, control of naval aviation had passed to the new Royal Air Force, formed on 'All Fool's Day', 1 April 1918. In 1939, the Royal Navy was looking forward to the most advanced aircraft carriers in the world, the fast armoured carriers of the Illustrious-class, but it lacked the high performance aircraft that were already in service with the United States Navy. Worse still, the naval airmen of the First World War had risen to high rank in the RAF, so that the Royal Navy was missing a generation of senior officers with experience and understanding of aerial warfare, in complete contrast to the United States Navy where their contemporaries had risen to the rank of captain or even higher, able to influence the development of tactics and strategy.

It was scant recompense for the loss of *Courageous* that, on 26 September, a Blackburn Skua fighter/dive-bomber flown by Lieutenant B. S. McEwen from HMS *Ark Royal* shot down a Dornier Do18 flying-boat, the first German aircraft to be shot

9

down by a British fighter. The Do18 was not the most agile or fleetest of aircraft, but then nor was the Skua, described by one naval officer as 'more dive-bomber than fighter'.

Action off Norway

During the first winter of war the opposing armies had sat facing each other in Europe in what the Germans called the 'sitting war', a more accurate term than the British 'phoney war' since the war was anything but phoney at sea. This came to an end with the German invasion of Denmark and Norway on 9 April 1940. It was clear from the outset that nothing could be done to help Denmark as German forces swept across the frontier of this small country that had placed its trust in neutrality, while other German forces sailed into the harbour at Copenhagen. Norway was a different matter, for despite its small population, the size of the country and the terrain meant that the invading Germans could not seize enough territory at the outset, while the operation was hampered by the loss of the heavy cruiser *Blücher*, carrying the German field headquarters staff, at Oslo. The King of Norway and his government were able to escape and organize resistance, buying sufficient time for the British and French governments to organize an expeditionary force with an initial 13,000 men, supported by air and naval forces.

The shortage of bases ashore and the difficult terrain meant that the Norwegian campaign was well suited to the aircraft carrier, had the Royal Navy had high performance aircraft. The elderly carrier HMS *Furious* was first on the scene, but was soon relegated to the role of aircraft transport, while the new *Ark Royal* and the older *Glorious* were hastily recalled from the Mediterranean. As it happened, it was shore-based aircraft from the Royal Naval Air Station at Hatston, on Orkney, left behind when *Ark Royal* had sailed for the Mediterranean in March, that were to strike the first blow when, on 10 April, twenty Blackburn Skuas of 800 and 803 Squadrons, attacked and sank the cruiser *Königsberg* as she lay alongside at Bergen. This was the first sinking of an operational warship by aircraft, and no small achievement since the Sea Skuas had nothing heavier than 500-lb bombs, which would have simply bounced off a battleship's heavy armour plating, or perhaps even have broken up.

When she arrived, *Ark Royal* sent Fairey Swordfish biplanes of

10

810, 820 and 821 Squadrons to attack targets ashore, striking at the German-held airfield at Vaernes and also maintaining anti-submarine and anti-shipping patrols. Meanwhile, the Royal Air Force had managed to base fighters ashore, Hawker Hurricanes and Gloster Gladiator biplanes. These forces were not sufficient to repel the German advance and the battle ashore was being lost, so when German forces invaded the Low Countries on their way to France, it was decided to evacuate Norway and reinforce France.

The evacuation was covered by aircraft from both *Ark Royal* and *Glorious*. The RAF squadrons ashore were ordered to destroy their aircraft as these did not have sufficient range to fly home, and evacuate their personnel. The Hurricane pilots decided to save their aircraft by flying them to the carriers. *Glorious* was chosen despite her shorter deck because her larger lifts meant that the aircraft could be struck down into her hangars without having to have their wings removed. The Hurricanes lacked arrester hooks and their pilots had never flown onto a carrier before, but sandbags were attached to weigh down the tailwheels and the aircraft were landed successfully aboard the ship.

Short of fuel, *Glorious* left Norway on 8 June and steamed westwards at a stately 17 knots, which her commanding officer considered fast enough to save the ship from submarine attack. She did not have radar and did not maintain aerial reconnaissance, indeed, did not even maintain a lookout from her crow's nest. All of her aircraft were struck down, while bombs and torpedoes were removed and returned to the magazines. Her sole protection was an escort of two destroyers. Onto this peaceful scene at 16.00, the two German battlecruisers, *Scharnhorst* and *Gneisenau*, as it happened amongst the few German ships to be fitted with radar, opened fire at 28,000 yards with their 11-inch guns. Outgunned, the only remedy available to *Glorious* was to increase her speed and launch her aircraft. As additional boilers were fired up, five Swordfish were brought up from the hangars and made ready to launch a torpedo attack, when, at 16.15, the Germans scored their first hit on the carrier, destroying the aircraft which were still without their crews. Having found their range, further shells then penetrated the flight deck and exploded amongst the Hurricanes in the hangar below. Within minutes, the hangar deck was an inferno as fuel left in the Hurricanes ignited and their ammunition exploded. At 17.00, a salvo destroyed the bridge, but by this time the ship was a pillar of smoke, despite having increased her speed to 27 knots. The destroyer escorts, *Ardent* and *Acasta,* were both lost in a desperate torpedo attack on the *Scharnhorst,* which was damaged by one of *Acasta's* torpedoes.

An hour later, *Glorious* slipped beneath the waves. It is believed that as many as 900 of her ship's company and embarked RAF aircrew of 1,500 may have survived the attack, but just thirty-nine men survived two days in cold water, without food or drink, before they were rescued.

For the second time in just ten months of war, a British carrier had been lost needlessly for want of taking sensible precautions against surprise attack. Worse still, when on 13 June, fifteen Skuas of 800 and 803 Squadrons aboard HMS *Ark Royal* were sent to attack the *Scharnhorst* and *Gneisenau* at Trondheim, they flew into heavy AA fire from the ships and a strong fighter defence, against which the Sea Skua stood little chance, so that eight of the fifteen aircraft were shot down and their crews either killed or taken prisoner. One survivor likened the operation to the Charge of the Light Brigade, but in fact the operation was far less successful since, when the *Scharnhorst* was struck by a bomb, it failed to explode.

Tackling Vichy France

The surrender of France in June 1940 meant more than simply having German forces just across the Channel from the south coast of England, a mere twenty-two miles; it also meant that an entire army and an entire fleet was lost to the war effort. In the Mediterranean, most of the coast of North Africa, all comfortably within easy reach of the main shipping lanes used by convoys for Malta and Alexandria, and the Suez Canal, was lost to the British. Worse still, the creation of what was effectively a puppet state by the Vichy French meant that the allegiance of the French Navy could not be taken for granted. Losing French ships and seamen was one thing, having them transferred to the enemy was something else again. A number of ships were in Portsmouth, and these were quickly seized on 3 July under cover of darkness, while measures were put in hand to neutralize the ships sharing Alexandria in Egypt with the Royal Navy. The big problem was the fate of the substantial number of major fleet units at ports in France's African territories.

The rest of the French fleet was divided between Oran, sometimes known as Mers El-Kebir, in Algeria and Dakar in West Africa.

Tackling the French fleet was an unwelcome task for the Royal Navy, whose personnel were all too aware that until recently this had been an ally. Vice Admiral Sir James Somerville, in command of Force H based on Gibraltar, was anxious to avoid a battle with the French. On 3 July, he presented his opposite number at Oran, Admiral Gensoul, with an ultimatum, demanding that the French warships be handed over or neutralized, by which he meant that they should be non-operational. Force H included the aircraft carrier *Ark Royal*, commanded by Captain Holland, who was sent to meet Gensoul, flying in a Fairey Swordfish seaplane from a battlecruiser. The British ultimatum was rejected, leaving Holland to fly back to his ship, on which the arrester wires were removed to allow the seaplane to land safely on her deck.

Somerville now had no option but to attack the French fleet and the shore installations. A single burst of gunfire from one of his battleships blew an army barracks off the crest of a hill. Supported by an attack by aircraft from *Ark Royal*, in just fifteen minutes Force H blew up the old French battleship *Bretagne*, crippled the battleship *Provence* and the battlecruiser *Dunkerque*, both of which had to be run aground to prevent them sinking, but the battlecruiser *Strasbourg* and six destroyers managed to escape to Toulon. Force H's ships were completely undamaged in this short action, although the thin flight deck of the British carrier would have been vulnerable to heavy shellfire.

On 8 July, the small aircraft carrier HMS *Hermes* and two heavy cruisers attacked the rest of the French fleet at Dakar, damaging the battleship *Richelieu*. On this occasion, the French did not attempt to escape, doubtless because this would have meant sailing past Gibraltar, a high risk strategy, and the force at Dakar remained intact until a further attempt was made to destroy it by the Royal Navy in September, when the French fought back and heavy damage was suffered by both navies.

II

NIGHT OF JUDGEMENT

'I want you in view of the desperate situation, to take *Illustrious* through the Straits of Gibraltar and join Andrew,' Admiral of the Fleet Sir Dudley Pound, First Sea Lord explained. 'He needs you badly out there.'

Pound was talking to Captain Denis Boyd, commanding officer of the Royal Navy's newest aircraft carrier, the fast armoured carrier *Illustrious*. Boyd had been summoned to the Admiralty after his ship had returned from a working up voyage that had taken her across the Atlantic to Bermuda. 'Andrew' was the officer commanding the Royal Navy's Mediterranean Fleet, Admiral Sir Andrew Browne Cunningham, known throughout the Royal Navy as 'ABC'.

By summer 1940, not only had Denmark, Norway, Belgium, the Netherlands and France been lost, and French territory as far apart as West Africa, Syria and Madagascar become hostile, but the strategic position had been made still more precarious by Italy's entry into the war, shortly before the fall of France. Cunningham was familiar with the Mediterranean having spent much time there before the war, including a spell as Flag Officer, Cruisers, when he had also been responsible for the Mediterranean Fleet's sole aircraft carrier, at that time the converted battlecruiser HMS *Glorious*.

The pre-war planners had intended that in the eventuality of war with Italy, the Mediterranean Fleet would be reinforced with ships from both the Home Fleet and the Far East, but their plans had failed to take into account the pressures under which the Home Fleet would be labouring in a war with Germany. In the same way, before long their plans for operations in the Far East which, they had confidently assured the Australians and New Zealanders, would be reinforced by units from the Home Fleet and the Mediterranean, would also be shown to be of little value.

At the time of Italy's intervention, the Mediterranean Fleet already had one aircraft carrier, the elderly and slow HMS *Eagle*, recalled from east of Suez to fill the gap left by the transfer of *Glorious* to Norway. *Eagle* had originally converted from a battleship that was being built for the Chilean Navy. Further west and based on Gibraltar, Force H under Vice Admiral Somerville had *Ark Royal*, and operated in the western Mediterranean and the Atlantic as required. *Eagle* had already seen action with the Mediterranean Fleet, taking part in the Battle of Punta Stilo, off the toe of Italy, on 9 July 1940. His two battleships, *Royal Sovereign* and *Malaya*, outpaced by the Italian battleships, Cunningham had sent aircraft from *Eagle* in an attempt to slow down the Italians, but the operation was unsuccessful, although eventually Cunningham managed a long-range gunnery duel between his flagship, the much modernized *Warspite* and the Italian *Guilio Cesare*. The Italian air force, the *Regia Aeronautica*, mounted an attack on *Eagle*, and although none of their bombs struck the ship, there were several near misses that were to impact on future operations by the carrier.

Now Cunningham's hand was being strengthened by the arrival of the Royal Navy's newest carrier.

Illustrious was a completely new carrier design, even a new concept, being fast and heavily armoured. Many have pointed out that the new carriers had inferior aircraft accommodation to the *Ark Royal*, but the truth was that the *Ark* suffered from a lack of armoured protection, so much so that on one occasion the flight deck was pierced when 20-lb practice bombs fell off an aircraft. The irony was that she was eventually sunk not by the bombs or shellfire that so worried many senior officers, but by a torpedo. Originally, there were to have been four ships of the Illustrious-class, intended to replace the four oldest carriers, *Furious*, *Argus*, *Eagle* and *Hermes*, but the class was increased to six as war loomed, and plans to decommission the older ships were abandoned.

The first three of the new ships, *Illustrious*, *Victorious* and *Formidable*, were true sisters, and although nominally part of the same class, the later ships differed considerably, with some having two hangar decks, so that many prefer to talk of the Illustrious and Implacable-classes, with the latter consisting of two, while the fourth carrier, *Indomitable* was a hybrid, with a hangar deck and a half.

Illustrious herself was 744 feet overall, with a 96 feet beam and a draught of 25 feet, and was powered by three turbines providing

110,000 hp and a speed of 30 knots. Her standard displacement was 23,000 tons, but at full load, with fuel, supplies and aircraft, this rose to 28,000 tons. The freeboard, that is the height between the waterline and the flight deck, was 43 feet compared with just over 60 feet for the *Ark Royal*. The flight deck armour was 3-inches thick over the hangar, but just 1½-inches at the ends fore and aft, with 4½-inch thick armour to the sides of the hangar and at the bulkheads fore and aft, and a 3-inch hangar deck. Heavier armour plating might, in the light of subsequent events, have been useful, but there is a balance to be struck between armour and becoming too top heavy. The only breaks in the armoured hangar and flight deck box were the two lifts. Further protection came in the form of armoured shutters or curtains to break the hangar up into three compartments in case of fire. Waterline armour plating was 4.5-inches, and the steering compartment, or flat, was protected by 3-inch armour. The bridge had light armour to protect against shrapnel or strafing.

Illustrious could accommodate thirty-six aircraft in the single hangar deck, with its 16-feet headroom, far less than in *Ark Royal*'s two hangar decks and, although the emphasis was on what today would be counted as strike aircraft rather than fighters, she also brought the new Fairey Fulmar fighter to the Mediterranean for the first time.

One naval officer with experience of the older carriers remarked that comparing *Illustrious* with *Courageous* was like comparing her with Noah's Ark!

Laid down in April 1937, *Illustrious* was launched in April 1939, and completed fitting out a year later. A shake down cruise to Bermuda was followed by a refit during which some problems were rectified.

The Fulmar was a monoplane with a Rolls Royce Merlin engine, the same power unit as the Supermarine Spitfire and Hawker Hurricane fighters that had given such a good account of themselves in the Battle of Britain, but there the similarities ended. The Fulmar was in the tradition of twin-seat fighters, so beloved of the Royal Navy which saw the provision of an observer, the Fleet Air Arm term for navigator, as far more important than aircraft performance. Having a two man crew made all the difference in terms of speed and manoeuvrability – it effectively crippled the aircraft.

Pound's enthusiasm for a strong carrier force in the

Mediterranean was strange, in that his view pre-war had been that aggressive aerial operations would be best conducted from shore bases in Malta, and that the life of a carrier in the Mediterranean was likely to be short. His planning for war with Italy made much of the fact that an aircraft carrier would be able to mount one offensive operation at most before being sunk or badly damaged. Like many other senior naval officers, he saw offensive air operations in the Mediterranean being conducted almost entirely by Royal Air Force units based on Malta – while both the RAF and the British Army saw Malta in a different light, not as an 'unsinkable aircraft carrier', but as a base that would be difficult to defend and that should be abandoned, rather as the Channel Islands had been partially evacuated and demilitarized. The Royal Navy saw Malta as being a suitable base for operations against the enemy by submarines and light forces. The loss of Malta would have made running convoys across the Mediterranean to Alexandria impossible, but as the war developed, this was likely to be the case anyway. On the other hand, keeping Malta also meant that Axis convoys linking Italy with North Africa also came under attack, and at times shipping losses far exceeded those getting through.

Illustrious Enters The Mediterranean

Illustrious arrived in the Mediterranean accompanied by the recently refitted and modernized battleship *Valiant*, a sister ship of Cunningham's flagship *Warspite*, and the two anti-aircraft cruisers *Calcutta* and *Coventry*. For the first time, the Mediterranean Fleet now had radar, which not only gave advance warning of an attack by day or by night, it also eased the lot of the ships' AA gunners who previously had spent long periods closed up at action stations on the guns just in case an attack materialized. Despite its shortcomings, the Fairey Fulmar fighter, slower than the Hurricane, was still a big improvement over the three Sea Gladiators that had been hastily pressed into service aboard *Eagle*, although these elderly biplanes had acquitted themselves well, eventually accounting for eleven Italian aircraft – a tribute to the skill of their pilots who had such a short time ago been flying the venerable Swordfish biplane torpedo-bomber.

The arrival of *Illustrious* was also welcome ashore, for in Malta the Fleet Air Arm's 830 Naval Air Squadron needed the

17

replacement aircraft flown ashore from the carrier, which also brought blind flying instrument panels and long-range fuel tanks to improve the capability of 830's Swordfish.

Despite the capability of the new carrier and the other ships that accompanied her, no chances were taken. When she entered the Mediterranean on 30 August 1940, *Illustrious* was escorted by Somerville's Force H, which left her south-west of Sicily to traverse the Pantellaria Straits, through which they steamed at speed through the night with paravanes deployed to cut mine mooring cables, just in case. The following morning, mine mooring wires were found on the starboard paravane; the carrier had come within a hair's breadth of striking a mine and suffering serious damage. The reinforcements were then met by Cunningham with *Warspite* and *Eagle* in an operation code-named 'Hats'. With his strengthened force, Cunningham also made sure that the Italians were well aware of their presence, sending aircraft from the two carriers to attack Italian airfields on the island of Rhodes as the Mediterranean Fleet steamed towards its wartime base of Alexandria.

Cunningham's major problem was that the Italian Navy, the *Regia Navale*, was reluctant to engage the Royal Navy in battle. With its six large battleships, the balance of power in the Mediterranean lay with the Italians, although Cunningham had been able to see these ships for himself when they visited Malta before the war and knew that they lacked radar and were unlikely to be a match for either *Valiant* or *Warspite*. The Italians also had a substantial submarine force, far larger than that of Germany in 1939, as well as destroyers and cruisers. This was a similar problem to that faced by Nelson at Copenhagen in 1801, when the enemy fleet refused to engage on the high seas. Nelson had solved the problem by sending in his frigates, but this option was not open to Cunningham in 1940 because of the layout of the major Italian naval base at Taranto and its strong defences.

While the Italians had several major naval bases, Taranto, in the instep of the 'foot' of Italy, was the most convenient for operations against Malta and against British shipping crossing the Mediterranean, and for convoys from Italy for Italian land and air forces in North Africa. The importance of Taranto had been recognized by the Royal Navy pre-war, when action against Italy was contemplated after that country invaded Abyssinia, present-day Ethiopia, and plans had been prepared for an air strike against the port by aircraft flown off the Mediterranean Fleet's carrier, HMS *Glorious*. At the time, the carrier was commanded by Captain Lumley Lyster, and now, some years later, Lyster was back, but this time aboard *Illustrious* as the Mediterranean Fleet's Rear Admiral, Carriers.

Almost as soon as they reached Alexandria, Cunningham called his commanding officers together to discuss a programme of oper ations against Italian bases and shipping.

Operation Judgement

The attack on Taranto was given the code-name Operation Judgement, prompting one naval aviator to declare that he hoped that 'it would be the Italians' hour of judgement, not ours!' Planning called for thirty aircraft from both aircraft carriers to be used, and for the operation to take place on the night of 21–22 October, the anniversary of Nelson's famous victory at Trafalgar in 1805. The number of aircraft planned to take part in the attack was below the total available since a number would also have to be available for reconnaissance and anti-submarine duties to protect the fleet.

At a time when monoplanes were entering service with the world's air forces, the raid was to be carried out by Fairey Swordfish biplanes, known affectionately to their crews as 'Stringbag', because supposedly the aircraft could carry a wider variety of items than could be found in a pre-war housewife's stringbag. First flown in April 1934, the first Swordfish did not enter service until July 1936 and was powered by a single Bristol Pegasus III provided 690hp, although later MkII and MkIII Swordfish had the more powerful 750hp Pegasus XXX. The aircraft had a wingspan of 45 feet 5 inches, and was 36 feet 3 inches long, with an overall height of 12 feet 10 inches – it was a fair size for the day, and had a maximum weight of 9,250-lbs. There were usually three members in the crew, each with his own open cockpit, with the pilot and observer both usually commissioned, and the rear cockpit occupied by the telegraphist-air-gunner, or TAG, who was a naval rating. The range was 450 nautical miles, but this could be increased to 896 nautical miles with additional fuel tanks. Aircraft assigned to act as dive-bombers could have the extra tank mounted under the fuselage, but for the torpedo-droppers this was not possible, and the extra

19

range was gained by placing a ninety-three gallon tank in the observer's cockpit, and relegating the observer, with his bulky Bigsworth chart board, to the confines of the TAG's cockpit. This not only provided cramped accommodation for the observer, with the extra duty of having to handle any communications that might be needed, he also had to contend with the all too real danger of being soaked in high octane aviation fuel as the aircraft took off or climbed, an unenviable position to be in, especially with the risk of the flimsy cockpit being pierced by AA tracer shells, or 'flaming onions' as they became known! The maximum speed was 125 knots, although most Swordfish aircrew would maintain that even 100 knots was seldom, if ever, achieved, especially on operations! For the raid, all of the aircraft, whether bombers or torpedo-droppers, would have just a pilot and an observer.

Intensive training was given to the aircrew, whose aircraft would be divided amongst torpedo-droppers and dive-bombers, and night flying skills were brought up to scratch. Unfortunately, fate intervened, and a serious hangar fire aboard *Illustrious* destroyed two aircraft while the others were doused in water and had to be stripped down and rebuilt. The operation needed a moonlit night for success, and this meant that it had to be postponed until the next full moon on the night of 11–12 November. Meanwhile, a fresh problem arose. Both carriers had been attacked several times by Italian bombers during their forays into the Mediterranean, and although escaping direct hits, there had been many near misses. In *Eagle's* case, the near misses during the Italian bombing after the Battle of Punta Stilo had had a similar affect to striking a mine, and had damaged her aviation fuel system. Rather than delay the operation further, it was decided to use just one carrier and transfer some of *Eagle's* aircraft to *Illustrious*, reducing the number available for the raid to just twenty-four.

On 6 November, *Illustrious* left Alexandria with a cruiser and destroyer escort, with departure timed to coincide with the departure of a convoy carrying reinforcements for Greece, to put the Axis agents in Alexandria off the scent. On 10 November, the ill-luck that had dogged the operation struck again, with a Swordfish suffering engine failure and having to ditch in the sea. The next day, another aircraft suffered the same fate and investigation showed that one of the ship's aviation fuel tanks had become contaminated by sea water. There was no alternative but to drain the fuel system in every aircraft.

Meanwhile, reconnaissance by Malta-based RAF aircraft showed that Taranto now had all six Italian battleships, rather than the five expected. A diversionary operation against targets in the Straits of Otranto by the Mediterranean Fleet's cruisers was set in hand, leaving the main force at noon on 11 November, while Force H was also present in the western Mediterranean approaching the coast of Sicily.

Down to twenty-one aircraft, the raid was to take place in two waves, with the first consisting of twelve aircraft led by Lieutenant Commander Kenneth Williamson and the second with nine led by Lieutenant Commander 'Ginger' Hale. About half the aircraft were to carry torpedoes for use against the battleships, while the remainder had flares and bombs, for use against cruisers and destroyers, and shore targets including a seaplane base and an oil storage depot.

The first wave took off starting at 20.30, whilst the ship was off the coast of Cephalonia and 170 miles from Taranto. One aircraft was forced to return after its fuel tank broke loose. Flying through cloud some of the aircraft fell out of formation, although navigation was eased when the AA defences at Taranto opened up after being disturbed by a patrolling RAF flying boat from Malta. The aircraft of the second wave followed, taking off at 21.20, by which time the Italian AA gunners were well and truly alerted.

While the period before the operation had been marked by a series of accidents that boded ill, unknown to the attackers, on the day of the raid their luck had changed. The Italians had been due to put to sea, and had spent the morning removing the torpedo nets that protected their major ships. The planned exercise was cancelled at the last minute, and the fleet stayed in port, but the torpedo nets were not reset. This oversight was to have serious consequences.

The aircraft of the first wave arrived over the harbour flying low and on the look out for the barrage balloons that reconnaissance photographs had located, although fortunately far enough apart for a Swordfish to fly between the cables. Charles Lamb remembers the aircraft '. . . flying into the harbour only a few feet above sea level – so low that one or two of them actually touched the water with their wheels as they sped through the harbour entrance.'

21

The slow and lumbering Swordfish, which many naval airmen maintained couldn't manage 100 knots when loaded with a torpedo, should have presented the Italian AA gunners with an easy target. Yet, the fact that so many of the aircraft were flying so low may well have saved them, as in order to depress their guns low enough to catch the aircraft, the AA gunners risked strafing their comrades on other ships. The Italians also wasted ammunition firing at the flares being dropped by some of the aircraft.

Williamson's aircraft dropped its torpedo and sunk the battleship *Conte di Cavour* in shallow water, but in turning to make his escape, his aircraft either put a wing into the water and crashed, or, more probably was shot down. Other aircraft torpedoed the *Littorio* and *Caio Duilio*, all of which ended up on the bottom of the harbour. Three cruisers and two destroyers had also been badly damaged, with two of the cruisers lying in a pool of oil, while two auxiliaries had also been crippled. The destroyers had been affected by near misses, with the *Libeccio* having a fractured bow, while the *Pessagno* had damage to her hull. The seaplane base and the oil storage tanks had also been damaged by six bombs. The cruiser *Trento* had a lucky escape as a bomb crashed through her and out through the bottom of her hull without exploding, possibly because it had been dropped too low to arm itself.

Just two aircraft were shot down, with Williamson and his observer becoming prisoners of war, although the crew of the other aircraft were killed. The remaining aircraft all returned safely to *Illustrious* and a warm welcome, while the Italian Navy moved its warships out of Taranto to Naples on 13 November.

This was the first attack on an enemy fleet by carrier-borne aircraft. It was completely successful in that the Italians suffered greater damage than had the German High Seas Fleet at Jutland in the First World War, and were forced to move their fleet to the less convenient port of Naples, while the Royal Navy had lost just two aircraft. It is questionable whether Pound's preferred means of attack, by Malta-based Bristol Beaufort torpedo-bombers would have been as successful, simply because the heavier and faster Beaufort might not have been able to operate as low as the Swordfish.

One of the most significant features of the attack on Taranto was the low number of casualties on both sides. The British lost just two airmen, with another two captured, the Italians lost just forty sailors. The Fleet Air Arm's low losses can be put down in no small part to the fact that attacking at such low level gave the Italian anti-aircraft gunners a major problem, for as they depressed their guns to target the attackers, they risked raking the decks of the other ships with their own fire. The flare droppers survived because the Italians seemed to concentrate on shooting at the flares. As for the crippled Italian warships, not one of these blew up. Miraculously their magazines all remained intact, although there were some very close shaves. Had even one of these ships blown up, the death toll would have been much closer to that experienced at Pearl Harbor a little more than a year later.

Retribution

While the Fleet Air Arm was still reflecting in the glory of the raid on Taranto, moves were already afoot to change the balance of power in the Mediterranean, which had swung so decisively in favour of the British. Germany's leader, Adolf Hitler, was outraged that his Italian ally could lose so many ships in a single night without even engaging in a major fleet action. At first, Italian air raids against Alexandria increased in intensity, although the Italians seemed reluctant to approach too closely when the Mediterranean Fleet, with its strong AA defences, was in harbour.

A little more than two weeks after the successful attack on Taranto, it was Force H's turn to engage the Italian Navy. Somerville was taking Force H eastwards to escort three fast freighters from Gibraltar to Alexandria, with the aircraft carrier *Ark Royal* and the battleship *Ramillies*, as well as the battlecruiser *Renown*, with five cruisers and fourteen destroyers. The Italian Admiral Campioni was detected south of Sardinia by British reconnaissance aircraft with the two battleships *Vittorio Veneto* and *Guilio Cesare*, six cruisers and fourteen destroyers. On 27 November, south of Sardinia, the battle of Cape Teulada commenced, initially with a cruiser action. Leaving the slower *Ramillies* behind, *Renown* entered the battle, forcing the Italian cruisers back into the cover of their battleships, which then joined battle. At this stage, *Ark Royal* sent her aircraft on unsuccessful sorties against the Italian battleships, but the threat of naval air power was enough to encourage Campioni to break off the engagement.

Anxious to maintain the pressure on the Italians, on 17 December, *Illustrious* once again sent her aircraft to attack Italian airfields on Rhodes.

In North Africa, British forces also advanced so that by January 1941, all of Cyrenaica, a substantial part of modern Tripoli, was occupied. These moves, on top of the Italian losses at Taranto, convinced the Germans that action was necessary.

At the start of 1941, the *Luftwaffe* moved General Geissler's powerful Tenth Air Corps, *Fliegerkorps X*, from Poland to Sicily. *Fliegerkorps X*, with its 150 Heinkel He111 and Junkers Ju88 medium-bombers, 150 Junkers Ju87 Stuka dive-bombers, as well as fifty Messerschmitt Bf109 fighters, was more powerful than the combined RAF and Fleet Air Arm strength in the Mediterranean. Unlike the British forces, scattered over more than 2,000 miles from Gibraltar to Alexandria, it was concentrated on one point, the *Regia Aeronautica*'s airfields in Sicily.

The *Luftwaffe* and *Regia Aeronautica* planned to attack British shipping, with *Illustrious*, whose fighters could provide air cover and whose Swordfish had already wreaked such havoc, as the prime target. Malta and Alexandria would be next, followed by sowing mines in the approaches to the Suez Canal. The raids on Alexandria and the mining of the Suez Canal would follow the occupation of Crete, since most *Luftwaffe* aircraft were short in range and there were limits to the trade-off between fuel and bombs or mines if an effective punch was to be landed on the enemy.

In wartime, luck is important. The Royal Navy had a run of bad luck immediately before the attack on Taranto, but almost everything had gone right on the night. Other lesser successes had followed, and as the year end neared, convoys were still getting through to Malta and Alexandria from Gibraltar. Now, the Mediterranean Fleet was to have a run of appallingly bad luck.

It was planned to run a convoy, Operation Excess, through to Malta and Alexandria at the end of 1940. Had all gone well, the convoy would have reached its destinations on time, but it was delayed by a sighting of the German heavy cruiser *Hipper* on Christmas Day, and the convoy scattered. Force H left Gibraltar to provide support. A heavy escort, the elderly battleship *Renown*, was damaged by heavy seas and was delayed in Gibraltar for repairs, while one of the cargo ships was driven ashore by the bad weather.

Running late, and down to just four ships, the convoy did not leave Gibraltar until 6 January 1941. The delay was to have serious consequences. As with the arrival of *Illustrious* herself the previous year, Force H was to cover the convoy as far as Sicily, and then it would pass to the Mediterranean Fleet, which left Alexandria on 7 January 1941. To keep the Italian Navy out of the way, on 8 January Malta-based Wellington medium-bombers raided Naples, damaging the *Cesare* and forcing her and the *Vittorio Veneto* to move further north.

As Force H escorted the convoy eastwards, ten Savoia Marchetti SM79s attempted an attack, but with little success and losing two aircraft to the *Ark Royal*'s Fulmar fighters. Handover of the convoy was fixed for dawn on 10 January 1941, with Force H leaving the convoy at dusk on 9 January with just the cruisers *Gloucester* and *Southampton*, with two destroyers, as escorts through the Sicilian Narrows.

Meanwhile, those aboard *Illustrious* were aware of the arrival of the Tenth Air Corps, *Fliegerkorps X*, in Sicily, and knew that it included many of the *Luftwaffe*'s most experienced anti-shipping aircrew. On the broad reaches of the North Atlantic, such work was left to flying boats and the long-range Focke-Wulf Fw200 Condors and Junkers Ju290s, for which the Fulmar could prove a match, but over the 'Med', this was for the more manoeuvrable medium-bombers and dive-bombers.

All went well at first, as an Italian reconnaissance aircraft had been shot down by a Fulmar from *Illustrious* as she sailed westwards. The worst the *Regia Aeronautica* seemed able to do was mount sporadic attacks.

Illustrious was ready to pick up the convoy at 04.30 on 10 January, steaming to the north-west of Malta with the battleships *Warspite* and *Valiant*, close to the Pantellaria Straits, in clear weather, without any clouds. It was dangerous, with limited room for manoeuvre, within easy reach of enemy aircraft and of shore based artillery and had previously only been passed through at night. Lyster and Boyd had argued that there was no need to expose the carrier to air attack, since she could cover the convoy from a distance, while her fighter squadron, 806, had suffered heavy losses. Cunningham insisted on sending *Illustrious* as the fleet's morale was always high when the ship was in sight. It is also likely that Cunningham was beginning to appreciate that there was a substantial degree of interdependence between major fleet units. The traditional ships needed the air cover that the carrier could provide, while the carrier needed the additional heavy anti-aircraft fire from the battleships and cruisers. This was later to be proven to be the key to successful defence against Japanese air attack in the Pacific, but whether the Mediterranean Fleet at the time had heavy enough AA armament for this to work, or whether the capital ships and cruisers were close enough to *Illustrious* to offer really worthwhile protection, must be open to question.

Just before 12.30, two Italian torpedo-bombers approached, flying just above the sea on the carrier's starboard quarter. The starboard side AA defences opened up, and the bombers dropped their torpedoes at 400 yards, while Boyd changed course to starboard successfully combing the torpedoes. The carrier's anti-aircraft gunners missed these aircraft, possibly because many were inexperienced after more than twenty of her experienced gunners had been posted away. Both bombers were shot down by two Fulmars, and it soon became clear that the true function of the Italians was to decoy the combat air patrol to a lower altitude, where they would have difficulty fending off a high level attack.

Believing that the danger was past, the carrier turned back into the wind to launch the six Fulmars that had been waiting, but as she did so the first Stukas were into their bombing dives. The last fighter to leave the deck was shot down.

Meanwhile, most of the aircrew not in the air had assembled in the hangar deck, their appointed place during action stations. It was to prove to be the worst place possible for them.

Shortly after 12.30, two waves with a total of forty-three Stuka dive-bombers led by *Major* Enneccerus and *Hauptmann* Hozel swooped down onto the Mediterranean Fleet from 12,000 feet. Ten aircraft attacked the two battleships, while the rest concentrated on the carrier.

'We opened up with every AA gun we had as one by one the Stukas peeled off into their dives concentrating almost the whole venom of their attack upon the *Illustrious*,' Cunningham later wrote.

At times she became almost completely hidden in a forest of great bomb splashes.
One was too interested in this new form of dive-bombing

26

attack to be frightened, and there was no doubt that we were watching complete experts. Formed roughly in a large circle over the fleet they peeled off one by one when reaching the attacking position. We could not but admire the skill and precision of it all. The attacks were pressed home at point blank range, and as they pulled out of their dives some were seen to fly along the flight deck of *Illustrious* below the level of the funnel.

I saw her hit early on just before the bridge, and in all, in something like ten minutes, she was hit by six 1,000-lb bombs, to leave the line badly on fire, her steering gear crippled, her lifts out of action, and with heavy casualties . . .

The Stukas could hardly miss, releasing their bombs at between 2,300 feet down to 1,600 feet, and scoring six direct hits on the carrier with another three very close misses. The 3-inch armoured flight deck was designed to withstand the force of a direct hit from a 500-lb bomb, but some of the Stukas were armed with 1,000-lb bombs. Even so, most of the damage was caused by the 500-lb bombs. One hit the un-armoured after lift, blowing the 300-ton lift platform into the hangar, and wrecking a Fulmar on the lift. Another exploded inside the hangar, setting fire to several aircraft. A third 500-lb bomb struck the forward lift, causing further serious damage. The sixth and final bomb, of 1,000-lbs, breached the flight deck and exploded inside the hangar. The damage knocked out many of the ship's systems.

The first bomb to strike the ship had come at 12.38, and a few seconds later came the first to cause significant damage. It was all over in just ten minutes, but then a second attack followed.

This time a bomb destroyed the wardroom killing many of the ship's officers while the entire after part of the carrier was on fire and the rudder jammed so that she could only to steam in circles. Damage control parties struggled to jam the rudder amidships leaving the engines for steering.

Aircraft in the air either had to ditch or, if they had enough fuel, make their way to Malta.

That night, *Illustrious* limped into Malta's Grand Harbour under cover of darkness. Most of her guns were still working while her speed had never dropped below 18 knots as the men in her boiler rooms and engine rooms had struggled to maintain power in temperatures as high as 140 degrees F, but she was useless as an aircraft carrier. Her flight deck was punctured and her lifts shattered, while her hangar was a blackened smoking mess, with the corpses of many of those who had been there plastered against the bulkheads. Most of her accommodation was unusable, the wardroom having suffered a direct hit and some of those seriously wounded by the blast subsequently drowned by the volume of water used in fighting the fires.

The fate of the carrier at this stage was uncertain. She needed a major refit and in naval terms she 'was beyond local repair', but she needed to be patched up to make her escape from the island. There was a brief respite as low cloud made enemy air attack difficult, but she then became a target for a renewed *Luftwaffe* and *Regia Aeronautica* assault. This became known in the history of the war in Malta as the 'Illustrious blitz', while the *Luftwaffe* Ju87 Stuka dive-bombers struggled to lift 2,500-lb bombs into the air, determined that the carrier should not survive. There was further damage to the ship as bombs blasted away the scaffolding surrounding her superstructure, and one bomb damaged her hull as it landed in the water alongside the ship. At its worst, most of the ship's company had to be evacuated to Hal Far, then an RAF base. Nevertheless, on 23 January she was able to sneak out of Grand Harbour and make a dash for Alexandria, the first leg in her voyage to the United States and a major refit. *Eagle*, no longer an asset, also left the Mediterranean for the time being.

Nevertheless, despite the damage inflicted on *Illustrious*, it was clear that a carrier was needed in the Mediterranean, and after some delay while mines and wrecks were removed from the Suez Canal, the departure of the two carriers coincided with the arrival of a replacement for *Illustrious*, the new HMS *Formidable*. Meanwhile, naval air power in the Mediterranean was dependent upon the occasional foray by Force H, which ventured into the Gulf of Genoa to raid Genoa and Leghorn on 9 February, with aircraft from HMS *Ark Royal* and heavy bombardment from the battlecruiser *Renown* and the battleship *Malaya*.

III

TREACHERY IN THE PACIFIC

'The flame and smoke erupted skyward,' recalled Mitsuo Fuchida. 'It was a hateful, mean-looking red flame, the kind that powder produces, and I knew at once that a big magazine had exploded.'

Mitsuo Fuchida was the leader of the Japanese Navy Air Force attack on the United States Pacific Fleet at Pearl Harbor in Hawaii. As mentioned in the previous chapter, one big difference between Pearl Harbor and Taranto was the way in which some of the ships blew up, and this more than anything else accounted for the far larger loss of life aboard the ships. There was yet another difference. In November 1940, Italy and Britain had been at war for five months, while, as in the Russo-Japanese War of 1904–1905, at Pearl Harbor the Japanese attacked first without any declaration of war. The Japanese force deployed at Pearl Harbor was also far larger than that at Taranto, and it was a daylight raid rather than under cover of darkness.

It is tempting to believe that the Japanese took Taranto as a blueprint. This is not true. The Imperial Japanese Navy had already war-gamed the attack on Pearl Harbor, unknown to anyone else, but Taranto did convince the Japanese that the attack was feasible.

As a former, but unreliable, ally in the First World War, Japan benefited from the presence of a British Naval Mission between 1919 and 1922. The mission included F. J. Rutland, who as Flight Lieutenant Rutland (a rank that originated with the Royal Naval Air Service) had flown a reconnaissance flight just before the Battle of Jutland. Japan had opposed the conditions of the 1922 Washington Naval Treaty, demanding a far larger total tonnage than the 315,000 tons allocated to her, in contrast to 525,000 tons for both the UK and USA, starting the cooling-off in relations between Japan and both the UK and USA.

Taranto and Pearl Harbor had one factor in common; both were intended to redress an imbalance of naval power. The Royal Navy was weaker than the Italian Navy in the Mediterranean but stronger overall, but its strength was spread over three potential theatres of war at once, the Atlantic and the Mediterranean, and, as the threat of war with Japan loomed, the Far East. By contrast, the Imperial Japanese Navy was stronger than the United States Navy in the Pacific, but not overall.

War between Japan and the United States eventually became inevitable, despite US isolationism, after the US imposed an embargo on the sale of scrap metal and war materials to Japan in December 1940, and followed this by freezing Japanese assets in July 1941, after the Japanese had seized upon the impotence of Vichy France and invaded Indo-China. The Imperial Japanese Navy included many senior commanders who realized the enormity of the task. One of the realists was the Commander-in-Chief of the Imperial Japanese Navy's First Fleet, Admiral Isoroku Yamamoto, who appreciated that Japan could not match the United States militarily or, no less important in modern warfare, industrially. Yamamoto felt that Japan could win a major victory in the first year of war, but that the United States would have recovered by the second year and could move to the offensive. Japan needed a 'knock-out' blow to the United States Navy in the Pacific before the Pacific and Atlantic fleets could combine to overwhelm them. Yamamoto decided to strike a crippling blow at the US Pacific Fleet through attacking its main base at Pearl Harbor, on the Hawaiian island of Oahu. It was important not just to sink as many major US warships as possible, but also to render Pearl Harbor unusable for a prolonged period, during which the United States would not have a forward naval base in the Pacific.

There were many in the Imperial Japanese Navy who had foreseen that war was inevitable and that the United States was the likely opponent. These included Mitsuo Fuchida, the leader of the raid on Pearl Harbor, who had chosen English as his compulsory foreign language while training as a naval officer. It was to prove useful.

Planning

The Japanese were able to bring a massive concentration of force to bear on Pearl Harbor, far beyond the wildest dreams of those attacking Taranto, with six aircraft carriers with 423 aircraft between them, of which 353 were to be used for the attack and for fighter cover.

Fuchida had been selected to lead the attack by his friend Commander Minoru Genda, one of the Japanese planners. Genda was strongly in favour of an aerial torpedo attack, although Fuchida was opposed to this, despite the excellence of Japanese torpedoes, because he felt that the Americans would have protected their ships with torpedo nets, while the water inside Pearl Harbor was also very shallow, at just forty feet deep in places. Genda felt that torpedo nets were unlikely, simply because the Americans would not be expecting an attack. A more likely problem would arise if the entire Pacific Fleet was in port, since many of the ships would be double berthed, and protected from torpedoes by the ship alongside, but Genda won the argument by pointing out that the bombs dropped by the dive-bombers would be wasted against the armoured decks and gun turrets of the battleships.

Japanese aircraft were far superior to anything that the Royal Navy could offer. The fighter, the Mitsubishi A6M, the famous 'Zero', was later evaluated by an American officer as being '. . . a light sports plane with a 1,300-hp engine,' but in contrast to the Fulmar, the Zero wasn't weighed down by an observer. The main strike aircraft was the Nakajima B5N, known to the wartime Allies as 'Kate', a single-engined monoplane with all-metal stressed skin construction, power-folding wings and retractable undercarriage, capable of a top speed of 230 mph against the 100 mph or so of the Swordfish. The attack would include forty of these aircraft armed with torpedoes, and another 103 carrying bombs. The dive-bomber was the Aichi D3A1, known to the Allies as 'Val', and heavily influenced by German thinking. Like the Stuka, this was a low-wing monoplane with a fixed spatted undercarriage.

Japanese aircraft carrier design suffered from the country's growing isolation between the two world wars. On many Japanese carriers, the hangar did not run the full length of the hull, and the forward end of the flight deck was often mounted on struts. Two ships, *Akagi* and *Hiryu*, had port side islands, ostensibly so that when operating abeam of other carriers, their air groups would not get in the way during landing and take-off, especially when getting into formation. Many did not have islands, but instead the bridge was under the flight deck. Like some of the early British carriers, the early Japanese carriers had a second flight deck running out of the hangar for aircraft to take-off, and again, like the British, found that this feature fell into disuse as aircraft sizes grew. They were also to find that having two hangar decks improved aircraft accommodation.

The port side islands were supposed to have doubled the accident rate, largely because, for reasons that are not fully understood even today, pilots when in trouble or taking evasive action tend to turn their aircraft to port.

Regardless of whether or not they had an island, and on which side it might have been, most Japanese carriers had the smokestacks on the starboard side and either horizontal or even pointing seaward. This must have been less satisfactory than a conventional vertical smokestack, although on the carriers without an island it did mean that there was nothing for an aircraft to hit. It also meant that there was no risk of a bomb dropping down the smokestack, as happened on at least one occasion with an Allied carrier.

The most conventional Japanese aircraft carrier and the last to be laid down before the attack on Pearl Harbor was the *Taiho*. It is generally believed that had the war continued for longer than was in fact the case, she could have been the lead ship of a class, but despite deciding to restart a carrier building programme half-way through the war using two standard designs, a shortage of shipyard capacity meant that the full programme could not be implemented.

A large fast carrier of 29,000 tons, the *Taiho* was laid down in 1941 and completed in March 1944. She had a service speed of 33 knots and accommodation for more than sixty aircraft. The starboard side island incorporated a funnel, which still angled outwards, but her bow was plated up to the flight deck, giving her a very British appearance. In contrast to the new British carriers, armour plating of the flight deck was limited to the area between the two lifts, although the hangar deck was also armour plated. End and side armour plating was minimal. An eccentric feature was the position of the anti-torpedo protection inboard of the hull. Extra concrete protection was fitted around the fuel tanks. The use of more extensive armour than was usual on Japanese carriers meant that her draught was more than thirty-one feet, which was considerable for her tonnage.

Given the increasingly tense international situation and the problems in US relations with Japan, hostilities should have been expected. Indeed, Admiral Husband Kimmel, the Commander-in-Chief of the United States Navy, had received a warning that war was possible and had been sufficiently concerned to ensure that the Pacific Fleet carriers were not in Pearl Harbor, but failed to ensure liaison and coordination with the United States Army in Hawaii and to order improved defensive measures, still less any state of alert. All of this was despite the fact that the Russo-Japanese War of 1904–1905 had started without a declaration of war by Japan. One reason for Kimmel's inaction was that he saw the Philippines as the most likely target for Japanese attack and invasion. While the Philippines would have been an easier target for the Japanese and would have helped to consolidate their growing hold on China, the advantage of striking in completely the opposite direction, at Pearl Harbor, was that it meant crippling the United States Pacific Fleet and making US communications across the Pacific to reinforce the Philippines, or anywhere else, much more difficult.

Ten days after the attack, Kimmel applied for early retirement and played no further part in the war.

The Attack

By mid-November 1941, everything was ready.

'Japan has faced many worthy opponents in her long history,' declared Admiral Yamamoto on his visit to the flagship *Akagi* on 17 November. 'Mongols, Chinese, Russians – but the United States is the most worthy of all. You must be prepared for great American resistance. Admiral Kimmel, commander-in-chief of the Pacific Fleet, is known to be farsighted and aggressive. You may have to fight your way to the target.'

The Japanese fleet sent to attack Pearl Harbor consisted of six aircraft carriers, the *Akagi*, *Kaga*, *Shokaku*, *Zuikaku*, *Hiryu* and *Soryu*, supported by the two battleships *Hiei* and *Kirishima*, as well as three cruisers and nine destroyers. Given the number of aircraft carriers, the number of escorting vessels was far less than might have been expected, and the fleet could have been vulnerable to surprise attack had American battleships got within range before aircraft could have been launched. It is also highly likely, given the Japanese inability to mount effective anti-submarine defences, that the fleet would have fallen easy prey to submarine attack.

Surprise Attack

On the morning of 7 December, an American destroyer claimed to have sunk a Japanese submarine, although the wreckage was not discovered and identified as such until 2002. Given this incident, there should have been no element of surprise, but not for the first time air forces and navies failed to speak to one another. Awareness might well have put Hawaii's air defences on a higher state of alert. In any event, given what would today be described as a 'deteriorating international situation', the United States should have been extremely suspicious of Japanese intentions.

Those aboard the Japanese carriers knew that war would break out on 8 December, but the date in the US would be a day earlier because of the position of the international date line.

The attack was to be made in two waves, with fighter escorts since the Americans were expected to put up fighters. Awake at 05.00, the first wave aircrew breakfasted as their ships were pitching and rolling to the extent that had it been an exercise, Fuchida would have asked to postpone the operation. Fuchida was being flown by Lieutenant Mutsuzaki, leaving him free to direct the operation. As he climbed into the aircraft aboard the *Akagi*, the senior maintenance crewman handed him a white scarf. 'All of the maintenance crew would like to go along to Pearl Harbor,' he explained. 'Since we can't, we want you to take this *hachimaki* as a symbol that we are with you in spirit.'

Fuchida tied the scarf samurai-fashion around his flight helmet.

At 06.15, the 183 aircraft in the first wave were airborne and formated on Fuchida's aircraft ready for the 275 nautical mile flight to Pearl Harbor. The weather remained poor, with dark clouds, but they were reassured by the forecast of good weather by a radio station in Hawaii, meaning that the target would not be obscured by cloud. Fuchida's English lessons had proven their worth! Below in Hawaii, in a radar station that was just about to close down for the day, an operator dismissed the Japanese aircraft as a flock of birds!

As the massive formation of aircraft approached Pearl Harbor itself, Fuchida fired a rocket to signal that the aircraft should now prepare for an attack, and then saw Murata, leading the torpedo-bombers, head down towards the ships at anchor in Pearl Harbor. A second rocket intended for the fighters was mistaken by the leader of the dive-bombers as a warning of enemy fighters, and immediately led his aircraft down towards their targets. The confusion made little difference to the outcome, but made the attack all the more overwhelming.

Fuchida's aircraft remained at around 10,000 feet as the attack developed. He could see that there were no aircraft carriers, but all eight of the battleships were there, with the USS *Pennsylvania* in dry dock. Japanese intelligence had counted the *Utah*, relegated to the role of target ship, as an active battleship. Most important of all, however, was the absence of the United States Pacific Fleet's aircraft carriers.

With no sign of fighter defences or AA fire at first, the Zero fighters were free to race across the airfield and the dockyards, in 'fighter ramrod' attacks. The few American fighters that struggled to get into the air were shot down. The dive-bombers swooped down towards Ford Island, hitting harbour installations, so that soon the clear blue skies were stained by smoke from the explosions of their bombs and the fires that they started. On Battleship Row, as at Taranto, the torpedo-bombers came in low so as not to damage their torpedoes and, as at Taranto thirteen months earlier, torpedo nets had not been deployed. They were followed by high altitude bombers, but by this time the first AA fire was starting and the bombers had to maintain their steady course through this. Fuchida's own aircraft received a single hit and was shaken by a near miss, but his pilot assured him that everything was well. Fuchida made three passes over his target, the battleship *California*, taking a considerable risk as experience later in the war was to prove that even a second pass over a target put attacking aircraft in a very vulnerable position, so that he could drop his bombs accurately. On the second run, he saw an explosion as the battleship *Arizona*, whose air defences had been enhanced the previous year with additional guns and radar, blew up. His plane was buffeted by the blast.

Fuchida remained behind as the first wave returned to the carriers, waiting for the 170 aircraft of the second wave. The second wave did not include torpedo-bombers since these were seen as highly vulnerable once the AA defences had been alerted, as their attack started fifty minutes after the first wave. The main reason for Fuchida risking loitering over the target was not so much that he was playing what the RAF would later describe as the role of the 'master bomber', but instead he had to assess the damage for his commander, Vice Admiral Nagumo. By this time

35

the *Arizona* was blazing, the *Oklahoma* and *Utah* had both capsized, and both the *California* and *West Virginia* were settling in the water. The light cruiser *Helena* was crippled.

The second wave flew into AA fire augmented by a number of American fighters that had managed to get into the air in the lull between the two waves of the attack. Most of the twenty-nine aircraft lost were from the second wave.

The Americans did what they could to fend off the attack. The captain of the battleship *Nevada* considered his ship would be safer at sea, since a fast moving ship in the open sea would be a much more difficult target, but he had first to get her into open water. Japanese aircraft swarmed around the *Nevada*, realizing that if she could be sunk in the harbour mouth, the entire base would be out of action for some time, with the surviving ships penned in. The attack was overwhelming, but the ship's officers managed to beach her in a position where she would not be an obstruction.

Other aircraft from the second wave damaged the *Pennsylvania* and two destroyers in dry dock.

Casualties amongst those aboard the ships and ashore were extremely heavy, with a total of 3,581 United States naval personnel either killed or wounded. In contrast to Taranto more than a year earlier, three American warships, the battleship USS *Arizona* and two destroyers, blew up, while another, the USS *Oklahoma*, capsized, and it was this as well as the sheer scale of the attack that made the casualty figures so high. No less than 188 United States Army Air Force and Unites States Navy aircraft ashore had been destroyed in the attack.

Fuchida returned to the *Akagi*. The carriers were busy landing aircraft and striking them down into hangars; any that caused an obstruction were quickly pushed over the side, losing a further fifteen aircraft in this way. Had the Americans known the location of the fleet and been able to mount an attack, at this stage all six carriers would have been highly vulnerable, as with their flight decks completely taken over by the returning aircraft, it would have been impossible to have put up fighters.

As Fuchida climbed out of his aircraft, someone pointed to a large shell hole behind the cockpit, through which the control wire was hanging by barely a thread. He had narrowly escaped being shot down.

The Japanese planners had considered that a third wave, and possibly a fourth wave, would find plenty of targets remaining to be attacked. But Nagumo decided not to mount another attack on Pearl Harbor, even though their aircraft had been refuelled and re-armed. Many had torpedoes to attack any American warships at sea giving chase. Fuchida protested, but was told curtly by Kusaka, Nagumo's chief of staff, that the attack's objectives had been met!

Nagumo thought that a third or fourth wave would suffer severe losses from the American defences, but undoubtedly he was even more worried about being attacked by the Pacific Fleet's carrier-borne aircraft. This threat was real, but with six carriers, he could have mounted a strong defence once the returning fighters had been re-armed. In any event, he should also have put reconnaissance aircraft into the air to maintain a watch for American ships. Losses would have been heavy if third and fourth waves had been sent, with the American defences now on a high state of alert, but without the further waves, Pearl Harbor remained an operational base, in contrast to Fuchida's belief that the main battle fleet would not be able to operate for six months.

The attack had failed to change the balance of power in the Pacific. When he heard of Nagumo's decision, Admiral Yamamoto felt that his subordinate had failed in not ordering a further attack.

If the tactics were at fault, so too was the Japanese strategy. Japanese commanders failed to follow up Pearl Harbor with measures designed to make it more difficult for the United States Navy to reinforce its Pacific Fleet. An attack on the Panama Canal or intensive mining of its Pacific end, would have been helpful, forcing the Americans to send their warships around Cape Horn and the entire land mass of South America. Sabotage of the Panama Canal's extensive lock system would have closed it for months, if not longer. Yet, the Canal escaped the war unscathed and always remained as a short cut between the Pacific and the Atlantic.

IV

CONFRONTING THE ENEMY
AT SEA

'They looked like giant vultures,' recalled Admiral Iachino.
'Flying around their prey until a favourable moment should
present itself to descend.'

The 'giant vultures' were none other than our old friends the
Fairey Swordfishes, this time pressing home their attack on
the Italian fleet at the Battle of Cape Matapan. The arrival of
the *Luftwaffe* in Sicily had created an unusual situation in the
Mediterranean. The Royal Navy had control of the sea, but
the *Luftwaffe* had control of the air, at least in the central
Mediterranean. The presence of the new aircraft carrier
Formidable and bases in Egypt, Crete and Greece meant that
some resistance to the *Luftwaffe* could be maintained in the
eastern Mediterranean. Meanwhile, Cunningham was as
anxious as ever to bring the Italian fleet to battle, and by this
time fully aware of the potential of naval aviation. By this time,
thanks to the success at Taranto, the two navies were more
evenly balanced, with both having three battleships, the British
ships being Cunningham's flagship, the *Warspite*, and the *Valiant*,
as well as the *Malaya*, which despite being the same class as the
other two had not enjoyed the same degree of modernization.
While the Italians were stronger in submarines, destroyers and
cruisers, they lacked an aircraft carrier, although in itself this was
probably not a major disadvantage given Italy's geographical
position, protruding into the Mediterranean and almost cutting
it in half. Of much greater significance was the lack of effective
communication and coordination between the Italian Navy, the
Regia Navale, and the Italian Air Force, the *Regia Aeronautica*, and
what seems to have been the inability of the Italians to take the
potential of naval aviation into account.

In late March 1941, British reconnaissance aircraft had discovered the Italian fleet at sea, exactly what Cunningham had been hoping for. The problem was that once the Mediterranean Fleet put to sea, the Italians would probably, on previous form, race for shelter. Alexandria was supposed to be full of Axis agents and so to fool them, on 27 March Cunningham went ashore with a suitcase, hoping to convince any spies that he intended spending the night ashore. Indeed, while the presence of Italian and especially German agents in Alexandria was doubtless exaggerated, the Japanese consul was known to pass on any fleet movements he observed, although no one could be sure that his information was passed on in time to be of use to the Italians. Cunningham made sure that he spent his afternoon on the golf course, the favourite post-meridian haunt of the Japanese consul, a short squat man of such elephantine proportions when he bent over that Cunningham's irreverent chief-of-staff had come to describe him as 'the blunt end of the Axis'.

'We intentionally sent principal staff officers away by air during the day so to allay all the Italian agents' apprehension; we kept our awnings spread and the Admiral invited people to dinner,' recalled S.W.C. Pack, one of *Formidable*'s senior officers. 'As soon as it was dark we furled our awnings, the officers returned, and the dinner was cancelled.'

The Mediterranean Fleet left Alexandria and slipped out to sea under cover of darkness. Cunningham had his flagship, *Warspite*, plus two other battleships, *Valiant* and the elderly and unmodernized *Barham*, which kept close company with the aircraft carrier *Formidable*. This force had as a screen nine destroyers. Unfortunately, while leaving this unsatisfactory harbour, with poor defences, badly maintained and poorly dredged, *Warspite* passed too close to a mud bank, filling her condensers with mud, and reducing her maximum speed to around 20 knots.

Also under cover of darkness, the one convoy at sea in the danger area was ordered to reverse its course.

Meanwhile, Vice Admiral Pridham-Whippell was ordered out of the Aegean Sea to be at a point south-west of Gavdo Island at dawn on 28 March. Pridham-Whippell was in the cruiser *Orion*, accompanied by the *Ajax*, *Perth* and *Gloucester*, escorted by just four destroyers.

Battle of Cape Matapan

By 06.00 on the morning of 28 March, there was sufficient light for *Formidable* to launch aircraft for reconnaissance and anti-submarine patrols as well as establishing a fighter combat air patrol over the fleet. First reports came at 07.20 when four cruisers and four destroyers were spotted to the north-east of the British ships, and at first this was assumed to be Pridham-Whippell's force, but doubts arose when this report was followed at 07.39 by a sighting of four cruisers and six destroyers. The immediate reaction was that this could have been the same force, then there was concern that one force could be Italian and the other the British cruiser force. Cunningham was also concerned because, as he noted in his memoirs, *A Sailor's Odyssey*, aerial reconnaissance had in the past confused Italian cruisers with battleships. Concerned that Pridham-Whippell could be facing Italian battleships and heavy cruisers, with the latter's high speed and 8-inch guns giving them superiority, at 09.39, Cunningham ordered *Formidable* to fly off six Fairey Albacores that had been ranged along her flight deck ready for just such an eventuality. This action saved the British light cruisers who were being chased by the battleship *Vittorio Veneto* and the Italian heavy cruisers, but not before the cruiser *Gloucester* was hit.

At 11.27, the aircraft from the carrier appeared, escorted by Fairey Fulmar fighters that shot down two Junkers Ju88 fighter-bombers and drove a third Ju88 off. Flying through heavy AA fire, the Albacores pressed home their torpedo attack and although they failed to score any hits, succeeded in forcing the *Vittorio Veneto* to break off the action. Meanwhile, a second strike of three Albacores and two Swordfish from the carrier's 829 Squadron had been flown off, in part to clear the decks for the return of the first strike, who landed at 12.44 just in time for a torpedo-bombing run by two Savoia-Marchetti SM79s against *Formidable*, which managed to avoid being hit.

'*Formidable*'s log for this day shows that flying operations were conducted on twenty-one separate occasions,' recalled S.W.C. Pack. 'Each operation might occupy only a few minutes but required an alteration of course into the wind which was upsetting when the whole fleet had to conform to these movements to ensure that the destroyer screen would remain effective. Essential routine operations severely limited the number of aircraft that could be made ready for the big strikes. She had a total of only twenty-seven aircraft on board: thirteen Fulmars, ten Albacores (of which only five were fitted with long-range tanks) and four Swordfish. These had to cover all routine requirements, such as fighter protection and anti-submarine patrol in addition to the shadowing, mass reconnaissance and offensive strikes needed in battle: a pitiably small force when compared with the large forces available in carriers in the Pacific Campaign of 1945.'

The Albacore was another biplane, albeit with an enclosed cockpit, and intended as a replacement for the Swordfish. In fact, the aircraft, with its Bristol Taurus engine of 1,065 hp on early versions, and 1,130 hp on later versions, was unreliable.

That afternoon, the RAF sent Bristol Blenheim bombers from Greek bases to make four attacks on the Italian ships, but the high altitude bombing resulted only in near misses and no hits. The second wave of aircraft from the carrier arrived, led by Lieutenant Commander Dalyell-Stead and, while his fighter cover machine-gunned the superstructure of the battleship in an attempt to force the AA gunners keep their heads down, three Albacores dropped their torpedoes, although the first aircraft was blown out of the sky by AA fire, just seconds before its torpedo struck the *Vittorio Veneto* just above the port outer screw and fifteen feet below the waterline. The stricken battleship shipped a massive quantity of water and within minutes her engines stopped. It took damage control parties ninety minutes to get the battleship moving again at reduced speed, so that at 17.00 she was moving at 15 knots.

A further air strike materialized at dusk, led by Lieutenant Commander Gerald Saunt with six Albacores of 826 Squadron and two Swordfish of 829 Squadron, as well as another two Swordfish from Maleme in Crete. These aircraft struck the heavy cruiser *Pola*, causing her to lose speed. Not anticipating a night battle, Admiral Iachino sent the two heavy cruisers *Fiume* and *Zara* with four destroyers to the aid of the *Pola*.

Cunningham, meanwhile, had mistaken the radar trace of the *Pola* for the *Vittorio Veneto*, and as his ships prepared to fire, the other two Italian cruisers, lacking radar, crossed the path of his ships and drew the fire of the three British battleships, hitting both the Italian cruisers and two destroyers with their 15-inch broadsides. All three cruisers and both destroyers were then sunk by torpedoes from British destroyers. In the heat of the battle, *Formidable* was picked up by *Warspite*'s searchlights and her gunnery officer was preparing to attack her with his 6-inch secondary armament when, just in time, he realized his mistake.

At daylight, the Mediterranean Fleet started to pick up Italian survivors, pulling 900 men from the sea before the arrival of the *Luftwaffe* forced them to withdraw, but many more Italian lives were saved when Cunningham communicated the position of the survivors to Rome, allowing the Italian Navy to mount a rescue.

While Matapan was a great success for the British, it did little to delay the German invasion of Greece, and during the battle for Crete that followed, on 26 May *Formidable* was badly damaged by Ju87 Stuka dive-bombers after mounting a successful raid on the German airfield at Scarpanto (known today as Karpathos) on Rhodes. The problem by this stage was that the British were desperately short of aircraft in the Mediterranean, afloat and ashore. The real success of Matapan had been that it enabled the British to control the seas around Crete, enabling British and Greek troops to be evacuated to Egypt and hindering the seaborne element of the German invasion, but at considerable cost, given German mastery of the air. Cunningham had in fact signalled to the Mediterranean Fleet on 22 May: 'Stick it out. Navy must not let Army down. No enemy forces must reach Crete by sea.' It might have been even better if Crete had only been used as a staging post rather than occupied and defended.

At the height of the battle it had been decided to attack Scarpanto on which many German aircraft were based. German aerial attack had seriously damaged the Mediterranean Fleet which had lost two cruisers and four destroyers, with a battleship, another two cruisers and four destroyers badly damaged. HMS *Formidable* had been deployed for the attack, with her squadron of Fulmars built up to twelve aircraft to attempt to provide air cover, although, as Cunningham himself noted, 'some were of doubtful utility'. Command of the operation had been given to Pridham-Whippell, who used the battleship HMS *Queen Elizabeth* as his flagship and also had the *Barham* as well as the carrier and eight destroyers. Sailing from Alexandria at noon on 25 May, between 05.00 and 06.00 the following morning, the carrier sent four Fairey Albacores and four Fairey Fulmars 100 miles to attack Scarpanto. This puny force achieved complete surprise and was able to destroy and damage a number of aircraft on the ground, but it was far from enough to put the airfield out of action.

Not surprisingly, alerted by this attack to the carrier's presence, later in the morning radar picked up enemy aircraft approaching. By this stage, *Formidable* had just eight serviceable Fulmars, and these were launched on no less than twenty-four sorties and engaged enemy aircraft twenty times, shooting down a number of the Axis aircraft. At 13.20, as Pridham-Whippell was withdrawing, twenty aircraft approached from North Africa, and in the dive-bombing attacks that followed, the carrier was hit twice by 2,200-lb bombs and badly damaged, while the destroyer *Nubian* had her stern blown off, yet could still manage to steam at 20 knots!

Once again, the Mediterranean Fleet had its carrier damaged 'beyond local repair'. It would take six months before *Formidable* would be ready for service again. This time, however, there could be no replacement.

Sink the Bismarck!

In contrast to the First World War, in the Second World War the German *Kriegsmarine* had no intention of seeking a major fleet action with the Royal Navy. It had a far more effective weapon at its disposal in the U-boat campaign, augmenting this by commerce raiders. German naval strategy was based on the premise that it took many more naval vessels to hunt down submarines and surface raiders and to protect convoys than it took to attack them, while the submarine campaign of the First World War had nearly brought Britain to its knees.

The two most impressive surface raiders were the battleships *Bismarck* and *Tirpitz*. *Bismarck* had an official net displacement of 46,000 tonnes and a full load displacement of 50,955 tonnes, although a post-war United States Navy assessment put the latter figure at closer to 53,000 tonnes. A broad beam ensured that she had the stability to act as an effective gun platform in the open seas and three screws gave her a maximum speed of 30 knots. Heavily armoured, the ship had two twin 38-cm, approximately 15-inch, turrets forward and another two aft. Her reconnaissance aircraft were four single-engined Arado Ar196 monoplane floatplanes, capable of flying at almost 200mph. Her ship's company in 1941 totalled 2,200 men, including an admiral's staff and war correspondents.

On 18 May 1941, *Bismarck*, in company with the heavy cruiser *Prinz Eugen*, put to sea from the German port of Gotenhafen under the command of Admiral Gunther Lutjens, to commence a raiding operation code-named Operation Rhine Exercise. Curiously, for such an operation, *Bismarck*'s fuel tanks were not completely full as a hose had given way and interrupted fuelling, and even when the ships called at Korsfjord in Norway, the opportunity to replenish them was not taken. On leaving Norway, the German ships were soon spotted by the Royal Navy and shadowed by two heavy cruisers, *Suffolk* and *Norfolk*, which managed to hang on to the Germans by using their radar despite heavy seas. Vice Admiral Holland took the battlecruiser *Hood*, between the two world wars the pride of the Royal Navy, and the new and still not fully worked up battleship *Prince of Wales*, intending to bring the Germans to battle. On 24 May, the four ships met in what was to be a classic naval engagement, in the course of which *Hood* blew up with the loss of 1,500 men, leaving just three survivors, generally believed to have been caused by a German shell penetrating one of her magazines. The *Prince of Wales* was forced to retire after taking several hits from the German ships. Nevertheless, the *Bismarck* herself was hit three times, breaking the connections from the forward fuel tanks and also causing a fuel leak that caused Lutjens to break company with the *Prinz Eugen* and head for St Nazaire, with Brest as an alternative, in occupied France. The failure to fill up completely was now being felt.

Throughout this drama, the cruisers *Norfolk* and *Suffolk* had continued to track *Bismarck*. At 21.30 GMT, 22.30 British Summer Time, nine Fairey Swordfish from HMS *Victorious* found the *Bismarck* and launched a torpedo attack.

'In seconds, every anti-aircraft gun on the *Bismarck* was ready for action,' recalled *Oberleutnant* Baron Burkhard von Mullenheim-Rechberg, the ship's adjutant and fourth gunnery officer.

> One after the other, the planes came towards us, nine Swordfish, torpedoes under their fuselages. Daringly they flew through our fire, nearer to the fire-spitting mountain of the *Bismarck*, always nearer and still nearer. Watching through my director, which, having been designed for surface targets, had a high degree of magnification but only a narrow field, I could not see all of the action . . . But what I could see was exciting enough.
>
> Our anti-aircraft batteries . . . fired into the water ahead of the aircraft, raising massive water spouts. To fly into

one of those spouts would mean the end. And the aircraft, they were moving so slowly that they seemed to be standing still in the air . . . the pilots pressed their attack with suicidal courage.

Bismarck increased her speed to 27 knots and started to zigzag, but the Swordfish had planned their attack from different directions so that to avoid one torpedo meant putting the ship in the way of another. One torpedo dropped at close range hit the ship before it could get to its set depth, hitting the armour belt at the water-line amidships, doing little damage but killing a warrant officer and injuring six engineers. The attack was followed by a brief gunnery exchange with the *Prince of Wales*, but this was broken off in the fading light.

On 25 May, Vice Admiral Sir James Somerville sailed from Gibraltar with Force H, including the aircraft carrier *Ark Royal*, the battlecruiser *Renown* and two cruisers. Contact with the *Bismarck* was lost early the following morning, but later an RAF Consolidated Catalina flying boat rediscovered the ship. Early in the afternoon, in rough weather, fifteen Swordfish took off from the *Ark Royal* while the cruiser *Sheffield* was ordered to maintain contact with the German ship. Unaware of the *Sheffield*'s presence, as the Swordfish dropped out of the clouds they attacked her by mistake and she was only saved by her high speed and prompt evasive action, as well as faults in the torpedo magnetic detonators. Meanwhile, closing in on the *Bismarck* was Admiral Tovey, commander-in-chief of the Royal Navy's Home Fleet, with the battleships *King George V* and *Rodney*, and a destroyer escort. Tovey signalled Somerville that unless *Bismarck*'s speed could be reduced, he would have to withdraw *King George V* to refuel and leave *Rodney* on her own.

At 19.15, again in low cloud and poor visibility, a further strike by fifteen Swordfish was launched from *Ark Royal*, and on this occasion the torpedoes were fitted with contact detonators which required a direct hit. Once again they appeared over the *Sheffield*, which pointed them in the direction of the *Bismarck*, but thirty minutes later the aircraft were back looking for fresh directions. This time the sound of heavy AA fire told those aboard the cruiser that the Swordfish had found the *Bismarck*.

'They approached even more recklessly than the planes from the *Victorious* had done,' recalled von Mullenheim-Rechberg.

Every pilot seemed to know what this attack meant to Tovey . . .

Once more, the *Bismarck* became a fire-spitting mountain. The racket of her anti-aircraft guns was joined by the roar from her main and secondary armaments as they fired into the bubbling paths of the torpedoes, creating splashes ahead of the attackers. The antique-looking Swordfish, fifteen of them, seemed to hang in the air, near enough to touch. The high cloud layer . . . probably did not permit a synchronised attack from all directions, but the Swordfish came so quickly after one another that our defence did not have it any easier . . . They flew low, the spray of the heaving seas masking their landing gear . . .

Von Mullenheim-Rechberg watched the rudder indicator in his position moving frantically as the battleship zigzagged, while the engine room was told repeatedly to stop, or to increase speed, or even to go astern, all in an attempt to avoid the torpedoes. Then, he heard two torpedoes strike the ship, one immediately after the other, and saw the rudder indicator jammed at left 12 degrees as the ship went into a continuous turn.

All fifteen aircraft returned safely to *Ark Royal*.

The situation aboard the battleship was critical. The rudder would have to be cut off or blown off to allow her to manoeuvre on her engines, and while using the hangar door as a makeshift rudder was considered, the rough seas prevented this. The steering rooms had in any case been flooded by the massive hole in the hull, which had also closed a safety valve shutting down the starboard engines, although this was quickly repaired.

Meanwhile, the two British battleships were fortunate to be passing *U-556* just as she was returning from a mission and had expended all of her torpedoes, otherwise one at least of them would have made a good target!

That night, British destroyers carried out a torpedo attack on the *Bismarck*, but did little further damage. It was left to *King George V* and *Rodney* to engage the *Bismarck* in a gunnery duel on the morning of 27 May, hitting her several times so that after ninety minutes she was burning fiercely. A further strike by Swordfish was put into the air, but had to turn back because of the heavy rate of fire from the two British battleships. Then, two cruisers also torpedoed the stricken ship. Eventually, Captain

Lindemann gave the order to abandon ship, with the British cruiser *Devonshire*, picking up some of the survivors before one of them told his rescuers that U-boats were coming, causing the cruiser to move away. Whether this was a ruse to avoid becoming a prisoner of war and in the hope of being rescued by a German ship, we will never know, but as a result, of the 2,200 men aboard the *Bismarck*, just 115 survived.

For HMS *Ark Royal*, the victory over the *Bismarck* was relatively short-lived. On 13 November 1941, the ship was torpedoed by *U 81* thirty miles east of Gibraltar. The ship remained afloat until the next day and preparations were made to tow her into Gibraltar, but a severe list developed and she eventually slipped beneath the waves. Just one member of her ship's company was killed. Many British naval officers blamed bad damage control for the loss of the ship, but while there may be some justification for this, the torpedo had knocked out her machinery making pumping difficult. The irony was that the ship had always been seen as vulnerable to aerial attack, so much so that when Britain's commander in the Mediterranean, Admiral Sir Andrew Cunningham, 'ABC' to his men, pressed for carriers to transport replacement aircraft for the RAF in Malta, he was reminded sharply by the First Sea Lord, Sir Dudley Pound, of what might have happened had it been *Ark Royal* rather than *Illustrious* that had been attacked off Malta in January of that year. It was also the case that this was a ship that German propaganda had claimed to have sunk on several occasions, so that the term: 'Where is the *Ark Royal*?' had become something of a joke. In fact, many ashore, with no knowledge of her weaknesses, had come to believe that the ship was unsinkable.

The loss of *Ark Royal* and similar problems with their own carriers under attack also led the Americans to displace the machinery on their new fleet carriers, the Midway-class, so that it would become increasingly difficult to cripple a carrier with one blow as at least one set of machinery would remain operational after an attack.

Petsamo and Kirkenes

Relief for those at home in the British Isles, and indeed for those in the besieged island of Malta in the Mediterranean, came with the German invasion of the Soviet Union in June 1941. Resources were moved from France and Italy to drive through Soviet occupied Poland and into Russia herself. The Soviet Union, which had been effectively a German ally at the outset, was now an ally of the British. But it was an unreliable and uncertain ally for the two nations had nothing in common. Russia was also a demanding ally, having failed to prepare for a German invasion, despite the warnings and despite the signals which had left little scope for misunderstanding German intentions, it expected the hard-pressed British to demonstrate their commitment to Russia's survival. The British, not without some cause, were concerned that Russia might try to reach an accommodation with Germany – ceding parts of the Soviet Union's territory was considered by Stalin before and immediately after the German invasion.

While the British wished to encourage the Russians, opportunities for doing so were limited.

German possession of the ports of Petsamo and Kirkenes, north of the Arctic Circle made it more difficult for Russia's new allies to send supplies, since the direct route through the Baltic was completely out of the question!

Kirkenes, in Norway, had been taken by the Germans as they advanced in the spring and early summer of 1940. Petsamo, or Pechenga to the Russians, had changed hands on a number of occasions. Originally part of Russia, it became part of Finland when that country became independent in the wake of the Bolshevik Revolution, but it was one of the towns lost again as the price of peace in the Russo-Finnish War of 1940–41, and then regained as the Germans advanced towards Moscow.

In 1941, still fresh from its victory at Taranto, the only possible means of making an impact on the German forces attacking the Soviet Union lay with the Royal Navy, and especially with naval air power. The Commander-in Chief, Home Fleet, was urged by Britain's wartime leader, Winston Churchill, to carry out an attack which would be ' a gesture in support of our Russian allies to create a diversion on the enemy's northern flank'.

For the operation, the Royal Navy deployed one of its newest aircraft carriers and its oldest. The new vessel was HMS *Victorious*, a sister of HMS *Illustrious*, while the other ship was HMS *Furious*, the first aircraft carrier. Aircraft still included the veteran Fairey Swordfish biplanes, but this time they were to be complemented by Fairey Albacore torpedo-bombers, and escorted by Fairey Fulmar fighters. Aircraft from *Victorious* included twenty Fairey Albacore torpedo-bombers from 827 and 828 Naval Air Squadrons, escorted by Fairey Fulmar fighters from 809 Squadron. The elderly *Furious* sent nine Fairey Swordfish of 812 Squadron and nine Albacores of 817 Squadron, escorted by the Fulmars of 800 Squadron.

The Albacore was intended as a successor for the Swordfish, yet this was another biplane, with its main concession to the changing times being an enclosed cockpit. If providing yet another museum-piece for the Fleet Air Arm wasn't bad enough, the Albacore was to prove to be notoriously unreliable, so that the Swordfish was to outlive both the Albacore and its successor, the Barracuda, a 'maintenance nightmare' in the words of one naval officer, in frontline operational service. Barracudas sent with the Fleet Air Arm when it returned to the Far East were soon withdrawn, especially as better American aircraft became available to the Royal Navy, but even in the less demanding climatic conditions of the North Atlantic, the Barracuda became notorious for some of its less desirable habits, such as not pulling out of a dive!

The Operation

This could not be a repeat of the Taranto raid using more modern and more capable aircraft. The raid had to take place in daylight because of the almost twenty-four hour summer daylight of the far north, while German aerial reconnaissance was far more methodical than that of the Italians, so that the presence of the carriers was soon known, and their intentions guessed, by German reconnaissance aircraft. Despite these additional problems, the targets were themselves far less worthwhile than Taranto as neither port had the mass of significant warships that had been waiting at Taranto. The final approaches to the targets were also far more difficult.

Aircraft were flown off late in the afternoons of 22 and 25 July 1941. *Victorious* was to send twenty Albacore torpedo-bombers to Kirkenes, escorted by Fulmar fighters, while *Furious* was to send nine Albacores and nine Swordfish, again escorted by Fulmars, to Petsamo, or Pechenga. The aircraft from *Victorious* had to fly over a German hospital ship on the way in to the target, and were ordered not to attack this, although, of course, those aboard could warn those ashore.

At Kirkenes the aircraft had to fly over a mountain at the end of the fjord before diving into the bay, where they found just four ships. After enduring heavy anti-aircraft fire from positions on the cliffs, the attackers were themselves attacked by German fighters, and most of them had to jettison their torpedoes in a desperate bid to escape. They managed to sink just one cargo vessel of 2,000 tons, and set another on fire. The slow and lumbering Fulmars did well to shoot down four *Luftwaffe* aircraft.

'We went from one side of Kirkenes Bay, and 827 Squadron went in from the other side,' recalls Petty Officer Francis Smith, a telegraphist-airgunner with 828 Squadron.

> . . . all of a sudden, there's flaming onions and God knows what else coming down at us – because we're flying up the fjord, and the Germans are firing down, from the cliffs with light ack-ack. Not funny at all.
>
> So we go in so far, and we have to climb over the end of the fjord . . . and over the mountain and down into the bay. And there's all this mass shipping – about four little ships. And before anything can happen, there were 110s and Stukas all over the place – they're all airborne . . . they're there, waiting for us.
>
> And they start . . . By now the ack-ack has stopped firing, they've left it to the Stukas and the 110s, and they're blasting away with cannon-shells and God knows what. Well, almost immediately, my last sub-flight all got shot down . . . Everyone jettisoned their torpedoes . . . nobody got a chance to fire at any ship.[1]

Petsamo was even worse, for the harbour was empty. Frustrated aircrew could do nothing more than aim their torpedoes at the wharves, hoping to do at least some damage.

Having received such a hot welcome, for so little of any value in the target area, the attackers attempted to make their escape. This was easier said than done, for the aircraft were easy prey for the German fighters. The normal defensive drill in such circumstances was for the Swordfish or Albacore pilots to go right down on the water and wait, with the TAGs watching for the cannon shells hitting the water, and at the last second calling out to the pilot, 'hard-a-starboard' or 'hard-a-port'. Flying just above the surface of the water also meant that the fighters had to pull out early or risk a high speed dive into the sea.

In the operation, *Victorious* lost thirteen of her aircraft, while *Furious* lost three. Altogether, forty-four aircrew were lost, seven of them killed, the remainder taken prisoner. Had the losses at Taranto been on a similar scale, seven aircraft would have been lost rather than just the two.

Tovey's reaction was simple and straightforward: 'The gallantry of the aircraft crews, who knew before leaving that their chance of surprise had gone, and that they were certain to face heavy odds, is beyond praise . . . I trust that the encouragement to the morale of our allies was proportionately great.'

In short, great risks had been taken and heavy losses suffered for no material or strategic benefit at all!

Notes
[1] Imperial War Museum Sound Archive Accession No. 10476/4

V

THE CONVOY WAR

In the First World War, the Royal Navy had been extremely slow to institute a convoy system, something for which it has been soundly criticized since, not least because the protection of merchant shipping has always been one of the service's primary tasks. Even before the Second World War broke out, the Admiralty Trade Division made the protection of merchant shipping an overriding concern. It was clear that in any future war, the submarine would be an ever greater threat than it had been in the earlier conflict.

Convoys are as old as maritime history, having originated to protect Roman shipping against Mediterranean pirates. Much later, convoys were used by the Spaniards to protect shipping to and from their American colonies. During the Napoleonic wars, the British used convoys, and it seems all the more strange that they were so slow to organize convoys during the Great War when shipping had not only to contend with surface raiders, but with the hidden menace of the submarine. After the entry of the United States into the Second World War following the attack on Pearl Harbor, the United States Navy and Coast Guard were reluctant at first to organize coastal convoys off the US eastern seaboard, but an upsurge in losses to U-boats soon changed this.

It soon became clear that the most effective anti-submarine weapon was the aeroplane, and both land-based and carrier-borne aircraft played a major role in keeping convoys safe. The limited range of maritime-reconnaissance aircraft at the outbreak of the Second World War meant that shipping was highly vulnerable in the so-called 'Atlantic Gap'; that stretch of ocean that was beyond the reach of shore-based aircraft on either side of the ocean. As successive aircraft types entered service, the gap began to shrink, but at the outset the most effective counter seemed to be to use carrier-borne aircraft. Regardless of their range, shore-based maritime-reconnaissance aircraft also suffer from having to provide many more aircraft to provide cover for a convoy than those accompanying a convoy aboard a carrier. For every aircraft patrolling above the convoy, there would be one on its way out to act as a replacement, one on its way back to base, and one on the ground being prepared for its next mission. Given the need for the crews to have time to eat and sleep, and aircraft needing more than the minimum of re-arming and refuelling, it could easily take six aircraft to ensure one maintained a presence over a convoy at all times.

The short range of many aircraft also meant that fighters in particular had to be shipped rather than flown across the North Atlantic, until the advent of the long-range escort fighter, by which time the Allies had secured bases in Iceland. One idea investigated was the creation of a large airbase made of ice in mid-Atlantic. It was found that by mixing ice with woodpulp, a concoction known as pykrete by its inventor, Hermann Mark, an Austrian-born chemist, the ice lost much of its brittleness. Tests proved that pykrete was weight for weight as strong as concrete, and did not shatter on being hit by a projectile. But that unless cooled to at least minus 15 degrees Celsius it tended to sag slowly under its own weight – not something that could be guaranteed. The Fleet Air Arm requirement was for a deck that was fifty feet above the waterline, 200 feet wide and 2,000 feet long. The Admiralty had even higher expectations, requiring it to be self-propelled with a hull at least forty feet thick to be able to withstand torpedo attack! If this seemed impossible, someone then demanded a cruising range of 7,000 miles. In the end, these requirements added up to a vessel that had a theoretical displacement of 2.2 million tons with a rudder the height of a fifteen storey building. The simple iceberg had developed to the stage that the United States Navy estimated that the volume of steel needed to freeze sufficient pykrete in a single winter was going to be greater than the amount needed to build a comparable ship of steel. Needless to say, the project was abandoned.

Convoys were never compulsory, but it was either a foolish shipowner or master who failed to take advantage of them, or one with a very fast ship. An impression of the importance of convoys can be gathered from the statistics. In the Second World War, there were 2,889 escorted trade convoys to and from the UK, with a total of 85,775 ships. Out of these, 654 were sunk, a loss rate of 0.7 per cent. There were in addition another 7,944 coastal convoys, comprising 175,608 ships, of which 248 were sunk, a loss rate of 0.14 per cent. This latter figure has to be put into perspective, for after the fall of France coastal convoys did not operate through the English Channel because of the danger of enemy attack, and instead their cargo became yet another burden for the railways.

Convoys were not universally accepted. Fast troopships such as the former liners, *Queen Mary* and *Queen Elizabeth*, sailed alone, relying on speed to keep them safe. To the convoy losses have to be added the independent sailing of ships not in convoy. In 1942 alone, these accounted for 840 merchant vessels lost to U-boats, against 299 from convoys, but at least a fifth of the convoy losses were stragglers; ships that for one reason or another could not keep up with the rest of the convoy.

The nature of the convoy and the protection afforded varied from one theatre to another. The most dangerous convoys were those across the Mediterranean in the struggle to sustain the defence of Malta, but the grimmest were those to Russia, sailing past occupied Norway and north of the Arctic Circle, the weather was as much an enemy as the *Kriegsmarine* and the *Luftwaffe*. A total of 811 ships sailed in the Arctic convoys to Russia, of which 720 completed their voyages, another thirty-three turned back for one reason or another, and fifty-eight were sunk, giving a loss rate of 7.2 per cent. Of the ships that reached Russia, 717 sailed back (some were being delivered to the Soviet Union), and of these, twenty-nine were sunk, a loss rate of 4 per cent. This was the price of delivering to Russia some 4 million tons of war stores, including 5,000 tanks and more than 7,000 aircraft. It is worth reflecting that the sinking of a 10,000 ton freighter, was the equivalent, in terms of lost equipment and ordnance, of a land battle.

The Second World War convoys across the North Atlantic saw the birth of Canadian and Dutch naval aviation, brought into being as part of the Royal Navy's Fleet Air Arm and at first fully integrated with it.

The seven aircraft carriers available to the Royal Navy on the outbreak of war in Europe were insufficient for protection, and often needed elsewhere. Such ships were occasionally assigned to protect a convoy – especially those to Malta – but these were desperate circumstances. On the other hand, some of the British losses in the early years were of ships that might have been better used as escort carriers, especially the small *Hermes*.

Despite the official US stance of neutrality as the war developed in Europe, the United States Navy soon took on the role of escorting convoys in the western Atlantic, ostensibly to ensure that neutral shipping was not engaged by German submarines. The rules of engagement were refined after a German U-boat attacked the destroyer USS *Greer* on 4 September 1941, while on passage from the United States to Iceland, and carrying mail and passengers. The destroyer attacked with depth charges. Although a second torpedo was fired, neither the destroyer nor the U-boat was damaged. For their part, the Royal Navy made facilities available to the United States Navy at Londonderry in Northern Ireland. The then commander of US naval forces in the Atlantic, Admiral Ernest King, had remarked on taking up his post that it was like being given a big slice of bread with 'damn little butter', reflecting on the shortage of ships. After the battleships *Idaho*, *Mississippi* and *New Mexico* had been transferred with the aircraft carrier *Yorktown* from the Pacific to the Atlantic, despite growing tensions with Japan, the President of the United States, Franklin D. Roosevelt, asked King how he liked the butter he was getting. Came the reply: 'The butter's fine, but you keep giving me more bread.'

The Merchant Aircraft Carriers

Recognizing that there would be a desperate shortage of aircraft carriers once war broke out, the Admiralty cancelled plans for its new fast armoured carriers to replace the older carriers of 1918 and the early 1920s, and also increased the order for the new carriers from four ships to six. Other measures were also considered as time began to run out. During the late 1930s, the Admiralty's Trade Division had advanced a scheme to provide small 'trade protection carriers'. Conversion of the new fast liners RMS *Queen Mary* and *Queen Elizabeth* to aircraft carriers was also considered, but rejected, partly because of the lack of suitable aircraft but also because these ships were seen as being invaluable as troop transports.

In 1940, Captain, later Rear Admiral, M. S. Slattery, Director of Air Material at the British Admiralty, proposed two solutions to the shortage of aircraft carriers, both involving the use of merchantmen. One idea was to use merchant vessels with simple flight decks placed over their holds; the other was to equip other merchant vessels with catapults for fighters. The problem with the first idea was that the ships would be too small and too slow to operate fighters, so anti-submarine Swordfish would be all that could be carried. As for the second idea, the catapult-launched fighters had to be expendable, for as with the fighters flown off lighters towed by destroyers in the First World War, there would be nowhere for these aircraft to land after their one and only sortie against German bombers and maritime-reconnaissance aircraft. Combined, these two ideas would provide an urgent and cost-effective solution to convoy protection.

True to Slattery's vision were the merchant aircraft carriers, or MAC-ships, of which there were two kinds; tankers, able to carry three Swordfish, and grain ships, which could carry four Swordfish. The grain ships had a hold aft converted as a hangar, with an aircraft hoist so that all four aircraft could, with wings folded, be struck down into it, affording some protection from the elements. The grain ships had a shorter flight deck, at between 413 and 424 feet, than the 460 feet of the tankers, but the extra length of the tanker deck was cancelled out because aircraft could only be parked on the deck, reducing the take-off run. Without a hangar, maintenance work was difficult and unpleasant in bad weather, and often dangerous, if not altogether impossible. On both types of ship, flight deck width was sixty-two feet.

Thirty-five merchant vessels were rapidly converted with catapults, becoming Catapult Aircraft Merchant Ships, CAM-ships, sailing under the Red Ensign and still carrying their normal cargo, with the aircraft usually flown by RAF pilots, although one Fleet Air Arm unit was formed. The Royal Navy was obviously reluctant to waste the carrier deck landing skills of its pilots.

Conversion of the first two MAC-ships, *Empire MacAlpine* and *Empire MacAndrew*, both grain ships, started in June 1942, and by October, ten more were in hand. Plans for thirty-two MAC-ships were cut back to nineteen as the more capable escort carriers were introduced. The simpler tanker conversion, of which the first was the *Rapana*, took much less time, and ships were converted in as little as five months.

Obviously, the size of the MAC-ships meant that aircraft were deployed as flights rather than complete squadrons, and for administrative purposes these were assigned to 836 Squadron, manned by Royal Navy personnel, and the smaller 860

Squadron, manned by the Royal Netherlands Navy, based at Maydown, near Londonderry in Northern Ireland. The Dutch had two ships, MV *Acavus* and *Gadila*. Flights disembarked to Maydown as the eastbound convoys approached the Clyde. On the other side of the Atlantic, the MAC-ships used Halifax, Nova Scotia, and their aircraft disembarked to RCAF Dartmouth.

Starting in May 1943, MAC-ships made 323 crossings of the Atlantic and escorted 217 convoys, of which just one was successfully attacked. The Swordfish flew 4,177 patrols and searches, an average of thirteen per crossing, or one per day at average convoy speed. As a rule simply sighting an aircraft forced U-boats to submerge, but sometimes U-boats caught on the surface, possibly while charging their batteries, did make a fight for it.

The small number of aircraft available aboard a MAC-ship meant that the best use had to be made of what were very - limited resources, and so a series of standard patrol patterns were established, each with a code-name to avoid unnecessary communications, which in themselves could alert the enemy to the presence of a convoy. Often, orders would be given using an Aldis lamp. All of the patrol patterns were suitable for a single aircraft. Even when escort carriers were used, with their larger complement of aircraft, the numbers of extra Swordfish for anti-submarine and anti-shipping patrols were often not much more than on the MAC-ships, as many escort carriers also carried fighters. Often, the aircraft would sink a U-boat in cooperation with one of the convoy escorts, and in many cases, the important role of the aircraft was to force the U-boats to remain submerged, as they were slower under water and also had a restricted view.

The main patrol patterns were:

COBRA 'Y': Patrol around convoy at a distance of Y miles, with Y being the distance from the convoy so that the instruction Cobra 12, would mean patrol at a distance of twelve miles.

VIPER: Patrol around convoy within sight.

ADDER: Patrol ahead of convoy at distance of eight to twelve miles, with the breadth of patrol fifteen miles on either side of the centre line.

'X' PYTHON 'Y' : Given when a submarine had been spotted, so that the aircraft would patrol on bearing 'X' at a distance of 'Y' miles, and would carry out a square search around the indicated position for twenty minutes.

'X' MAMBA : Search along bearing 'X' to a depth of thirty miles and return.

'X' LIZARD 'Y' : Search sector bearing 'X' to a depth of 'Y' miles.

FROG 'Y': Patrol astern of convoy at distance of 'Y' miles. Length of patrol would be 2 'Y' miles, that is 'Y' miles on either side of the centre line. This was to stop U-boats trailing the convoy, often shortly before dusk. It was also essential prior to any change of course so that the U-boat commander would keep his craft submerged and not realize that the change had taken place until it was too late.

ALLIGATOR . . . port or starboard: Patrol on side indicated at distance of ten miles from the convoy along a line parallel to the convoy's course. The length of patrol would be twenty miles, that is ten miles ahead and astern of the aircraft's position on the convoy's beam.

CROCODILE 'Y': Patrol ahead of convoy from beam to beam at radius 'Y' miles, in effect a half COBRA. This was popular with fast convoys since they had little to fear from a U-boat sneaking up from astern.

Patrols generally took around two and a quarter hours to allow for an aircraft always to be on station, recognizing that this was important both for the morale of those in the merchant ships and to keep the U-boats submerged. Later U-boats were equipped with better anti-aircraft armament, and some commanders would take a chance and attempt to fight off a Swordfish, and on some occasions even stand and fight against a heavily armed Sunderland flying boat or B-24 Liberator bomber.

The Atlantic Convoys

The German *Kriegsmarine* used auxiliary cruisers, as well as U-boats and surface raiders such as the *Graf Spee*, in its campaign against British shipping in the North Atlantic. The auxiliary crusiers were converted fast merchantmen and included *Atlantis*, *Orion*, *Pinguin*, *Thor* and *Widder*, while the auxiliary cruiser *Komet* managed to steam around Siberia in August 1940 to attack British shipping in the Pacific. The German U-boat fleet in 1939 and 1940 was not strong, with just fifty-nine submarines in service at the outbreak of war, but it was put to good use and rapidly grew in strength under a massive wartime construction programme, with sixty-five U-boats under construction in September 1939, and a further 1,097 completed by the end of the war in Europe. The fall of France also helped the U-boat campaign, cutting out the long and dangerous passage around the north of the British Isles to bases in Germany as bases became available in the west of France, such as Brest and St Nazaire. From the end of August to the end of September 1940, the U-boats sank twenty-two ships from four convoys, a loss of 113,000 tons of shipping. This was just a start.

There were two main areas for the U-boats. The first was the 'Atlantic Gap', that part of the mid-Atlantic out of reach of shore-based maritime-reconnaissance aircraft from either the British Isles or North America. Convoys from the United States and Canada, and from the Caribbean, some of which would have come through the Panama Canal from the Pacific, were the targets in this vast area of ocean. The other was the Bay of Biscay and the Atlantic off Portugal. On this route passed convoys to and from Gibraltar, which itself was the dividing point from where convoys would either proceed across the Mediterranean or south to the African territories of the British Empire. Often, a Mediterranean and a South Atlantic convoy would sail as one from the UK as far as Gibraltar. As the situation in the Mediterranean became increasingly difficult, convoys for the Middle East and Australia would be routed past the Cape of Good Hope, and indeed, British forces in Egypt were also served by this route and the Suez Canal.

The escort carrier first became involved in convoy protection with Convoy HG76 which sailed from Gibraltar to Britain on 14 December 1941, with thirty-two ships escorted by the Royal Navy's first escort carrier, HMS *Audacity*, three destroyers and nine smaller escorts, mainly corvettes. Twelve U-boats attacked the convoy as it steamed north off the coast of Portugal, but the carrier's Fairey Swordfish helped the escorts sink five of the U-boats. Only three of the merchantmen were sunk, but the U-boats also accounted for *Audacity* and one of the destroyers. An idea of how slow convoys could be, when faced with bad weather and heavy attack can be gained from the fact that the convoy did not reach the UK until 23 December.

Audacity had been a British prize, having started life as the Norddeutscher Line cargo ship *Hannover*, 5,500 grt, and captured by the British in the West Indies in March 1940. The Admiralty was under pressure to provide additional carriers and concerned lest pressure grow so that much-needed battleships and cruisers might have to be converted, so approval was given for the captured ship to be converted to act as an escort carrier. The conversion was quick and distinctly rough and ready, as the ship had no hangar, meaning that her aircraft had to remain permanently on deck, while only the most rudimentary platform on the starboard side was available for both navigation and air control. She was sunk by *U-751* on 20 December.

Convoy SL125 was another convoy that suffered a cruel fate when off Morocco during 27-31 October 1942, with just four escorts to look after thirty-seven merchantmen. Ten U-boats found the convoy and sank eleven merchant vessels. It is hard not to believe that this convoy was a 'tethered goat', there to attract the wolf pack, as the rush of U-boats to the convoy enabled the troop transports for the Allied landings in North Africa to pass completely unscathed.

While the escort carriers were awaited, the merchant aircraft carriers bore the brunt of convoy protection. The aircraft were painted white, this being found to be the best camouflage for day flying over the sea, and certainly the colour scheme chosen for the maritime-reconnaissance flying boats of Royal Air Force Coastal Command. Small units on detachment have often developed a somewhat 'piratical' manner of their own. Those aboard the MAC-ships were no exception. Operating from ships that were still merchant ships, the airmen and maintainers had to sign on as members of the ships' companies, and although they claim never to have received the promised shilling (5p, or US 20 cents at the then rate of exchange) a day pay in addition to their naval pay, they did get a bottle of beer a day! To the anger of many senior officers, several insisted on wearing merchant navy badges in the lapels of their naval uniform. Others went even further, painting out the words ROYAL NAVY on their aircraft and substituting MERCHANT NAVY!

Security on convoy work was tight, not least because the base at Maydown was close to the border with the Irish Republic, and many Irish Republicans, if not active sympathizers with the Axis, worked on the basis that my 'enemy's enemy is my ally'. The men allocated to convoy protection duties were never told in advance of their sailing date, but the fact that leave was cancelled was a clue that it would not be far distant.

An Irishman, Lord Kilbracken, then Lieutenant (A) John Godley, RNVR, (*Bring back my Stringbag – A Swordfish Pilot at War*, Peter Davies, London, 1979), remembers his first operational crossing of the Atlantic on the MAC-ship *Acavus*, a converted tanker.

> During this first crossing of mine, we flew fewer than the average number of sorties because we ran into a gale, which grew into a storm with winds of sixty knots and over. You can't fly when the wind speed is greater than your stalling speed – you'd be taking off backwards – and *Acavus* was pitching so heavily that the forward end of the flight deck often dipped under water. But these same conditions, which continued off and on for half the trip, also immobilised the U-boats. All our three Stringbags were damaged in the battering they took and work on repairing them was extremely difficult, often impossible, without protection from the elements . . . .

Taking off from the short decks of the MAC-ships, which were in any case slower than even the escort carriers, entailed rocket assistance, offering the spectacle of an antique biplane being rocket-propelled off the deck!

It was not until spring 1943 that escort carriers first appeared on the North Atlantic convoys in substantial numbers. Most came from the United States, effectively mass-produced on merchant hulls by a number of shipyards, and intended to be capable of conversion back again after the war. A few were built by the British, as the Admiralty was convinced that their riveted hulls would be more suitable for operations in Arctic waters than the welded hulls of the American product. Radar aboard the escort carriers and now in many of the anti-submarine aircraft as well, meant that by this time the convoy battle was being won. Shore-based aircraft with much longer ranges and greater endurance were also entering service, and between them, these developments started to close the 'Atlantic Gap'.

Between 4 and 6 May 1943, the well-defended convoy ONS5 was attacked by no less than thirty U-boats which managed to sink twelve ships with a total tonnage of 56,000 tons, but in the process seven U-boats were also accounted for. The remaining U-boats then turned their attention to the double convoy HX237/SC129, protected by the escort carrier HMS *Biter*, which provided air cover, and although five merchantmen were lost, another five U-boats were sunk. An attack on Convoy SC130 lasting for five days in mid-May saw no merchantmen lost, but five U-boats were accounted for. Such U-boat losses could not be sustained, no matter how massive the construction programme, while gradually the overall level of experience amongst U-boat commanders and their crews fell sharply.

Typical of the escort carriers was HMS *Biter*, one of the Avenger-class, built between 18 December 1940 and 1 May 1942 by the Sun Shipyard in the United States and converted by the Atlantic Basin Ironworks. Entry into service was delayed by a number of modifications, including some lengthening of the flight deck to 440 feet on arrival in the UK. Displacement was 10,366 tons and maximum speed from a single Doxford diesel engine was 16.5 knots, while fifteen aircraft could be accommodated and struck down into the hangar deck by a single lift aft. The ship survived the war, despite being torpedoed by one of her own aircraft after it had ditched. Apart from taking part in Operation Torch, the Allied invasion of North Africa, her entire British service was spent on escort duties. Less fortunate was her sister, *Dasher*, which blew up during aircraft refuelling in the Firth of Clyde on 27 March 1943 with heavy casualties.

In October 1943, in another five day battle, a pack of U-boats managed to sink just one ship in the double convoy ON206 and ONS206, but six U-boats were lost, four of them to aerial attack. By the end of 1943, the Battle of the Atlantic had been won.

The Arctic Convoys

The main convoy routes were across the North Atlantic, terminating usually on the Clyde or at Liverpool; from Scotland and Iceland to the Soviet Union, which needed the larger aircraft capacity of the escort carriers for both anti-submarine and fighter protection; from Southampton and Plymouth to Gibraltar; to Malta from Gibraltar; and from Gibraltar to Cape Town. CAM-ships appeared on the Atlantic and Arctic convoys. Coastal convoys were usually looked after by RAF Coastal Command, often aided by Fleet Air Arm shore-based squadrons under RAF control who concentrated on ships close to home waters.

The only route for the Arctic convoys lay around the northern tip of occupied Norway to the Soviet ports of Murmansk and Archangel. In summer, almost constant daylight left the ships open to attack from the air, as well as from U-boats and surface raiders. In winter, with almost constant darkness and just three hours of weak twilight in the middle of the day, the weather was another hazard. One officer having difficulty eating a meal as his cruiser rolled to angles of 30 degrees consoled himself with the thought that life must have been even more difficult in the destroyers and corvettes, which rolled 50 degrees or more! The cold meant that airmen tried to wear as much as possible, limited only by the need to get into and out of the cockpit. Metal became so brittle that tail wheels could, and did, break off on landing.

After the terrible fate that had afflicted the ill-fated convoy PQ17, the last Arctic convoy to be without its own air cover, the first Arctic convoy to have an escort carrier was PQ18 in September 1942.The carrier was the US-built HMS *Avenger*. She carried three radar-equipped Swordfish from 825 Squadron for anti-submarine duties as well as six Sea Hurricane fighters, with another six dismantled and stowed beneath the hangar deck in a hold, for fighter defence. The fighter aircraft were drawn from 802 and 883 Squadrons. The CAM-ship, *Empire Morn* carried another Hurricane, one of the expendable standard aircraft operated by the RAF's Merchant Service Fighter Unit. Other ships protecting the convoy included the cruiser *Scylla*, two destroyers, two anti-aircraft ships converted from merchant vessels, four corvettes, four anti-submarine trawlers, three minesweepers and two submarines. The presence of a rescue ship meant that the escorts would not be distracted from their work to rescue survivors, an urgent matter in such cold seas, and three US minesweepers being delivered to the Soviet Union also acted in this role.

Even getting to the convoy assembly point off Iceland was difficult. Rough seas swept a Sea Hurricane off *Avenger*'s deck, while steel ropes failed to stop aircraft breaking loose, crashing into one another and into the sides of the hangar. Fused 500-lb bombs stored in the lift well broke loose, and had to be captured by laying down duffle coats with rope ties, to be quickly tied up as soon as a bomb rolled on to the coats! On her way to the assembly point, *Avenger* suffered engine problems due to fuel contamination. Even Iceland was not completely safe, with the carrier bombed by a Focke-Wulf Fw200 Condor long-range maritime-reconnaissance aircraft, which dropped a stick of bombs close to the ship, but without inflicting any damage.

The engine problems meant that the convoy, already spotted by a U-boat whilst on passage to Iceland, left without the carrier. On 8 September, PQ18 was discovered by another Condor. *Avenger* had caught up with the convoy by 12 September, when a Blohm und Voss Bv138 flying boat dropped through the clouds, and the carrier was able to launch a flight of four Sea Hurricanes, although not quickly enough to catch the flying boat before it disappeared. In addition to protecting the ships, the fighters also had to cover the Swordfish. The Swordfish maintained a general reconnaissance for the convoy, spotting Bv138s dropping mines ahead of the ships. Sometimes, U-boats were discovered on the surface, but attempts to attack them were foiled by heavy AA fire from the U-boats.

At 04.00 on 13 September, Sea Hurricanes were scrambled after Swordfish on anti-submarine patrol were discovered by another two *Luftwaffe* aircraft, a Bv138 and a Junkers Ju88 reconnaissance aircraft, but these disappeared into the low cloud before the fighters could reach them. Later that day a formation of Ju88 medium-bombers made a high-level bombing attack on the convoy. Again, the convoy's fighters were unable to shoot down a German aircraft, largely because the early Sea Hurricane's machine guns could not concentrate enough fire on the bombers to have any effect. While the fighters refuelled and re-armed, the *Luftwaffe* attacked at 15.40. As twenty Ju88s flew over the convoy in a high-level attack, distracting the defences and causing the ships to take evasive action, twenty-eight Heinkel He111 and eighteen Ju88s made a low-level torpedo attack, followed by a second wave of seventeen Ju88s. Sweeping in at around twenty feet above the waves, the attackers ignored the escorts and concentrated on the merchant vessels, the correct strategy. The Sea Hurricanes were still on the carrier's deck and could not take off.

A mass 45 degree turn was attempted, but the inexperience of many of those aboard, and the large size of the convoy, meant that not all of the ships managed this manoeuvre. Inexperience also showed in the wild anti-aircraft fire against the low-flying aircraft which exposed the anti-aircraft crews on other ships to fire from shells and bullets. Pressing home their attack with considerable courage, the Germans sank eight ships, the more fortunate crews being able to jump direct from their ships onto the ice-encrusted decks of the escort and rescue vessels. The less fortunate had minutes in which to be rescued or die in the cold sea. The temperature of the sea was academic for the unfortunate crew aboard the *Empire Stevenson*, loaded with explosives, as they disappeared with the ship in one huge explosion. The AA fire accounted for five aircraft.

The Sea Hurricanes drove off a later attack by Heinkel He115 floatplanes, but one was shot down.

A change of tactics saw the Sea Hurricanes rotated, each spending twenty-five minutes in the air before landing to refuel, keeping a constant CAP over the convoy.

On 14 September, the first Swordfish of the day found *U-589* on the surface, but she dived leaving the Swordfish to mark the spot with a smoke flare. Once the aircraft had gone, the submarine surfaced and continued charging her batteries. Alerted by the Swordfish, the destroyer *Onslow* raced to the scene. Once again, *U-589* dived, but she suffered for her impertinence when the destroyer attacked with depth charges and destroyed her.

The Germans also changed their tactics. Reconnaissance Bv138s and Ju88s were sent to intimidate the Swordfish, forcing them back onto the convoy, until the Germans were driven away by heavy AA fire. The Swordfish would then venture out, only to be found and driven back again.

A further attack by Ju88s later that day saw *Avenger* herself become the target, moving at her maximum 17 knots. The Sea Hurricanes broke up the attack, and no ships were lost, but eleven Ju88s were shot down, again mainly by AA fire. Further attacks that day, including dive-bombing, saw another German aircraft shot down without any losses to the convoy. In a final attack, three of the four patrolling Hurricanes were shot down by friendly fire, although all three pilots were saved, after five *Luftwaffe* aircraft were shot down and another nine damaged beyond repair with five of these credited to the Sea Hurricanes. In this attack, *Avenger*'s commanding officer, Commander Copeland, successfully managed to comb the torpedoes dropped by the Germans, but the ammunition ship, *Mary Luckenbach*, blew up, again with the loss of all of her crew, but taking her attacker with her as the aircraft had flown so low to ensure accuracy that it was caught in the explosion.

The following day, the remaining Sea Hurricanes and the Swordfish were again in the air, with the former breaking up further attacks. The day after, 16 September, the Swordfish were relieved of their patrolling by shore-based RAF Consolidated Catalina flying boats operating from Russia. The break was short-lived as later that day, the convoy crossed the homeward convoy, QP14, with the survivors of the ill-fated PQ17, and *Avenger*, with her aircraft and some of the other escorts transferred to this convoy. The brief interval after shore-based aircraft had started to provide cover was used by the ship's air engineering team to assemble five Sea Hurricanes, more than replacing the four lost on the outward convoy. All in all, the Sea Hurricanes had accounted for a total of five enemy aircraft and damaged seventeen others.

The Malta Convoys

Italy's entry into the Second World War on 10 June 1940, found Malta isolated. The situation was not unexpected, and the British government and armed forces had already considered what to do once Italy entered the war. It was clear that Malta would be a target, sitting astride the crossroads of the Mediterranean, roughly halfway between Gibraltar and Alexandria, and between southern Italy and Italian forces in North Africa. This was a vital strategic situation, but Malta was a fortress of the past, not the present. Her extensive fortifications had been built with earlier conflicts and armaments in mind, while at best the island could only provide a quarter of the food needed to feed its own people, even without taking the needs of a garrison into account.

The British Army and the Royal Air Force agreed that the Maltese islands could not be defended. The sole dissenting voice in this debate was that of the Royal Navy, seeing Malta as of vital strategic importance in control of the Mediterranean, and as a base for light forces and submarines. Most British civilians were evacuated, but the Royal Navy had won the argument, and the armed forces stayed. Initially, it seemed as if the worst fears over the fate of Malta were exaggerated, as during the first six months of Italian involvement in the Second World War, convoys continued to arrive, despite the *Regia Navale* venturing out to sea and the bombing of the *Regia Aeronautica*. The successful raid on the naval base at Taranto also persuaded the Italians to move their fleet further north, initially no further south than Naples. This hopeful strategic position could not last, and changed abruptly following the arrival of substantial German air forces in Sicily, *Fliegerkorps X*, at the start of 1941.

While the Germans and the Italians planned an invasion of Malta, using both paratroops and sea-landed troops, fortunately this was delayed as a much higher priority was accorded to the invasion of Crete. The invasion of Crete proved so costly, with massive losses amongst paratroops and glider-landed troops, and with a number of sea convoys wiped out, that Hitler initially banned any further massive airborne invasions.

Given the small population of Malta, at just over 300,000 in 1940, Malta convoys were far smaller than on the Arctic routes, and escorting warships often outnumbered the escorted merchantmen, due mainly to the heavy losses, which meant that at times convoys simply could not get through, despite the protection of large attack carriers and battleships. The island also lacked the port facilities capable of unloading large merchant vessels as in peacetime her supplies had often arrived in small craft, many of them powered by sail. The limited port facilities meant that when four ships reached Grand Harbour on 23 March 1941, two were sunk at their moorings before they could even be unloaded.

Aircraft were flown from carriers, including two trips by the USS *Wasp*, to provide Malta with a fighter defence, but initially many aircraft were destroyed as they landed to refuel and re-arm in the middle of almost continuous Axis air attack. Even the Royal Navy's great achievement at Taranto still left Malta convoys vulnerable to air attack. This point was brought home with a vengeance as we saw in an earlier chapter when Operation Excess ran into trouble early in 1941.

Most famous of the Malta convoys was that of 10-15 August 1942, known to the Allies as Operation Pedestal, but to the Maltese as the Santa Maria Convoy, arriving in Malta on 15 August, the feast day of the Assumption of the Virgin Mary.

Operation Pedestal was the largest of the Malta convoys; it had fourteen merchant vessels, reflecting both the desperate plight of those on Malta and the reality that not all of the ships could make it. Under the command of Vice Admiral Syfret, the escorts included the battleships *Nelson* and *Rodney*, with their 16-inch guns in three triple turrets forward, the aircraft carriers *Eagle*, *Furious*, *Indomitable* and *Victorious*, seven cruisers and twenty-seven destroyers. *Furious* was carrying forty-two Supermarine Spitfire fighters to be flown off to augment Malta's defences.

The fleet itself was largely dependent on forty-three Sea Hurricanes for its air defence, although it also had a number of Fulmars and Grumman Martlets. *Victorious* had sixteen Fulmars of 809 and 884 Squadrons, five Sea Hurricanes of 885 and twelve Albacores of 832 Squadrons. *Indomitable* had nine Martlets in 806 Squadron, twenty-two Sea Hurricanes in 800 and 880 Squadrons, and sixteen Albacores in 827 Squadron. *Eagle* had sixteen Sea Hurricanes in 801 Squadron and another four in 813. In addition to her Spitfires, *Furious* had four Albacores of 823 Squadron as spares.

The operation got off to a bad start when, after passing Gibraltar on the night of 10–11 August, the *Eagle* was torpedoed at 13.15 on 11 August by *U-73*. All four torpedoes hit the carrier, sinking her quickly, and her four Sea Hurricanes flying CAP at the time had to land on the other carriers. The elderly carrier, regarded as too slow for front-line duty, was no stranger to the Malta run, and had flown 183 fighters safely to the island from her deck.

Later that day, the *Luftwaffe* started the series of heavy aerial attacks that the convoy was to suffer on its run across the Mediterranean. At 20.45, thirty-six aircraft attacked from bases in Sardinia. The following morning, at 09.15, twenty German aircraft attacked, before a combined *Luftwaffe* and *Regia Aeronautica* force of seventy aircraft attacked at noon. The fighters on patrol succeeded in bringing down some of the attackers. The escort vessels sank a U-boat at 16.00, before another combined strike of 100 aircraft attacked at 19.00, sinking a merchantman and so seriously damaging *Indomitable* that she was put out of action, leaving her aircraft to be recovered by *Victorious*. An hour later, twenty *Luftwaffe* aircraft attacked, sinking the cruiser *Cairo* and two more merchant vessels, as well as damaging the cruiser *Nigeria* and three other ships, including the tanker *Ohio*. Those ships sunk had been badly damaged in earlier attacks.

Darkness brought no respite. An attack by E-boats sank another five ships, and so badly damaged the cruiser *Manchester* that she had to be sunk later.

On 13 August, at 08.00, twelve *Luftwaffe* aircraft flying from Sicily sank another ship and caused still more damage to the *Ohio*. After an Italian air raid at 11.25 damaged the tanker further and fires burned out of control, her master ordered her to be abandoned. Before they could be picked up, the crew reboarded the ship as she was still afloat. By this time the convoy was badly scattered. The leading ships reached Malta on 13 August, but *Ohio*, aided by an escorting destroyer, did not arrive until 15 August, one of just five out of the fourteen merchant vessels to survive the ordeal. Her master and crew were valiant, but they were also lucky; as another straggler behind the main convoy was promptly dispatched by a U-boat. *Ohio*'s cargo of fuel was to prove invaluable in the defence of Malta. Strangely, this time there were no attacks on the ships as they unloaded!

The operation cost one aircraft carrier sunk, a cruiser and a destroyer, with serious damage to two carriers, *Indomitable* and *Victorious*, and two cruisers. Part of the problem was the quality of fighter. While the Sea Hurricanes could tackle a Stuka, the Ju88s were far more difficult, making 'the fleet fighters' task a hopeless one', according to Syfret. Yet, this marked the beginning of the lifting of the siege. The tide was turning against the Axis Powers, and nowhere sooner and more sharply than in the Mediterranean theatre and North Africa.

On the Attack

The convoy war was not simply one-sided. Germany had few true overseas trade routes, but the invasion of Norway and Denmark had been largely to secure supplies of Swedish iron ore. The ore was shipped through Norwegian ports after a railway journey from Sweden because the Gulf of Bothnia froze during the winter.

On several occasions, the Home Fleet sent carrier-borne aircraft to attack coastal shipping off occupied Norway, accounting for 100,000 tons of shipping. Further losses came from mines laid by the aircraft. These attacks also helped to foster a belief amongst many in the German leadership, including Hitler, that the planned invasion of Europe would start in Norway. This was not entirely wild thinking, for at one stage Churchill had favoured an invasion through northern Norway rather than directly through northern France.

In the Pacific, Japanese ships, especially tankers, often fell prey to the Fleet Air Arm's attacks, especially in Sumatra and then, towards the end of the year, in Japanese ports, where the Fleet Air Arm earned its second VC of the war. Nevertheless, the bulk of Japanese shipping losses during the war were to American submarines and mines as for the most part, US carrier aircraft concentrated on operations against Japanese naval vessels and in attacks against Japanese ports and airfields rather than seeking to tackle the Japanese convoys.

Japan had entered the war with a substantial submarine force and with torpedoes that were far better than anything possessed by the British or the Americans. Some of the submarines had ranges as long as 16,000 miles, which could doubtless have been considerably extended by refuelling at sea. Part of the submarine force included aircraft-carrying submarines, with hangars for one, and in some cases two, aircraft, but there is only one recorded instance of these being used operationally, when a submarine launched its aircraft on two sorties to bomb the forests of Oregon, hoping to start a forest fire. Eventually, some of the aircraft-carrying submarines were converted to carry *Kaitan* suicide midget submarines – the underwater equivalent of a Kamikaze aircraft.

The inability to appreciate the potential of the submarine in attack was matched by Japanese refusal to see convoy escort as a vital part of the Imperial Japanese Navy's role in wartime. Typically, a convoy of up to eight merchantmen would be escorted by a single destroyer. Not only was this an inadequate escort, the Allies had found that larger convoys suffered disproportionately lower losses than smaller convoys, provided, of course, that adequate protection was provided. There was never any attempt to provide carrier cover for a convoy. On one occasion, the First Fleet had the chance to escort a convoy; it was taking the same route, but the request was turned down abruptly on the grounds that the First Fleet's freedom of movement was sacrosanct. Contrast this with the United States Navy's decision to transfer three battleships and the aircraft carrier USS *Yorktown* from the Pacific to the Atlantic despite growing tension with Japan.

Japanese inability to take convoy protection seriously arose from the prevailing culture that aggressive war was the only way. As fuel and raw materials became scarce, and people in the home islands began to starve, the error of this attitude soon became apparent. Belatedly in the war, a new class of convoy escorts was laid down, but too little, too late, and still without air cover. In any case, Japanese anti-submarine measures were hopelessly inadequate, usually consisting of no more than a destroyer chasing down the track of a torpedo in the hope of finding a submarine at the end of it! While at the outset, Japanese sonar technology had been as good as anyone else's, here again technology entered a stalemate with little further advances once hostilities started.

The Japanese failure to provide an equivalent to the escort or auxiliary aircraft carriers favoured by the Royal Navy and United States Navy is all the more strange since a number of ships were converted to carry aircraft that could have provided an equivalent to the MAC-ships or escort carriers – but these were mainly for the Japanese Army Air Force to use as aircraft transports! Before the outbreak of war, the Japanese Army Air Force had concluded that in any rapid advance across the Pacific it would need its own assault ships and aircraft transports, from which aircraft could be flown off to ensure that shore-based fighter and fighter-bomber units could be established quickly. No details survive of the first two of these ships, the *Akitsu Maru* and the *Nigitsu Maru*, which entered service early in 1943 and in spring 1943 respectively. The conversions were crude, with the smokestacks moved to the starboard side and the flight deck built over the superstructure, and just twenty aircraft could be carried. *Akitsu Maru* was torpedoed off Kyushu, one of the home islands, on 15 November 1944, by the USS *Archerfish*, while *Nigitsu Maru* had already pre-deceased her, sunk by the submarine USS *Hake* on 12 January 1944 east of Formosa. A further ship, the *Kumano Maru*, was also converted, but entered service too late to be of use.

71

A more serious attempt to provide convoy protection was also instigated not by the Imperial Japanese Navy but by the Imperial Japanese Army, but this was not until 1944. That year, two tankers, *Yamishiro Maru* and *Chigusa Maru*, were acquired as escort carriers, not to protect the convoys from submarines but for air defence of the convoys using Ki-44 fighters. In common with the MAC-ships operated by the British and Dutch, neither ship had hangars or lifts, but eight aircraft could be carried. Both were intended to carry their own anti-submarine weapons as well, with provision for up to 120 depth charges each. Although *Yamishiro Maru* was commissioned at the end of January 1945, she was sunk within three weeks by American aircraft before she could be used operationally, while *Chigusa Maru* was never completed and was converted back to a tanker post-war. The Imperial Japanese Navy finally got round to the concept of escort carriers in late 1944, when it also acquired two tankers, *Shimane Maru* and *Otakisan Maru*, for conversion, but the first of these was sunk by American aircraft in July 1945, before she could be deployed operationally, while her sister drifted on to a mine at Kobe as the war was ending and was so badly damaged that she was later scrapped.

That these conversions took place so late in the war, when even the Japanese Army Air Force aircraft transports were unlikely to be needed as first one Japanese outpost and then another fell to the advancing Americans, speaks volumes about Japanese efficiency and the inability to ensure that the right type of warship was being made available at the right time. It is highly unlikely that these ships, had they been deployed earlier, would have made a substantial difference to the outcome of the war, but they may have delayed defeat, including the day when American bombers were close enough to begin the heavy bombing campaign against Japanese cities. Would they have delayed this enough to have postponed the use of the atomic bomb against Hiroshima and then Nagasaki? One can only conclude that this would have been highly unlikely, for these ships, even if available a year or two earlier than was the case, would have still been too little, too late, with no aircraft capable of operating anti-submarine patrols from them in the manner of the Swordfish.

VI

THE ADVANCE IS CHECKED

After the attack on Pearl Harbor, Japanese forces spread eastwards, taking the Philippines, Malaya and Singapore, then the Dutch East Indies, with the carriers *Akagi*, *Kaga*, *Shokaku* and *Zuikaku* providing supporting air cover. Anxious to make the best use of their resources, carrier air cover was not provided when land-based aircraft were within range, as at the invasion of the Philippines in late December 1941, although Mitsuo Fuchida protested at the use of the large carriers and their aircraft for the attack on the Royal Australian Air Force base at Rabaul, at the northern end of New Britain island in January 1942. In his own words, Fuchida felt like 'a hunter sent to stalk a mouse with an elephant gun,' while for want of targets, since the bases had only token garrisons, aircraft had to jettison their bombs over jungle rather than risk landing back on the carriers with live explosives. Fuchida convinced Nagumo of the waste of such operations, but Yamamoto still insisted on sending the carriers to Palau, a small atoll off the south-western end of the Marianas. Probably more effective was the support provided by aircraft from *Soryu* and *Hiryu* for the invasion of the Dutch East Indies. In February, *Akagi*, *Kaga*, *Hiryu* and *Soryu* were sent to attack Darwin in the belief that Allied defences in the town and port were being strengthened, but as at Petsamo and Kirkenes, there were no major fleet units in the port, although at least it did have some Australian and American transports and a destroyer and a corvette. The raid had no strategic benefits, other than reminding the Australians that they were engaged in a war.

Despite the speed at which Japan had managed to acquire what amounted to an empire in little more than a month after the attack on Pearl Harbor, there were disagreements over the best strategy. Many Japanese officers believed that Japan should isolate Australia from the United States by taking Fiji, Samoa and ultimately Hawaii, while instead of attacking Darwin, Sydney should have been the target. Fuchida and Genda belonged to this school of thought, which also anticipated a major battle with the United States Navy's carriers, whose aircraft had already attacked Japanese bases in the Marshall Islands. Certainly, such a strategy would have caused a massive diversion of Allied resources to protect Australia, and would have given Japan dominance of the Pacific for far longer than was in fact to be the case.

The problems of high intensity operations were also becoming apparent. In a raid on Java, *Kaga* scraped a reef and had to return to Japan for repairs. By this time, Japan was also faced with increasingly long distances between its major bases and what might be described as the front line, always a fluid term in naval warfare. Singapore to Japan was a distance comparable with Southampton to New York, and so ships had to be rotated out of operations for far longer than was desirable.

Next on Japan's wish list was Burma, seen as a route into India. India was the supposed 'jewel in the crown' of the British Empire, although in reality, of the colonies, Malaya with its rubber and tin was by far the most valuable. Japan also by this time had the oil-fields of the Dutch East Indies. Burma was too close to the Royal Navy's Eastern Fleet for comfort, and so the destruction of this fleet was seen as an important pre-requisite for any invasion of Burma. On 26 March 1942, Yamamoto sent five aircraft carriers, *Akagi*, *Shokaku*, *Zuikaku*, *Hiryu* and *Soryu*, to attack British bases on Ceylon, now Sri Lanka, off the southern end of India.

The British Eastern Fleet was by this time under the command of Vice Admiral Sir James Somerville and included three aircraft carriers, the modern *Indomitable* and *Formidable* and the elderly and small *Hermes,* by this time more of a liability than an asset as she was unable to keep up with the rest of the fleet, unlike the two fast armoured carriers. Her aircraft complement was just a dozen Fairey Swordfish, meaning that she was of little use other than as an escort carrier, and as such she would have been in-valuable on the Atlantic convoys.

On 4 April, the advancing Japanese fleet was spotted by an RAF Consolidated Catalina flying boat which managed to transmit a warning just before it was shot down by Zero fighters. The next day, at 08.00, Mitsuo Fuchida led a massed attack against Colombo, Ceylon's major port, fully expecting a repeat of his success at Pearl Harbor. The Eastern Fleet was absent, but the harbour was very busy with merchant shipping. The RAF put its small force of fighters into the air to protect the port, but the Hawker Hurricane was no match for the agile Zero and almost all were shot down. Japanese bombers were able to inflict serious damage on the port installations, and amongst the ships hit were an armed merchant cruiser and a destroyer. Nevertheless, effective AA fire also meant that the Japanese suffered their first serious losses in the war.

Alerted to the Japanese advance, but not knowing where and when they would strike, the British had decided that their ships would be safer at sea, and had moved most of their warships out of Colombo and Trincomalee. The two large carriers had gone to Addu Atoll, now known as Gan, where a secret refuelling anchorage had been hastily constructed.

Returning from the raid, Fuchida suggested to Nagumo that they send reconnaissance aircraft to locate the British warships, and on this occasion Nagumo agreed. Fuchida remained aboard his ship while a strong force of aircraft was readied in case a further raid on Colombo proved necessary. At noon, a strong force of aircraft from the *Soryu* discovered the two heavy cruisers, *Cornwall* and *Dorsetshire*, without air cover, and in twenty minutes sunk both ships.

Hermes had left Trincomalee and headed north, but returned to the port on 6 April. On 8 April, following intelligence reports that Trincomalee was likely to be the next target for the Japanese, *Hermes* went to sea again, but on this occasion headed south. Early the following day, she was spotted by Japanese aircraft and ordered to return to Trincomalee where it was felt that the heavy AA defences would be able to protect her. Shortly before 07.30, Fuchida led a force of 100 aircraft against Trincomalee, but once again found the British Eastern Fleet missing. Again, the RAF sent its Hawker Hurricanes into battle, but nine of the eleven aircraft were shot down. While Fuchida's aircraft wreaked havoc on the shore installations and airfields, shooting parked aircraft, only one ship, a merchant vessel, was sunk by the first wave, although further ships fell prey to the second wave.

As he returned to the *Akagi*, Fuchida learned that a British carrier had been spotted. On landing, his aircraft were hastily re-armed and refuelled, while the *Akagi* was attacked by nine Bristol Blenheim bombers, which failed to hit her. The Japanese planned to attack *Hermes* with dive-bombers, escorted by Zero fighters in case the carrier put up fighters, while a force of horizontal bombers was fitted with torpedoes in case the initial attack failed. They needn't have worried. *Hermes* was completely without aircraft that day, and her sole defence, apart from her own AA armament was the Australian destroyer, HMAS *Vampire*. Fuchida was not in time to lead the attack, which was led by another officer called Egusa, but he arrived in time to find the carrier sinking and the destroyer dead in the water, crippled by explosions from her magazines.

'The planes seemed to have no fear,' recalls Donald Farquharson-Roberts, a young Royal Marines officer serving in *Hermes*. 'They came in at masthead height and at least one was reported as being below the fighting top . . . Marine Youle . . . told me he was firing downwards . . . I saw a plane coming straight for my gun. I saw the bomb swing clear and come straight for ME. I was standing about six feet behind the gun and it hit the deck a foot in front of me . . . and went straight through the deck!'

Farquharson-Roberts' gun had jammed before this event, and no doubt with eighty bombers attacking, the guns had overheated. Farquharson-Roberts again:

'I never heard the command to abandon ship, although I am told it was given. I took leave of the old girl by stepping into the water on the port side . . . There was then only a drop of about ten feet. I swam clear but the stern was swinging away from me as she had full helm on and the engines were still going full ahead . . .'

The first bomb had hit the carrier at 10.55 and she sank in less than twenty minutes. Fortunately, the Japanese had failed to detect an Australian hospital ship, the *Vita*, which arrived shortly afterwards and rescued most of the survivors, while a few had managed to swim the short distance to the shores of Ceylon.

This was a loss for the British, but once again Fuchida felt that excessive resources were being devoted to minor operations, while the losses that were being incurred could not be replaced easily for the major battles that had to lie ahead if the Imperial Japanese Navy was to defeat the Americans at sea. Like many of his fellow officers, Fuchida was impatient for a confrontation with the United States Navy – and he was to have his wish fulfilled even sooner than he expected.

Shangri-La

For the Americans, the problem was fundamentally one of distance. The aircraft of the day could not operate from Hawaii, let alone the mainland United States, and take the war home to the Japanese. American pride had been affronted by the attack on Pearl Harbor, but at least the Pacific Fleet's aircraft carriers had not been present and their survival meant that they were a constant worry to the Japanese naval planners. There was another problem, which was that the Japanese had been able to devote most of their resources to attack and largely ignore defence. This fitted in well with the national character and was to prove a fatal weakness as the war progressed with, for example, inadequate resources devoted to convoy protection or to developing fighters that could protect the homeland once United States Army Air Force heavy bombers had bases within striking distance.

The first American attempt to strike back at the Japanese was on 1 February, less than two months after the attack on Pearl Harbor. Vice Admiral F. Halsey, who had been at sea aboard the USS *Enterprise* at the time of the Japanese attack, took this carrier and the *Yorktown*, escorted by five cruisers and ten destroyers, to attack Japanese bases on the Marshall and Gilbert Islands, causing relatively slight damage but nevertheless doing much for the battered morale of the United States Navy. Further raids were planned as the Japanese continued their advance westwards, taking Singapore on 15 February while landings at Palembang on Sumatra on 13 February were covered by the aircraft carrier *Ryujo*. Bali was seized by the Japanese on 18 February.

Yorktown was the lead ship of a class of three carriers, which also included *Enterprise* and *Hornet*. The first two were constructed under the terms of the US National Recovery Act, which was a measure aimed at lifting the United States out of the depression years by stimulating employment. These ships reflected growing concerns within the United States Navy that its first carrier to be designed and laid down as such, the USS *Ranger*, was too small, at 14,000 tons, and possibly too slow as well. It was decided that 20,000 tons would be a far better figure, and the new class finally weighed in with a displacement of 19,872 tons each, with a speed of 32.5 knots. Unusually, these ships were fitted with arrester wires fore and aft, although the former was

77

seldom if ever used, while in addition to the two catapults or accelerators on the forward flight deck, another was placed athwartships on the hangar deck able to launch aircraft on either side. To the British, their 6-inch thick wooden flight decks were a weakness and a potential fire hazard. These ships each had three lifts, although in the early designs four were envisaged. At the time of construction, up to ninety-six aircraft were to be carried, but this figure fell as aircraft sizes grew. *Yorktown* had joined the fleet at the end of September 1937, followed by *Enterprise* in May 1938, and *Hornet* in October 1941, much later than the first two as under the terms of the Washington Treaty only these plus the much smaller *Wasp* could be built, but *Hornet* was built as an emergency addition to the carrier force as the Washington Naval Treaty had effectively lapsed by September 1939. Building another carrier to an existing design avoided the delays inherent in waiting for a new design to be completed.

On 20 February, a task force centred on the aircraft carrier USS *Lexington*, attempted to attack Rabaul in New Britain, but enemy reconnaissance aircraft discovered the carrier and the attack was not pressed home as the all important element of surprise had been lost and at this early stage in the Pacific War it was better for the United States Navy to husband its resources. Four days later, Halsey attacked Wake Island, while on 4 March, Marcus Island was bombed by aircraft from the *Enterprise*. There were further raids on 10 March when Vice Admiral Wilson Brown used aircraft from the *Lexington* and *Yorktown* to attack the ports of Salamaua and Lae on New Guinea.

Putting aside inter-service rivalry, a United States Army Air Force officer, Colonel James 'Jimmy' Doolittle, put forward the idea that United States Army Air Force bombers should be flown off an aircraft carrier to strike a blow at Japan that would be both a gesture of defiance and also force them to divert resources to the defence of their cities. There was some initial resistance to the plan, which seemed to be virtually impossible since it would mean flying twin-engined North American B-25 Mitchell bombers from the deck of a carrier, bearing in mind that to send a sizeable force would mean that the lead aircraft would have very little deck space. Generalissimo Chiang Kai-shek, leader of the nationalist forces in China, also objected to the operation, fearing that the attack could result in reprisals against the Chinese. Nevertheless, the overwhelming need to strike a blow at the enemy meant that eventually the plan was approved.

Doolittle has been described as having had an aggressive and expansive nature. He had left the then United States Army Air Corps in the 1930s and had only returned in 1940, anticipating American involvement in the war in Europe.

The United States Navy allocated two carriers to the operation, forming with their escorts Task Force 16, the USS *Hornet* was to carry the bombers, while her sister carrier the USS *Enterprise* was to provide fighter cover and anti-submarine protection. *Hornet* would be able to do very little to protect herself as the bombers could not be struck down into her hangar and crowded the flight deck to the extent that no other aircraft could be operated until after their departure. The plan was that the bombers would not return to the ship, but fly on from their targets to bases in mainland China, giving rise to the code-name of Operation Shangri-La for the fictional land beyond the clouds. The operation was kept so secret that only seven people knew exactly what was intended until the day before, and even the President of the United States was not given the full information until Admiral Ernest King visited the White House shortly before the operation.

When *Hornet* left Pearl Harbor with sixteen B–25 bombers crowded on her flight deck, everyone assumed that she was simply being used as an aircraft transport – the idea of operational flying seemed to be ridiculous. Her own aircraft were not simply struck down into the hangar deck below, they were 'stuck down' as until the deckload of twin-engined bombers departed, it would be impossible to range the carrier's own aircraft on the flight deck. The Japanese became aware of the approach of the two carriers on 10 April when the radio intelligence unit at Hagashishima picked up signals as the two ships attempted to rendezvous. Their presence raised little concern, for two or even three US carriers could be handled by Japanese forces ashore, while a network of picket ships had been established at 700 miles off the Japanese islands and the Japanese knew that the carriers would have to come within 300 miles if American naval aircraft were to attack any of the islands. The Twenty-Sixth Air Flotilla's force of sixty-nine bombers would be sent against the American ships when they crossed the picket line.

Japanese confidence was in fact excessive, since their main carrier force was still returning from its raids on Ceylon, and would not be back in home waters until 19 April, with another three ships involved in the attack on Port Moresby and only *Kaga* in Japan, but not operational. Had the Japanese carriers been used more effectively, and so much effort not expended on unnecessary 'side shows', Fuchida's hopes for a carrier fleet action would have been achieved earlier, and the Americans would have been at a disadvantage with *Hornet* unable to fight back.

After 10 April, the Americans maintained complete radio silence, depriving the Japanese of any information on their position. The American commander, Admiral William 'Bull' Halsey knew about the picket line of ships and assumed that when it was crossed the Japanese would be immediately aware of his position. This timed the operation to take place as soon as the ships crossed the picket line early in the morning of 18 April. The bombers were launched at 550 miles from Tokyo, and the carriers then withdrew. Halsey had taken a wise decision, not hazarding his ships and assuming the worst, but in fact the Japanese had not noticed his ships crossing the picket line, and the first indication that anything was happening came when a patrolling aircraft spotted the sixteen bombers in the air – but its radioed report was immediately rejected as the Japanese knew that the Americans did not have any twin-engined aircraft aboard their carriers! This was a mistake on a par with that of the radar station in Hawaii on the morning of the Pearl Harbor raid.

Led by Doolittle, the B-25 formation penetrated Japanese air defences with ease, missed completely by fighters patrolling at 10,000 feet as they raced across the coast at just 150 feet. No doubt the fighter pilots felt that they were simply going through the motions and that an American attack was highly unlikely. Not one aircraft was shot down. The Japanese response was also marred by a failure to realize that the aircraft would not be returning.

The targets for the bombers included Tokyo, Yokosuka and Nagoya, and they created considerable alarm and panic as they sped across the targets dropping bombs and machine-gunning, and this strafing attack killed two schoolchildren. The aircraft flew on to land in China, but the bases chosen were ill-suited for what were relatively large aircraft, and all of the aircraft were badly damaged or destroyed in crash landings. By this time, having been assigned different targets, the aircraft had become scattered, and one which overshot its assigned Chinese landing ground to land instead in the supposedly 'friendly' Soviet Union had its crew arrested. Unluckier still, another two bombers crash-landed near Japanese-occupied Hankow and when the Japanese commander in Shanghai informed Tokyo of their capture, he was ordered to send them to Japan where they were prosecuted for the deaths of the schoolchildren and executed. It was only when they heard of the crashed bombers that the Japanese realized the nature of the attack, but the presence of prisoners became a propaganda coup allowing the authorities to claim that nine bombers had been shot down.

While the raid was a boost to American morale at a dark period of the war before the major battles that would soon restore national confidence, the raid was also criticised by many Americans as meaningless bravado and a waste of aircraft and experienced aircrew. Chiang Kai-shek was later proved right, as on 21 April the planned advance of the China Expeditionary Army was brought forward and Operation Chekiang launched against Chekiang and Kiangsi provinces, with Japanese troops slaughtering every man, woman and child, a quarter of a million Chinese in all.

If the raid is to be criticized at all, the failure was not to concentrate all of the bombers on a single target, where they could have had a serious impact. As it was, too few aircraft with just 4,000-lbs of bombs each made little impression on any target. What it did do, however, was change Japanese strategy, which now became more defensive, and naval strategy in particular was to be inhibited for the rest of the war for fears of further raids on the homeland and on the emperor. Had the raid concentrated solely on Tokyo, and especially on the Imperial Palace, it would have had an even more profound impact on Japanese thinking. As it was, Yamamoto now ruled out the more adventurous course of taking first Fiji, then Samoa and finally Hawaii, which would have seriously hampered US efforts and also isolated Australia from the United States. Nevertheless, it also has to be appreciated that the entire operation gave American confidence a tremendous boost, showing that no matter how distant, Japan was not safe from American attack.

Battle of the Coral Sea

The Japanese advance had finally been stalled in territories as far apart as Burma and New Guinea, but further landings were planned in the latter as well as an advance northwards to the Aleutians. New bases were planned in the Solomons and at Midway Island. The Aleutians and Midway were seen as important stages in an outer defensive ring. Given the limited range and airlift capability by today's standards of the aircraft then available, the one strategic asset the Japanese possessed was the mobility of their naval forces and especially the carriers, but it was a strategic asset also possessed by the United States Navy.

Returning from the operations against Ceylon, Nagumo was ordered to detach towards Truk the Fifth Carrier Division under the command of Vice Admiral Takagi with two of his best ships, *Zuikaku* and *Shokaku*, with a total of 125 aircraft, to cover the planned strike towards Port Moresby, where the landings would be covered by the smaller *Shoho*, a converted submarine depot ship of just 13,000 tons. Meanwhile, Admiral Chester Nimitz, the commander in the Pacific, sent Rear Admiral Frank Fletcher with Task Force 17, including the aircraft carriers *Yorktown* and *Lexington*, with 141 aircraft, to the Coral Sea. Both carrier forces had supporting ships, the Japanese with two heavy cruisers and six destroyers, while the Americans had five cruisers and nine destroyers of their own, as well as three cruisers and two destroyers of the Royal Navy. Other Japanese ships were with *Shoho* for the landings.

On 3 May, the Japanese landed unopposed on Tulagi and Guadalcanal in the eastern Solomon Islands, but on 4 May aircraft from the *Yorktown* surprised Japanese warships lying off Tulagi and sank a destroyer and three minesweepers as well as destroying several seaplanes. Task Force 17 then turned its attentions to the Port Moresby assault force, and set off in pursuit, while the main Japanese force with the two larger carriers entered the Coral Sea the following day.

Both fleets refuelled at sea on 6 May while they were only seventy miles apart, and, despite both putting up aerial reconnaissance, remained unaware of each other, although later in the day United States Army Air Force aircraft located the Port Moresby assault force and passed this on to Fletcher. The following day, aircraft from both the American carriers found the Port Moresby invasion force including the *Shoho*, on which they concentrated their efforts. Despite the Japanese carrier circling desperately to avoid the American aircraft, she was sunk within three minutes for the cost of just three United States Navy aircraft, and the Japanese immediately recalled the assault force including the troopships. At much the same time, Japanese reconnaissance aircraft had discovered a destroyer escorting a tanker, and mistook them for an aircraft carrier and a cruiser, prompting Takagi to send no less than sixty bombers to attack both ships, and, not surprisingly with such force, both ships were sunk within minutes.

By this time, it was clear to both naval commanders that their opponents had carriers, but their location remained unknown, even though that night the Japanese and American ships were so close that six Japanese aircraft attempted to land on *Yorktown* in the dark. Finally, on 8 May, reconnaissance aircraft from both fleets discovered each other almost simultaneously while they were some 200 miles apart. The two admirals hastily arranged air strikes, with the Japanese sending ninety aircraft against the Americans, who sent seventy-eight aircraft at much the same time. *Zuikaku* was able to escape into a rainstorm, but three bombs struck *Shokaku* forcing her to return to Truk. *Lexington*'s Devastators dropped torpedoes but failed to hit the *Shokaku*, largely because US torpedoes at this stage of the war were both slow and unreliable, with one Japanese officer under interrogation later contemptuously claiming that they could 'turn and run away from them!'

In anticipation of a Japanese attack, Fletcher had arranged fighter cover for his fleet to be standing by, with reconnaissance aircraft sent out to provide advance warning. Soon reports began coming in, with first the Japanese aircraft being right ahead at sixty miles, then at 17,000 feet in four groups of nine aircraft each, with dive bombers and Zero fighters going 'awfully fast', then torpedo-bombers 'spilling out of the clouds eight miles out' at 6,000 feet in a steep dive.

By this time, *Lexington* was steaming about two miles ahead and to starboard of *Yorktown*, with both ships having a cruiser and destroyer screen. The torpedo-bombers attacked in three groups each of six aircraft, with two groups attacking *Lexington* from both sides and another attacking *Yorktown*. *Lexington*'s commanding officer, Captain Sherman, took evasive action to avoid the torpedoes while his AA gunners put up an intense barrage, blowing up a Nakajima B5N 'Kate' torpedo-bomber on its run towards the ship. It has been claimed since that as many as eleven torpedoes were dropped before two eventually struck the *Lexington*, suggesting excellent ship handling at what was still an early stage of the war. The first torpedo struck at 11.20 on the port bow, followed by a second torpedo also on the port side, but amidships, shortly afterwards.

'I arrived on the main deck – two below the flight deck – to find dust and smoke drifting through the passageways coming from further aft,' explained Stanley Johnson, who was a war correspondent with the *Chicago Tribune* later.

> In the passageway amidships I found four men who were nearly naked . . . they were horribly burned. A Filipino cook . . . assisted me to get the men on to the cots in the passageway and take off the remainder of their clothes, give them a drink of water and a morphia injection. A hospital corpsman . . . treated their burns with tannic acid jelly and took over their care. Men kept coming in from the 5-inch gun galleries, sometimes alone, others with the help of comrades. We had about twelve men on the cots and during a brief lull I went to the gun galleries to see what had happened. There I saw several bodies, they seemed to have been frozen or charred into grotesque statues.

A fight was going on to stop the ship sinking, and at first they succeeded.

'We've got the torpedo damage temporarily shored up,' reported Commander Healey, the ship's damage control officer, to his CO. 'The fires are out and soon we'll have the ship on an even keel. But I would suggest, sir, that if you have to take any more torpedoes, you take 'em on the starboard side.'

These were probably the last words he ever spoke, for no sooner had he completed his report than a blast, far greater than any bomb or torpedo strike, ran through the ship, coming from close to Commander Healey's central control station and killing him and a large number nearby. An aviation fuel tank had blown up. Streams of flame and sparks raced along passageways and through compartments, tearing off watertight doors and opening up decks and deckheads, overwhelming the damage control parties with the destruction. Many more were killed and much more damage followed when a second blast came twenty minutes later, shattering the water mains and ending all hope of fighting the fires, then the electricity failed, plunging the ship into darkness. The only means of communication throughout the ship was by messenger, and a chain of men had to be established so that instructions from the bridge could be sent 500 feet and four decks aft to the auxiliary steering position.

Lexington's death throes were not apparent to the returning aviators at first, but at 13.45 the smoke over the flight deck was so dense that all operations had to be suspended, and *Yorktown* had to recover *Lexington*'s aircraft. In a final desperate attempt to save as many lives as possible, at 14.30 all damage control and firefighting parties were withdrawn from the worst areas, leaving the fires to burn behind watertight doors. At 14.45, a further major explosion wrecked the ventilation system for the engine rooms and boiler rooms, causing these areas to be evacuated as temperatures soared. The ship had lost speed due to the damage taken, but now lost almost all movement, but it was not until 15.00 that other ships were asked for assistance, with the destroyer USS *Morris* coming alongside. The destroyer's firefighting capabilities were not up to the tremendous task as fuel-fed fires raged out of control, and the order was given to abandon ship. At 20.00, another destroyer, *Phelps*, torpedoed what was left of the carrier, by this time a floating burning wreck, and tomb to 216 of her crew, although, incredibly, more than 2,700 survived the ordeal.

Yorktown was hit just once, by a bomb that exploded close to the island, so that flying operations were unaffected.

On the face of it, in losing one of the two largest carriers in the world, the United States had come off worst in this encounter, but it had sunk the *Shoho* and caused such damage to the *Shokaku*, that she would not be available for the planned invasion of Midway Island, in effect really a small coral atoll. This was to be an important factor. More significant still, the Japanese expansion had come to an end, within six months of the war in the Pacific starting, as they were forced to abandon the assault on Port Moresby. There was now no question of Japan isolating Australia from the United States.

Admiral King wrote shortly after the battle to his opposite number in the Royal Navy, Sir Dudley Pound:

> The Battle of the Coral Sea was merely the first round of an engagement which will continue, with increasing strength on the part of the enemy, which we shall have difficulty in

matching . . . On the whole, we had rather the better of it and we seem to have stopped the advance on Port Moresby for the time being.

King's assessment was cautious, and with hindsight unduly pessimistic, but intelligence assessments of enemy strength, especially at some future date, have always been notoriously difficult. The fact was that still only months into the Pacific War, the Japanese had already lost a quarter of the Navy Air Force's frontline aircraft and had also lost many experienced naval aircrew and lacked the training mechanisms to replace them quickly. This was a consequence of the long period that the Japanese had had to prepare for the war and their experience of air operations over China – there had not been the need to create an organization that could produce aircrew and maintainers quickly and efficiently. Japanese industry also lacked the resources and manufacturing capability of the United States. Combined, these were to be fatal weaknesses as the war progressed.

VII

THE TIDE TURNS IN THE EAST

Luck plays an important part in warfare, almost as much as sound judgement. In less than six months after Pearl Harbor, the Imperial Japanese Navy had finally come to realize that it had failed in its principal objective, to prevent the United States Navy using its main forward base in the Pacific for at least six months. That was due in no small part to Nagumo's serious error of judgement in not sending a third, and perhaps even a fourth, wave of aircraft to attack Pearl Harbor. But it was simple bad luck that saw Mitsuo Fuchida succumb to appendicitis shortly before the planned Japanese attack on the small atoll of Midway, so that he was not available to lead the operation and, even more importantly, to oversee the organization of the reconnaissance. At this time, Fuchida was almost certainly the world's most experienced and successful leader of a carrier air strike.

At the Imperial Japanese Headquarters in Tokyo, opinions were divided over the future course of Japanese strategy. Many still wanted to pursue the original option of driving a wedge south to isolate Australia from the United States, effectively splitting the Pacific in two. They were opposed by those who wanted to establish a defensive line and whose arguments had been both strengthened and influenced by the Doolittle raid. The occupation of Midway fitted into this more cautious strategy, and it was also expected that the move would lure the United States Pacific Fleet beyond the atoll to be destroyed by the Japanese. The assault on the atoll would have its own aircraft carrier, *Zuiho*, to provide close air support and afterwards join *Hosho* to escort the main Japanese fleet commanded by Admiral Yamamoto in person flying his flag in the giant battleship *Yamato* with her nine 18-inch guns. Nagumo's First Air Fleet was assigned to support the landing from a distance and be ready to attack the US Pacific Fleet once it arrived in the area. Yamamoto's main fleet would be 300 miles away, and ready to destroy whatever was left of the Pacific Fleet following the attack by Nagumo's airmen. To distract the Americans, the Japanese also sent a raiding force including the carriers *Ryujo* and *Junyo* to attack US forces in the Aleutians, close to Alaska.

Given the ambitions of the Japanese, it seems odd that Nagumo was not party to these plans, and was simply ordered to execute them. Even before the Battle of the Coral Sea, a debate was aroused by the plans. Nagumo's own chief of staff, Kusaka, objected on the grounds that the fleet was not ready for another operation so soon after Pearl Harbor and its support for Japan's massive push westwards. The ships needed to refit rather than simply refuel and replenish. Aircrew losses needed to be made good, and the new arrivals trained to combat readiness, while the hard-worked veterans needed rest. His misgivings were shared by Minoru Genda, who felt that the pool of experienced pilots was far too low, especially after a number had been withdrawn to other theatres after the operations off Ceylon. An additional concern was that the Aleutian raiding force divided the main fleet. Fuchida had further objections; that the base on Midway was of little use and that the big guns of the main fleet would be too far away to be of any use. Fuchida and Genda were supported, not for the first time, by Yamaguchi, in command of the Second Carrier Division, but they were overruled. Fuchida even tried to reach Yamamoto through one of his staff officers, Commander Akira Susaki, but without success. No one considered consulting these officers with their experience of naval air warfare, and even Fuchida's concern about the main fleet being too far away were swept aside by senior officers who were convinced that the US Pacific Fleet was already a broken reed. No one seemed to appreciate the value of the heavy ships with their AA armament as close escorts for the carriers.

This sense of complacency, of under-estimating an opponent, was all the more serious because the United States had already broken the Japanese codes, giving them invaluable early warning of Japanese movements and intentions. Intelligence assessments apart, the commander in the Pacific, Admiral Chester Nimitz, was convinced that Midway would be the next Japanese objective, and he communicated his concerns to King in Washington. Both men felt that after Midway, Hawaii would follow. This left them with a problem, whether to send their carriers deeper into the Pacific to stop the Japanese at Midway, or to concentrate on protecting Hawaii, a far more important location and in addition to its strategic importance as a major base, the islands had a very large number of American civilians resident. A third option was to divide the still limited forces available. King decided that everything available should be used for the defence of Midway. If necessary, they could fall back on Hawaii.

A major planning conference was held aboard the *Yamato* on 28 and 29 April 1942. Here the way in which the objections raised by Genda, Fuchida and others had been treated were all the more surprising as senior officers were anxious to heap praise on the naval aviators for their exploits thus far in the war. They even reviewed the record of Nagumo's forces to see if any lessons could be learned. This gave Fuchida the opportunity to argue yet again that there should be a single force, with the First Fleet fighting as a single unit under Yamamoto with all six aircraft carriers and the battleship and cruiser force operating closely together. It was no good, and even the damage to *Shokaku* at the Battle of the Coral Sea a little more than a week later did nothing to change minds. The Battle of the Coral Sea should have acted as a timely reminder that the United States Navy was far from broken, and indeed was proving to be increasingly potent. The Japanese failure to take everything into account, and especially the growing forcefulness of the United States Navy is all the more strange given Yamamoto's recognition of American industrial superiority. It was also by now clear that the Americans were growing in both confidence and competence in the way in which they exercised naval air power.

Not the least of the Japanese assumptions was that the United States Navy had just two aircraft carriers in the Pacific when in fact there were three. Rear Admiral Spruance had *Enterprise* and *Hornet* in Task Force 16, while Task Force 17, led by Rear Admiral Fletcher, had the *Yorktown*.

The Battle of Midway

The Americans knew both the objective and the likely date; early June 1942. Information like this meant that Admiral Chester Nimitz, commander-in-chief of the US Pacific Fleet did not have to spread his forces but instead could risk concentrating them to defend Midway atoll. The Japanese did at least anticipate a strong defence and, apart from the Aleutian raiding force, concentrated the rest of their available naval forces in the hope that this would be the long sought decisive battle with the Americans. Realizing Japanese intentions, the Americans were not too concerned by the activities of the Aleutians raiding force when, on 3 June, *Junyo* and *Ryujo* sent aircraft to attack Dutch Harbour, and consciously took the decision to defend Midway, even when, two days before the battle began, they temporarily lost track of the Japanese fleet.

The first move by American forces took place on 3 June, when, during the afternoon, United States Army Air Force Boeing B-17 Flying Fortress bombers were sent to attack the Midway invasion force, but the heavy bombers enjoyed little success against ships under way at sea.

Aboard *Akagi*, Fuchida had refused the offer of a destroyer to take him to a naval hospital and had instead placed himself in the hands of the ship's chief surgeon so that he would be available to advise his superiors. He was still in the ship's sick bay, deep in the carrier's hull below the waterline, on 4 June, the day chosen for the main attack. Fuchida had only had his stitches removed the previous day and was still weak from the operation, but was anxious to see his airmen before they took off. This was easier said than done. With the ship closed up for action stations, all of the watertight bulkheads were closed and the only means of access through the ship was by means of the small manhole on each watertight door, which entailed unlocking the manhole using a wheel and then locking it again by the same means after passing through. There were ten manholes between the sick bay and Fuchida's cabin, where he rested briefly to regain his strength before shaving and changing into his uniform. He then had to get from his cabin to the flight deck, which meant passing through several more manholes.

Despite these difficulties and his still frail state, Fuchida arrived in the ship's control centre before the aircraft took off. He found that Lieutenant Tomega was to lead the attack in his absence, but less happily, he found that the reconnaissance missions were already being flown off and when he was shown their search patterns, he realized that these would leave large areas of sea uncovered. Despite their expectations of a strong American defence, the Japanese seem to have discounted the presence of the Pacific Fleet's carriers.

The first wave of Japanese aircraft left the carriers at dawn, with more than 100 aircraft heading for Midway to destroy the

1. HMS *Courageous* was torpedoed and sunk just two weeks after the outbreak of war in Europe, with the loss of a third of her crew.

2. Pride of the Royal Navy in 1939 was HMS *Ark Royal,* seen here with all three lifts down. The British public thought that she was unsinkable, but the Admiralty knew that she was vulnerable to bombing, although in the end she succumbed to a torpedo!

3. The most modern carrier on the outbreak of war, but with aircraft that looked as if they belonged in a museum! The Fairey Swordfish was to prove its worth, and not only at Taranto, outlasting its supposed successors.

4. Only the fact that none of the Italian warships blew up at Taranto kept the death toll relatively low. This is the *Caio Duilo* resting on the harbour bed.   *(IWM HU2058)*

5. Badly damaged, the USS *Lexington* burns fiercely before she finally slips beneath the
   waves. *(IWM OEM1570)*

6. A sunny August morning in the Mediterranean, but this is the famous Malta convoy
   Operation Pedestal. Two Sea Hurricanes of 885 Squadron are ranged aft on *Victorious*
   while an Albacore of 827 Squadron takes off from *Indomitable*, with *Eagle*, shortly to
   be torpedoed and sunk, next in line and *Furious*, acting as an aircraft transport,
   bringing up the rear. *(IWM A15961)*

7. The USS *Ranger* was an attempt to squeeze as many aircraft carriers as possible out of the tonnage limits imposed by the Washington Naval Treaty, but she soon proved to be too small. *(IWM FL18153)*

8. The need to get more aircraft to sea meant that escort carriers were invaluable. This is HMS *Avenger* with Hawker Sea Hurricane fighters ranged on her deck. The carrier's merchant origins are obvious. *(IWM FL1268)*

9. A Sea Hurricane on *Avenger*'s lift - note the absence of folding wings. *(IWM A10982)*

10. The height of the attack on Pearl Harbor, with ships on fire and heavy AA fire.
(IWM MH6014)

11. HMS *Hermes* sinking within sight of the coast of Ceylon. By this time she was too old, too slow and too small to be of use for anything other than escort work.

(FAAM CARRIER H/11)

12. USS *Ranger* with Grumman Wildcat fighters during an exercise - note the wooden decks.

(IWM A19330)

13. *Hiryu*, with much of her flight deck blown away by US bombing, was one of four Japanese carriers lost at the Battle of Midway. Her unusual port side island can be clearly seen – she was one of only two carriers to have this feature. (IWM MH6492)

14. The only ship lost by the Americans during the Battle of Midway was the *Yorktown*. *(IWM OEM3672)*

15. Aboard *Yorktown*, her crew found it increasing difficult to keep on their feet as a serious list developed. *(IWM OEM3673)*

16. The Fleet Air Arm managed to damage the German battleship *Tirpitz* but her armour plating was proof against their bombs and the steep sides of the fjord ruled out air-dropped torpedoes. Here she is leaking oil after an attack. *(FAAM CAMP/568)*

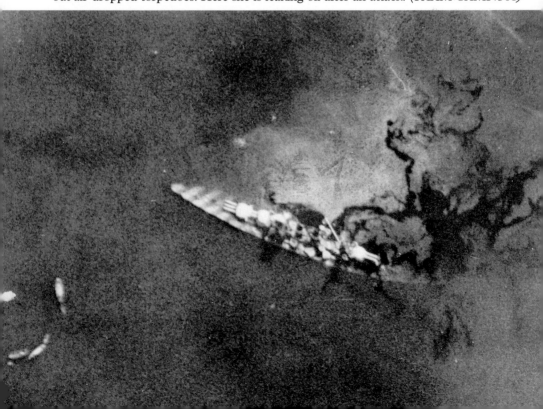

17. To get the Royal Navy and United States Navy used to working together, *Illustrious* and *Saratoga* operated against targets in Sumatra. The two ships are seen here at Trincomalee, or 'Trinco', in Ceylon.　　　　　　　　　　　　*(IWM A23475)*

18. *Saratoga* as seen from *Illustrious* with a Grumman Avenger in the foreground.
　　　　　　　　　　　　　　　　　　　　　　　　　(IWM A24265)

19. One of the many differences between British and American practice was the batsman's signals, which had to be standardized. Here a Corsair lands on *Illustrious* approaching the carrier at a tight angle. Note the two twin 4.5-in AA turrets almost flush with the flight deck. *(IWM A20995)*

20. *Ryujo* was typical of one Japanese approach to carrier design, completely without an island and with the bridge under the forward edge of the flight deck. *(IWM MH5927)*

21. More conventional to western eyes was *Unyru*.   *(MH5929)*

22. Here is *Shoho*, along with her sister *Zuiho*, clearly showing that she was a conversion, in her case from a submarine depot ship.   *(IWM5930)*

23. The Japanese also did half-conversions, such as the battleship *Ise*, with a flight deck in place of her aft turrets. Operations would have been difficult due to the turbulence from her superstructure. *(IWM MH5924)*

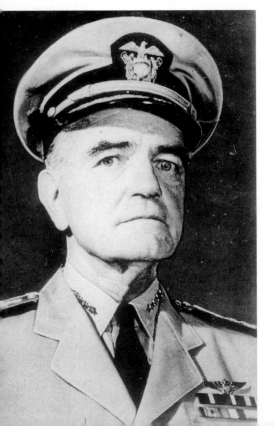

24. Commander of the US Third Fleet was Admiral William 'Bull' Halsey, so named because of his short temper. Halsey allowed himself to be lured away by a Japanese decoy force at Leyte Gulf and risked the safety of the landing fleet. (IWM NYF4736)

25. The designation of the US fleet at sea varied between Third and Fifth Fleet according
    to the admiral, but the carrier force, which alternated between being TF38 and TF58,
    was usually under the command of Vice Admiral Marc Mitscher. *(IWM NYP31440)*
26. So-called escort carriers had many important roles in the Pacific. Here Wildcats fly
    over *Ruler* - note the two-tone blue roundels to avoid confusion with the Japanese red.
                                                                      (FAAM Carrier R/6)

27. Described by many as the 'best fighter-bomber of the Second World War', the Corsair was a large aircraft and found the hangar decks of the British carriers a tight fit. *(FAAM Crosair/109)*

28. A Japanese torpedo-bomber crashes in flames as it succumbs to heavy AA fire. *(IWM NYP11545)*

29. Both Allied navies suffered from Kamikaze attacks on their carriers, although the armoured steel decks of the British ships offered greater protection. This is the flight deck of *Formidable* on 4 May 1945. *(FAAM CARS F/36)*

30. A largely wasted asset were the Japanese aircraft carrying submarines, some of which could carry two aircraft. An attack on the Panama Canal was planned, but never carried out, and two raids on the forests of Oregon seem to have been the only action. *(IWM MH6694)*

31. As the war progressed, new aircraft entered service, including the Curtiss Helldiver dive-bomber. *(FAAM US MIL/199)*

32. The United States fleet off the Marshall Islands in February 1944, with an Independence-class carrier in the foreground (note the four smokestacks), and in the distance the distinctive 'pyramid' islands of the Essex-class. *(IWM NYF 22732)*

defences, but while this operation was underway, shore-based aircraft of both the United States Army Air Force and United States Navy flew from Midway and, finding the Japanese carriers, attacked, disrupting the formation of the fleet and killing a number of crewmen working on the open decks in strafing attacks. The Japanese mounted an intense AA barrage and scrambled Zero fighters, with these defences accounting for seventeen American aircraft.

'This is fun', exclaimed Fuchida, as a Martin B-26 Marauder missed the *Akagi*'s bridge by thirty feet or so and, heading towards *Hiryu*, plunged into the sea. By this time, Fuchida was on the flight deck, propped up against the base of the island and taking notes.

The Japanese attack on Midway's shore installations caused considerable damage, but failed to put the airfield or the AA defences out of action. Tomanga radioed the carriers with a report and Nagumo decided to send a second wave to complete the operation and keep the US forces under pressure. The second wave could not be sent off immediately, however, as the aircraft had been armed with torpedoes expecting to launch an attack against US warships, and these had to be removed and replaced with bombs for the second attack on Midway itself. As this was being done, a reconnaissance aircraft finally discovered American warships, and radioed with a report that there were ten, sufficient to cause Nagumo to change his mind and reverse his order so that the bombs now had to be replaced with torpedoes. At this stage, there was still no indication that the Americans had an aircraft carrier, and because of the lack of fighter cover for the earlier attacks, the Japanese continued to assume that none was present. After consulting his staff officers, it was also decided that the second wave should wait until the first wave, by now returning with aircraft short of fuel, had been safely recovered. Meanwhile, in the hangar decks of the carriers, in their frantic attempts to follow first one order and then the counter-order, the armourers had left the bombs on the decks rather than sending them back to the magazines.

As they waited for the first wave to land, at 09.00 a reconnaissance aircraft radioed that it had seen an American aircraft carrier, which it believed to be the *Yorktown*.

The first wave finally landed and the aircraft were struck down into the hangars while the second wave aircraft were brought up and ranged on the flight decks, ready to take-off. None of the

Japanese ships had radar and there was no time to react when the first of the American aircraft were spotted. Spruance had put up the entire force from the *Enterprise* and *Hornet* while Fletcher had sent half of the *Yorktown*'s aircraft, making a force of 156 aircraft in all.

Leading the attack in the first wave were forty-one Douglas Devastator torpedo-bombers, seen as the ideal means of attacking ships at sea for, as one American admiral put it: 'It is easier to get water into a ship from the bottom than from the top.' Even if the Japanese ships had been fitted with radar, the low flying torpedo-bombers might still have escaped detection, at least until the last minute. Flying low over the sea towards the Japanese ships, no less than thirty-five of the Devastators were shot down, with their crews having little time to escape before their aircraft crashed into the sea. Most of the aircraft were accounted for by the carriers' AA defences, but a few Zero fighters managed to get into the air. Worst affected was *Yorktown*'s VT-3 squadron (VT for torpedo-attack squadron, 3 for the ship's pennant number), of which just one aircraft escaped. Those aboard the Japanese carriers who had feared a repeat of the Battle of the Coral Sea, were jubilant as confidence flowed back and they started to anticipate yet another great victory. They had accounted for more than fifty American aircraft in a single morning. The numbers involved in the first wave did nothing to shake their conviction that there was just a single American carrier present.

Radar would have caught the second wave of American aircraft as they flew high towards their targets, but the Douglas Dauntless dive-bombers remained unnoticed as they approached at 19,000 feet and the Japanese remained distracted by the low-level attack. At 10.22, the first dive-bomber peeled off and began its dive towards the *Kaga*. Twelve 1,000-lb bombs were dropped at the ship, and of these four hit her.

Aboard *Akagi*, still taking notes, Fuchida was amongst the first to notice the start of the American attack and yelled a warning to the control centre. Within seconds, the carrier's AA defences burst into life. From his vantage point, Fuchida could see that the first bomb was going to miss, but guessed that the second pilot would see this and correct accordingly. His judgement was correct, as the first bomb missed its target by around thirty feet, exploding in the sea and creating a large black geyser of water that washed over the bridge and blackened the faces of everyone there.

Anticipating a hit by the second bomb, Fuchida spreadeagled himself on the deck right by the island just before the bomb hit the flight deck, crashing through the amidships lift and into the hangar. A third bomb smashed through the flight deck to port and also went into the hangar. Below in the hangar where the bombs exploded, amongst the aircraft of the first strike and the bombs intended for the second strike, each of around 1,750-lbs. The bombs were caught by the explosions from the American bombs and a chain reaction started. Above, on the flight deck, aircraft fully armed and full of fuel, exploded in flames from the fires and explosions below, and a second chain reaction started as each aircraft set its neighbour alight. Flames swept across the flight deck while below the hangar had become an inferno.

The full impact of what was happening hit Fuchida as he went to the briefing room, and saw sailors bringing in the wounded but not making any attempt to get them to the sick bay. On asking why this wasn't being done, he was told that it was impossible.

'The entire ship is on fire and no one can get through', one of the rescuers told him.

The news hit Fuchida like a bombshell. Just a few hours earlier he alone had left the sick bay for his long ascent to the flight deck, leaving thirty-one sick and wounded men behind him. He attempted to reach his cabin in the hope of rescuing some of his belongings, but even this was impossible as fire and smoke turned him back.

Looking out to sea at the rest of the fleet, Fuchida could see that both *Kaga* and *Soryu* were in a similar plight, huge balls of smoke and flame. Only *Hiryu*, steaming well ahead of the other three ships, seemed unaffected. The four 1,000-lb bombs that had struck *Kaga* had exactly the same impact as those that had hit the flagship, while *Soryu* had taken three 1,000-lb bombs from *Yorktown*'s aircraft in a straight line along her flight deck, with these too smashing their way through into the hangar deck where the same scene of aircraft and discarded bombs awaited. The whole operation had taken just four minutes.

Amidst these scenes of chaos and destruction, down in the water, hiding behind a seat cushion hoping not to be spotted by the Japanese ships, was a witness to the destruction, Ensign George Gray, the only survivor of *Hornet*'s Devastator squadron,

VT-8. Later, Gray described the Japanese carriers as 'burning like blow torches', when he was rescued by a Midway-based Catalina flying boat after thirty hours in the sea.

The order was given to abandon *Akagi*, but Nagumo decided that he wanted to go down with his flagship and was only persuaded with difficulty that his real duty would be to continue to direct the battle. He transferred his flag to a light cruiser, *Nagara*. Fuchida followed, but broke both his legs leaping from the carrier to the light cruiser and had to be taken to the *Nagara*'s sick bay.

Destruction had been far beyond the worst fears of the Japanese, who were still supremely confident in their abilities. Even Fuchida, who had objected to the operation, had never doubted that Midway would have been taken and that if they found the US Pacific Fleet, it would have been destroyed. Fuchida's reservations had been centred on whether or not Midway was the right choice, since he doubted its value as a base, and he was also concerned at the number of relatively minor operations, in strategic terms 'side shows', on which the carrier force had been expending its energies, including trained and experienced manpower.

Rear Admiral Yamaguchi immediately ordered a strike against the *Yorktown*, and the aircraft took off from *Hiryu* at 11.00. Just eight Aichi D3A Val bombers managed to penetrate *Yorktown*'s fighter screen and intense AA fire, but they succeeded in dropping three 500-lb bombs onto the carrier. The first bomb exploded amongst parked aircraft ranged on the flight deck and set them alight, while the second hit the funnel and blew out the fires for five of the carrier's six boilers. The third actually penetrated the flight deck and travelled down three decks to ignite an aviation fuel tank. Prompt damage control saw the aviation fuel fire smothered with carbon dioxide while the magazines were flooded as a precautionary measure. It looked as if the *Yorktown* would survive.

That afternoon after lunch, Yamaguchi ordered his remaining aircraft to make a second attack on *Yorktown*, sending Tomonaga, who had led the first raid on Midway and then had been one of the few to return to *Hiryu* after the first strike against *Yorktown*, with just ten Nakajima B5N Kates and six Zero fighters. By this time the carrier was again operational, refuelling aircraft on deck. When the Japanese aircraft were spotted, refuelling stopped as the aviation fuel system was quickly drained, but this meant that only six Grumman F4F Wildcats were available to provide fighter cover with whatever fuel was left in their tanks.

'We only had forty gallons of gas apiece,' recalled Lieutenant (later Captain) J.P. Adams in a BBC documentary, *Pilots at Sea*. 'But nonetheless, they wanted to get us off to try to oppose the torpedo attack. Lieutenant Thach (later Admiral) and myself and four others manned the planes . . . All the guns in the Fleet were firing. I vividly remember taking off, trying to crank up my wheels and charge the guns, which we had to do manually and then trying to catch the torpedo planes. I did catch one and possibly another.'

In all, the fighters shot down five torpedo planes, but four managed to get within range of the crippled carrier. *Yorktown* avoided two torpedoes, but another two hit her on the port side. Three bombs also found their target. Adams saw the torpedoes strike the ship and realized that there was no way he could land, but nevertheless managed to reach the deck of the *Enterprise* about forty miles away with just a few gallons of fuel left in his aircraft's tanks.

It was now the turn of the *Yorktown*'s captain to give the order to abandon ship. When Tomonaga reported the hits on the *Yorktown*, Yamaguchi immediately jumped to the conclusion that a second American carrier had been hit and that there were now no American carriers in the Pacific. *Hiryu* prepared yet another strike against the Americans, but before this could be flown off, Dauntless dive-bombers from *Enterprise* and *Hornet* found her and attacked, with at least four bombs hitting the ship as she manoeuvred in a desperate bid to escape, and another four were near misses. Once again, aircraft burst into flames and fires swept across the flight deck and the hangar.

Later that afternoon, *Soryu*, abandoned and burning, blew up. Fifteen minutes later, *Kaga* blew up as the fires reached her magazines. *Akagi* survived the night and was sunk in a torpedo attack by Japanese destroyers at dawn, with a similar treatment dealt out to *Hiryu*, but the ship remained afloat and also survived an attack by Boeing B-17 Flying Fortress bombers before finally slipping beneath the waves at 09.00 with her captain and Yamaguchi still aboard.

On learning of the loss of all four carriers, Yamamoto abandoned the invasion of Midway and withdrew westwards.

Spruance then gave chase, with *Enterprise* and *Hornet*, hoping to catch the seven Japanese battleships at sea. On 6 June, *Mikuma* and *Mogami*, two heavy cruisers, from the assault group, collided and were seriously damaged, falling behind the rest of the Japanese fleet. United States Army Air Force and United States Navy aircraft from Midway attacked, but caused little damage. Later, US carrier aircraft attacked both cruisers, sinking *Mikuma* and badly damaging *Mogami* and two destroyers.

Meanwhile, efforts to save the crippled *Yorktown* continued with a destroyer providing an escort , but on 7 June, both ships were found by the Japanese submarine *I-168* and torpedoed, delivering the *coup de grâce* to the carrier and also sinking the destroyer.

The Americans might not have won the war in the Pacific at Midway, but the Japanese had lost any chance of winning. The early advantages of surprise attack and superior forces had been lost, as had the impression of Japanese invincibility created in the first few frantic weeks of war as the Emperor's forces spread rapidly across the Pacific and westwards through south-east Asia and Indonesia. The process of change from aggressor to defender had taken exactly six months!

King was later to write:

> The battle of Midway was the first decisive defeat suffered by the Japanese Navy in 350 years. Furthermore, it put an end to the long period of Japanese offensive action, and restored the balance of naval power in the Pacific. The threat to Hawaii and the west coast was automatically removed, and except for operations in the Aleutian area, where the Japanese had landed on the islands of Kiska and Attu, enemy operations were confined to the South Pacific. It was to this latter area, therefore, that we gave our greatest attention. (*US Navy at War, 1941-1945*)

VIII

ALLIES ON THE OFFENSIVE

German defeat was not inevitable before the end of 1943, by which time it had become only a matter of time, but the year 1942 marked the turning of the tide in every theatre of war. In the convoy war on the North Atlantic, the first escort carriers closed the Atlantic Gap, and the great American victory at Midway had dealt the Japanese a severe blow from which they never recovered. Nevertheless, these hopeful moves did not stop Joseph Stalin, the Soviet leader from demanding a second front, despite the pressures on his allies who were fighting an all-out war in both hemispheres, including mounting a major bomber campaign against strategic targets and major cities in enemy occupied Europe. An invasion of mainland Europe was impossible at this stage. Many in the United Kingdom and United States, and indeed some Germans, argued that the 'second front' was indeed the Allied bombing campaign.

Many Americans wanted the war in Japan to be pursued first, understandably given the nature of the attack on Pearl Harbor. Nevertheless, others, including both Ernest King and George Marshall, realized that Germany had to be given priority, not only because it was possible to attack Germany directly from bases in Great Britain, but because not until the war with Germany had been won could adequate forces be diverted to finish the war in the Pacific. King has often been portrayed as seeing the war against Japan as his priority, and to some extent it had to be because of the very real threat Japan posed first to Hawaii, then to the sea lanes linking the United States and Australia, and then to the west coast of the United States. Nevertheless, he never seriously challenged the need to defeat Germany first. A plan for the invasion of occupied Europe was prepared by the Operations Division of the US War Department which, it was felt could be launched in late spring 1943 with forty-eight divisions, although an emergency plan was prepared for an invasion using just five divisions during September 1942 if the position on the Russian front were to deteriorate suddenly. In either case, the landing site at the time was not seen as Normandy but as an area between Le Havre and Boulogne. At this stage, as in the Pacific, the restriction on action was the shortage of suitable transports, including not just landing craft for the invasion but also transports to move large numbers of US troops across the North Atlantic. In fact, the 'emergency landing' considered for September 1942 would have had to depend entirely on British troops. The stark truth was that the 1942 option was recognized from the start as being 'sacrificial', since success with such a small force was seen as unlikely – it could only serve to reduce the pressure on the Russian front. An alternative British plan was for an invasion of Norway. Landings in North Africa were also considered.

The British were to prove reluctant to tackle an invasion of France at this early stage, on the grounds that sufficient resources were not available. Norway was doubtless favoured because the difficult terrain would make it difficult for German reinforcements to be sent quickly. North Africa was favoured by the British as it would at a stroke relieve pressure on the Suez Canal and on Malta, on the verge of starvation at the time, and provide a jumping off point for an invasion of Italy, always seen as the weak link in the Axis. In one sense, the British strategy mirrored the step-by-step approach favoured by King in the Pacific. On the other hand, King felt that the resources needed for an invasion of North Africa would delay his plans for the Pacific theatre. In the end, Churchill's view prevailed, but Churchill also pressed ahead with a plan to seize and briefly hold a port on the French coast. The complete failure of the Dieppe raid on 19 August 1942, with half of the 5,000 troops landed being killed or captured, was to show just how difficult landings in France could be without adequate forces supported by overwhelming air power.

Madagascar

Even before the Battle of Midway, the Allies had started to secure their position in the east. The large island of Madagascar off the coast of East Africa, was of vital strategic importance. Under Vichy French administration, it provided a base for Axis commerce raiders in the Indian Ocean, and with the Mediterranean now all but impassable, Madagascar was close to the long convoy route around the Cape of Good Hope and through the Suez Canal to Egypt. Despite its potential importance, the Axis Powers were unable to give Madagascar the strong defence that it needed, simply because the Suez Canal was closed to them, as were the Straits of Gibraltar to all but submarines. The long sea route from Europe was also vulnerable to attack by British ships and aircraft from Gibraltar, Britain's West African colonies and, of course, from South Africa. Had Japan been so minded, it is possible that she could have seized and held Madagascar, at least for a time, but cooperation between the European and Asian arms of the Axis was never strong, and in any case before long the Japanese were to have difficulty maintaining seaborne communications even within their Asian empire.

On 5 May 1942, in Operation Ironclad, British forces were landed at Diego Suarez, in the far north of the island. Aircraft from eight Fleet Air Arm squadrons provided air cover and ground attack, operating from two carriers *Indomitable* and *Illustrious*, with the latter now back from her extensive repairs in the United States following her sufferings off and in Malta in January of the previous year. The carriers were part of a balanced naval force that included the battleship *Ramillies*, as well as two cruisers and eleven destroyers. While the landings took until 8 May to become fully established, little local resistance was met.

Nevertheless, while securing Madagascar was a step in the right direction and provided additional security for the Cape route, mainly for ships heading north towards the Suez Canal, it was well away from the harsh realities of the war and the vital objective of securing Axis defeat. This had to come through North Africa and southern Europe before a head-on clash in northern Europe could be contemplated.

Operation Torch
–the Landings in North Africa

In North Africa, the British Eighth Army inflicted a major defeat on the German *Afrika Korps* at the Battle of El Alamein, which lasted from 23 October to 5 November 1942. This was to be the first major British victory on land, although the Japanese were to be held in Burma, but it was also the last in which Britain fought alone.

By this time, even before El Alamein, the Allies had planned landings in North Africa, to squeeze the Germans between British and American forces. The North African landings were known as Operation Torch, and involved landing almost 100,000 men in Vichy French territory, on the Atlantic coast of French Morocco and in Algeria. In between these two large areas of Vichy territory lay neutral Spanish Morocco. Responsibility for the operation was divided between the British, with the Eastern Task Force, and Americans, with the Western Task Force. The Allies now had General Dwight Eisenhower as Supreme Commander while Admiral Sir Andrew Cunningham was Allied Naval Commander. Force H under Vice Admiral Syfret, with the aircraft carriers *Victorious* and *Formidable*, and three battleships, including the new *Duke of York*, defended the eastern flanks of the invasion force from the Italian fleet and German U-boats. The Eastern Task Force under the command of Rear Admiral Sir Harrold Burrough had three cruisers, sixteen destroyers and the elderly aircraft carriers *Argus* and *Furious*, with two escort carriers, to cover sixteen transports and seventeen landing craft to put ashore Major General Ryder's 33,000 British and American troops near Algiers. The landings to the north and south of Casablanca in French Morocco were covered by a Western Task Force, TF34, from the United States which had twenty-three transports to land 34,000 troops commanded by Major General Patton, protected by three American battleships, seven cruisers and thirty-eight destroyers, with air support provided by the USS *Ranger* and four American escort carriers.

In between these two major task forces, was a Centre Task Force that had sailed from England under the command of Commodore Troubridge, with two escort carriers, three cruisers and thirteen destroyers escorting twenty-eight transports and nineteen landing craft to put 39,000 men ashore at Oran in Algeria under the command of Major General Frendall.

Landings started at around 01.00 on 8 November at Oran, and then a little later at Algiers, while those in Morocco started at 04.30, with further landings at Safi, almost 200 miles to the south of Casablanca. In the days that followed, there were additional landings further east in Algeria at Bougie on 10 November, and after troops fighting east from Algiers joined up, at Bone on 12 November. The Algerian coastline extended well over 500 miles, while the landings in French Morocco were separated from those in Algeria by some 350 miles of Spanish Moroccan coastline. Coordination was helped by Troubridge maintaining a signals team of more than 100 personnel using a dozen radio wavebands located in a former armed merchant cruiser, *Large*. An idea of the tight timescale in which this, the first big Allied invasion, had been put together can be gathered from the fact that *Large*'s staff officers had to use umbrellas when sheltering in what was supposed to be their accommodation aft of the bridge!

Despite the size of the operation, almost complete surprise was gained. Nevertheless, the rapid expansion of both navies also meant that there were problems with inexperienced aircrew. Aboard the American escort carrier USS *Santee*, there were just five experienced pilots, and she was to lose twenty-one out of her thirty-one aircraft during Operation Torch, with just one of the losses possibly due to enemy action.

The uncertain position of the Vichy French forces was highlighted by the campaign, as the commander-in-chief of the Vichy Navy, Admiral Darlan was present in Algeria at the time. Darlan agreed to surrender if Marshal Petain, the Vichy French dictator agreed, but Petain was pre-occupied with stopping German forces occupying Vichy France. In the end, Darlan accepted surrender, but the lack of firm orders from Vichy meant that many of his subordinate commanders continued to fight, and gained time for German forces to enter neighbouring Tunisia.

While the battleships and cruisers attacked French ships and shore installations, the aircraft from the carriers were sent to attack airfields.

'We thought that we had taken the French Air Force by surprise as we caught their bombers on the ground, and this was just before the sun came up over the horizon,' recalled Lieutenant (later Captain) George Baldwin[1] who was senior pilot, or second in command, of 807 Squadron, flying Supermarine Seafire L2s.

> It was just light enough to see targets for strafing and we went in rather over-confidently. I certainly made at least three strafing runs, which was later a forbidden . . . tactic . . . it became doctrine that you only ever made one run on a strafing attack because the danger rose so rapidly after the first run. I was sure that I had done very heavy damage to three bombers.

After pulling out of the . . . attack, I was horrified to see a French Dewoitine fighter coming straight at me head on at about a thousand feet. I managed to evade him and turn in behind him, and give two bursts of machine-gun fire, because all my cannon ammunition had been used in the strafing. Saw hits and his undercarriage fell down.

I then decided it was time to get home as quickly as possible . . . but just as I was making my way back to the coast, I saw a second Dewoitine at right angles to me on my port side. And as I saw him, I saw machine-gun fire coming underneath me, and this was followed . . . by a huge explosion behind my seat, and I expected the aircraft to go out of control, but curiously nothing seemed to happen . . .

He was soon to discover that his aircraft's radio wasn't working as he attempted to return to *Furious*, and this was followed by the realization that the pneumatic system had also failed. He flew past the ship, signalling that he would have to land without flaps, meaning a faster than usual approach onto the elderly carrier's short flight deck. Fortunately, his undercarriage worked. On landing, he found that he was the centre of attention for a large number of aircrew and naval ratings who surrounded his aircraft. It was not until he climbed down from the cockpit that he discovered why – there was a large hole about two feet in diameter on the port side immediately behind his seat and inside he could see that the fuselage was full of acid as a result of the accumulator blowing up. His radio was in pieces. Potentially most serious of all, only one of the control wires to the rudder had not been severed, and this had got him back safely, otherwise he would have been in trouble, losing control at just 1,000 feet. Indeed, he could see that his Seafire had looked after him very well, as the armour plate behind his seat had been peppered with shrapnel and yet he escaped unscathed.

Baldwin's squadron commanding officer was the only person shot down from the squadrons aboard *Furious*, and was taken prisoner by the Vichy French. He sat in a French general's office while they decided what to do with him, and when they eventually surrendered, he was returned, going aboard the carrier just two days after being shot down and one of the shortest spells as a prisoner of war on record!

Meanwhile, at Casablanca aircraft from the USS *Ranger* and

gunfire from a US battleship, caused severe damage to the French battleship *Jean Bart*.

Vichy resistance in North Africa ended on 9 November in Oran. The surrender persuaded the Germans that they should finally occupy Vichy France, which they did, reaching Toulon on 27 November. Italian forces took the opportunity to invade Corsica.

The landings in North Africa marked the end of German and Italian ambitions in that continent, turned the balance of power in the Mediterranean and considerably eased the plight of Malta. They laid the foundations for the next step in the war, taking ground forces into Axis territory for the first time. These plans were not without controversy – the American Admiral Ernest King wanted specific tasks to be allocated to both the British and the Free French, with the British Eastern Fleet at the time serving little useful purpose when he felt that it could be used to sever Japanese shipping links with Rangoon. At the Casablanca Conference in January 1943, King explained that according to his estimates, just fifteen per cent of the total Allied effort was being devoted to the war against the Japanese in the Pacific, and that this would not be enough to stop them from consolidating their gains. His view was opposed by General Sir Alan Brooke, Chief of the Imperial General Staff, who felt that the Japanese were by this time on the defensive in the Pacific. The First Sea Lord, Admiral Sir Dudley Pound, felt that the British could not send naval units eastwards without strong carrier air support.

Given Churchill's reluctance to engage in either a major assault in Burma or a direct assault on Europe from the British Isles, and King's concern that the troops in North Africa should not be left idle, eventually it was decided to mount a campaign against either Sicily or Sardinia. King strongly favoured the former.

Operation Husky
–The Landings in Sicily

Some time elapsed between the landings in North Africa and the first invasion of Axis territory, Operation Husky, the Allied landings in Sicily. This was not simply because of the time needed to consolidate the Allied position in North Africa and finally defeat the Axis forces there, it was also due to the need to avoid the winter weather which even in the Mediterranean can be unpredictable and stormy. The irony was that when the operation did take place, it was hindered by unseasonably bad weather.

There had also been some disagreement amongst the Allies over exactly what the next step should be. The Americans and Russians would have preferred an invasion of France in 1943, but the British argued successfully at the Casablanca conference in January 1943 that the time was not right. The British saw an invasion of Sicily not simply as a stepping stone for the invasion of mainland Italy, it would also clear the shipping lanes through the Mediterranean, finally relieving the pressure on Malta and in allowing shipping to the Middle East and Australia to use the Suez Canal once more, it would at a stroke free a considerable volume of shipping, on one estimate giving the Allies the equivalent of more than a million tons of merchant shipping.

As a preparation for the operation, the small Italian islands of Pantelleria and Lampedusa, to the west of Malta, were taken on 11 and 12 June 1943 after the garrisons had surrendered following a heavy naval bombardment accompanied by raids by Malta-based aircraft of the RAF and the Fleet Air Arm. The scene was set for Husky, scheduled for 10 July.

For Operation Husky, two aircraft carriers were assigned, *Indomitable* and *Formidable*, from Force H, now under the command of Vice Admiral Willis. The carriers were able to give close air support, but most of the 3,700 aircraft available to the Allies were based ashore with Malta, less than twenty minutes flying time from Sicily. Allied aircraft heavily outnumbered those available to the Axis forces, which had just 1,400 aircraft. The Allies gathered together a force of almost 3,000 ships for the invasion, including 2,000 landing craft which included for the first time the new LST, Landing Ship Tank. Where the balance of power lay heavily with the defenders was in manpower, with 180,000 Allied troops facing 275,000 in General Guzzoni's Italian Sixth Army.

Once again the Allied forces were divided into a Western Naval Task Force, this time under Vice Admiral Hewitt USN, to land Lieutenant General Patton's US Seventh Army on the southern coast of Sicily, while an Eastern Naval Task Force under Admiral Ramsay RN landed the British Eighth Army under Lieutenant General Montgomery on the south-east point of the island. The main bases for the attack had to be in North Africa – Malta was far too small to host an operation of this size although the island's three airfields were very much in the fray.

The weather on 10 July was bad with high winds and heavy seas, so that at one stage postponement was considered. While the adverse weather may have lulled the defenders into a false sense of security, it also resulted in heavy losses amongst the paratroops and glider-borne forces. As before, Force H provided fighter cover for the landings, but apart from a single Ju88, discovered by two Seafires but which shot down one of the fighters, many Allied pilots did not recall seeing an enemy aircraft for the first four days after the invasion. The reason for the sluggish response from the Axis forces was quite simple, they had believed that Sardinia would be the most likely location for an Allied landing, even though Sicily was the most obvious springboard for an invasion of Italy itself and much closer to the Allied bases in North Africa and Malta. The only advantage of Sardinia would have been that it would have offered bases from which bombers could have attacked Italy and the South of France more easily than from Sicily, and perhaps also allowed the later invasion of the Italian mainland to take place further up the 'leg' of Italy, but again, this would have meant a bigger leap than necessary for the Allies.

Nevertheless, a counter-attack did come on 11 July spearheaded by German panzer divisions, but this was successfully countered by the invasion forces with the support of air power and a heavy bombardment by the major fleet units in Force H.

Unfortunately, it seems that the Allies became too relaxed, with an Italian aircraft successfully attacking and seriously damaging *Indomitable* with an air-launched torpedo after those aboard mistook the aircraft for a Swordfish. Some at least of those aboard the carrier put the Italian success down to carelessness as the carrier was supposed to have the protection of a battleship acting as radar guardship. A chief petty officer spotted the aircraft approaching in the moonlight and called up to the bridge, 'enemy aircraft approaching', only to be told that he shouldn't worry as it was a returning Swordfish. The torpedo was dropped close to the carrier and blew a 30 feet gash in her side, forcing her to divert to Malta for emergency repairs and there found that the Axis air forces were still capable of mounting a heavy aerial attack. Her squadrons were disembarked prior to *Indomitable*'s arrival in Grand Harbour, and spent an uncomfortable spell in poor tented accommodation at the height of the Mediterranean summer while the Axis mini-blitz extended to the airfields.

It took just over a month for the Allies to secure Sicily, and it would have been an encouraging start to the assault on the Axis strongholds in Europe had not most of the German and Italian forces on the island been able to slip away across the Straits of Messina over several nights, so that 100,000 troops remained free to fight another day!

Onto the Mainland
–The Salerno Landings

If carrier borne aircraft had been useful, but not essential, for the invasion of Sicily, they were vital for the next stage, the invasion of mainland Italy with landings at Salerno. Although Salerno was within range of aircraft operating from airfields in Sicily, it was only just within range for fighter aircraft, leaving a Spitfire with just enough fuel for twenty minutes on patrol above the beachheads, and far less if engaging enemy aircraft. The obvious solution was to station aircraft carriers off the coast to provide fighter cover.

Salerno was an attempt to shorten the war in Italy, and in this, as we shall see, it was unsuccessful for reasons that might not have been fully foreseen at the time. Montgomery's Eighth Army had already crossed the Straits of Messina into Calabria on 3 September 1943, a relatively easy operation but one that left them at the very tip of the 'toe' of Italy with some considerable distance to move through hilly terrain fighting German and Italian rearguard actions. Salerno was some 200 miles further north. The prospects at first seemed extremely bright, for on the same day that Montgomery moved into Calabria, an armistice was signed in secret at Syracuse with Marshal Badoglio's new Italian government, formed after Mussolini had been deposed in July. Negotiations for the armistice had been prolonged as at first the Allies were suspicious of Italian objectives, but this did at least give the Allies time to plan their assaults on Salerno and Taranto, fully recognizing that the Germans were likely to continue to resist whatever the Italians decided. This was another reason for choosing Salerno; the hope that a substantial number of German troops would be cut off and unable to withdraw. The armistice was announced on 8 September, on the eve of the Salerno landings, but it might have been as well to have waited another twenty-four hours as the Germans were able to move quickly to seize Italian airfields, although the Italians for their part were able to move most of their fleet to prevent it falling into German hands. Had the Germans not known about the armistice in advance, the landings at Salerno could have been easier.

The landings at Salerno, Operation Avalanche, on 9 September were coordinated with a British airborne landing at Taranto to seize the port and enable enemy shipping there to escape to Malta. Vice Admiral Henry Hewitt USN landed Lieutenant General Mark Clark's US Fifth Army in a landing fleet covered by an Independence-class light fleet carrier and four escort carriers, as well as eleven cruisers and forty-three destroyers, while Force H, still under Vice Admiral Willis, had the battleships *Nelson* and *Rodney* with the aircraft carriers *Illustrious* and *Formidable*, as well as Force V with the maintenance carrier *Unicorn* operating in the combat role with another four escort carriers, known in the Royal Navy as auxiliary carriers, *Attacker*, *Battler*, *Hunter* and *Stalker*. Force V was under the command of Rear Admiral Sir Philip Vian. Meanwhile, the Mediterranean Fleet had escorted Italian warships to Malta before supporting the Taranto landings with heavy gunfire from the battleships *Warspite*, *Howe*, *Valiant* and *King George V*, after which *Warspite* and *Valiant* were redeployed to provide heavy gunnery support for the Salerno bridgehead. While the two large armoured carriers were intended to defend the fleet and look for enemy shipping, the carriers in Force V were solely concerned to provide fighter support, with each escort carrier carrying a single squadron of thirty Supermarine Seafire LC2s, with their engines tuned to provide maximum power at 5,000 feet instead of the usual 15,000 feet, making it a very different aircraft from those at the North African landings almost a year earlier. *Unicorn* carried two squadrons with a total of sixty Seafires. As in the North African landings, the aircraft would be used to provide air cover and also to provide ground attack against German troops and airfields.

The Seafire was a big improvement in performance over anything that the Fleet Air Arm had operated before, being faster than the Sea Hurricane, although less manoeuvrable and more difficult to repair, and it had folding wings. The modifications necessary for carrier operation meant that it was slightly heavier than the Spitfire, from which it was derived, and so slightly slower. George Baldwin was once again one of the fighter pilots involved and was a former naval test pilot himself, having flown with the Naval Air Fighting Unit at RNAS Yeovilton. He visited the RAF to discover the latest in fighter tactics and up-to-date intelligence on German aircraft. The RAF personnel were helpful, but this couldn't disguise bad news. The latest versions of the Messerschmitt Bf109 and the new Focke-Wulf Fw190 were indeed formidable opponents, with the latter aircraft also having the manoeuvrability that the Bf109 lacked. Anxious to squeeze the last ounce of performance out of the aircraft, a programme of 'local modifications' was put in hand. The exhaust manifolds were removed and replaced with exhaust stubs to reduce drag and increase the thrust from the exhaust. The knobs for catapult (known at the time as 'accelerators') operation from carriers were also removed, further reducing drag. Good quality furniture polish was somehow obtained, despite wartime rationing and restrictions on production of quality materials, and everyone, pilots included, spent hours polishing the leading edges of the wings to make the aircraft more slippery. Introduced between May and June 1943, in time for the invasion of Sicily, these changes gave the aircraft another 15 knots maximum speed. The Seafire rarely needed catapult assistance during take-off, but at Salerno the question was academic for most of the Seafire pilots as the escort carriers lacked catapults or accelerators, despite having a much lower maximum speed than the purpose-built carriers, known as fleet carriers in Royal Navy parlance. The Seafire suffered from two shortcomings. The first was that, in common with many British fighters early in the war, it was short on range. The second was its tendency to pitch forward on landing, at best damaging the propeller, at worst the aircraft could be damaged beyond repair.

The British carriers made a feint towards Taranto after leaving Malta, although the assault on Taranto was covered by six battleships from Force H and the Mediterranean Fleet, and by aircraft from Malta. The announcement of the armistice saw the Italian Navy leave its ports of La Spezia, Genoa, Castellamare and Taranto and steam towards Malta, being escorted by four of the Royal Navy's Mediterranean battleships, leaving the other two to accompany *Illustrious* and *Formidable* to Salerno. Despite the escort, the *Luftwaffe* mounted a heavy aerial attack against the Italian ships, sinking the new battleship *Roma* and damaging the *Italia*.

The aircrew aboard the carriers of Force V were awakened at

04.30 on the morning of 9 September. Several of those present recalled not having had much sleep and few had any appetite for the breakfast of eggs and bacon put before them in the wardroom. Amongst the first into the air before dawn were eight Seafires drawn from *Unicorn*'s 809 and 887 Naval Air Squadrons, with four aircraft providing high cover and another four low cover, looking out for enemy dive-bombers and torpedo-bombers respectively. The practice was for aircraft to carry extra fuel in drop tanks, extending their patrol time, and to use this first as the tanks would have to be dropped to reduce drag before engaging in aerial combat. That first day, there was little sign of the *Luftwaffe*, but the troops landing encountered fierce resistance. In the days following the invasion, a strong counter-attack was mounted by mainly German forces accompanied by heavy aerial attack by the *Luftwaffe*, so that the entire operation soon appeared to be in difficulty.

Life was difficult aboard the carriers, with Force V given a 'box' offshore in which to operate, flying off and recovering their aircraft. In practice, this box was far too small for the ships, giving the carrier commanders great difficulties as they charged from one end to the other, but the situation was even worse for those in the air, with large numbers of aircraft circling within a confined space, the danger of a mid-air collision was very real as they waited to land on ships steaming close to one another. At times a light haze added to the difficulties. As luck would have it, the whole operation took place in conditions of complete calm, with little wind – never more than 3 knots – and the Seafire needed 25 knots of wind over the deck for a safe take-off or landing, but the escort carriers could only manage 17 knots. Arrester wires had to be kept even tighter than usual, as were the crash barriers two-thirds of the way along the flight decks.

'Judgement of speed over the water, and height above the water, on the approach to land was extremely difficult,' recalls George Baldwin, by this time an acting lieutenant commander with the role of Naval Air Wing Commander and responsible for the four squadrons embarked in the four British escort carriers.[2]

Looking at ways around the problems, Captain Henry McWilliams, commanding officer of the escort carrier HMS *Hunter*, asked Rear Admiral Vian for permission to saw nine inches off the wooden propeller blades of the Seafires. Vian wisely decided that the personnel aboard the carriers knew more about the problem than he did, and gave his permission. The modification was relatively easy for the ships' carpenters to do and had little effect on the performance of the aircraft, while propeller damage during landing was much reduced. After initial trials, the entire stock of replacement propellers aboard the carriers was also treated in the same way.

In other ways too, it often seemed to be a case of learning through trial and error. The casualty rate amongst the Seafire pilots seemed to be unduly high in the air, not just in landing, as many seemed to be unable to bale out quickly enough. Learning the hard way, it was soon discovered that the RAF-recommended method of escaping from a Spitfire, rolling the aircraft and opening the canopy before undoing their seat belts and 'ejecting' (in other words, falling out) from the aircraft, didn't work. Possibly this was due to the higher weight of the Seafire. Eventually pilots were advised to jump over the side of the aircraft, and the survival rate amongst those shot down improved immediately.

Turning their attention to the carriers, the *Luftwaffe* mounted intensive attacks during 11 September, forcing the carriers to operate at full speed even when not flying-off or landing aircraft, and fuel consumption increased considerably. For the first time, the Germans used glider-bombs, saving their aircraft from the intense AA fire put up by the fleet offshore. That evening, Vian was forced to signal Vice Admiral Henry Kent Hewitt in overall command of the operation: 'My bolt will be shot this evening, probably earlier.'

Hewitt had just been briefed by Lieutenant General Mark Clark on the situation ashore, and guessed that more air attacks were imminent. He signalled back, 'Air conditions here critical. Can your carrier force remain on station to provide earlier morning coverage tomorrow?'

'Will stay here if we have to row back to Sicily,' Vian confirmed.

Hewitt's guess proved to be right. He wasn't surprised to learn that the carriers were low on fuel, but he didn't realize that they were already on their emergency supplies. The reason for the difficulty was not so much the German attacks forcing the carriers to operate at maximum speed throughout the day, but that the planners had assumed that the Fleet Air Arm would be needed for two days, or three days at worst if the invasion met stiff resistance. After that, it was expected that airfields ashore would have been taken and would be available. As so often happens in warfare, everything was not going to plan. The airfields were not available that would allow the Royal Air Force and United States Army Air Force to bring aircraft forward from their bases in Sicily.

In the end, the carriers remained on station until 14 September, by which time the 180 Seafires had been reduced to just thirty, more by accident than the efforts of the *Luftwaffe*. One consequence of this was that many senior officers blamed the Seafire for the losses, rather than a combination of factors that had to include the difficulty in operating high performance aircraft off escort carriers with their short decks, lack of accelerators and low speed, in light wind conditions. The aircraft had its weaknesses, and as one naval officer put it, 'was too genteel for the rough house of naval flying', but it had its strengths, as Baldwin had discovered earlier during Operation Torch. It was also true that the naval air squadrons had carried out far more than the planned number of sorties, despite the high accident rate.

Even with land-based aircraft to support the ground forces, German resistance proved strong and was joined by a number of Italian units who had refused to surrender. In a further attempt to bypass German resistance, further landings were made at Anzio in January 1944, this time without carrier air support, which may have contributed to the difficulty the invasion forces had in breaking out of their new bridgehead. It took four months.

Landing in the South of France

By August 1944, the entire strategic situation in Europe had been transformed. Not only had German resistance been broken and Rome liberated, but Allied forces had landed in Normandy in June. This had been another major operation without carrier air cover, but on this occasion the reasons had been simple; it wasn't necessary. The Normandy beachheads were within range of airfields in the south of England and the sheer size of the invasion force and the constant stream of vessels across the English Channel meant that there would have been no room for carriers to operate their aircraft. A number of Fleet Air Arm aircraft had flown from shore bases in the south of England in support of the landings and the bridgehead, while naval aircraft also flew reconnaissance sorties and operated in the spotter role for the heavy guns of the battleships and cruisers covering the landings. The Italian campaign was maintained throughout this period because it forced the Germans to divert ground and air forces from the Normandy campaign.

Landings in the south of France were an easier option than landing in Normandy, although logistically it would have been difficult to have put the same quantities of men and *matériel* into such an operation as had been achieved in the Normandy landings, which had even included the construction of two ports to keep the invaders supplied. Serious consideration had been given to an invasion of the south of France as early as August 1943, but the British had objected declaring that it would divert resources from the advance through Italy, which they believed would lead to an invasion of Germany through Austria – a highly optimistic assumption given the intervening terrain! The south of France had then slipped down the Allied order of priorities as attention focussed on the invasion of Normandy, through which France and the Low Countries could be liberated, and meanwhile further landings in Italy at Anzio had proved necessary. The original name for the invasion was Operation Anvil, but this was later changed to Dragoon.

The south of France was seen as being easier than Normandy as the Germans had not taken Vichy territory until late 1942, and not only did they not have the time to build anything on the scale of the famous 'Atlantic Wall' fortifications along the English Channel coastline, but the resources were also becoming increasingly scarce. By this stage in the war as well, interference from enemy naval forces could also be discounted. As a consequence, the fast armoured carriers of the Royal Navy were sent to the Pacific to join the United States Navy in taking the war ever closer to Japan, and instead the entire air defence and ground attack needs of the landing force was entrusted to the two navies using nine escort carriers, with the five British ships carrying Supermarine Seafire L2Cs again, and the four American ships carrying the new Grumman Hellcat, a true carrier fighter aircraft. Heavy fire support was provided by three US battleships plus one each from France and the UK, while the United States Navy also provided three heavy cruisers.

The overall invasion fleet was under the command again of Vice Admiral Henry Hewitt who was to land Lieutenant General A. M. Patch's US Seventh Army and General de Lattre de Tassingny's II Free French Corps along the French Rivieras between Baie de

Cavalaire and Calanque d'Antheor. Rear Admiral Tom Troubridge commanded the British carriers and Rear Admiral Durgin the US ships.

Landing on 15 August, more than 56,000 troops came ashore on the first day, and by 28 August, the key naval base of Toulon had been surrendered as well as the major port of Marseilles. The most notable feature of these landings was the limited effort from the *Luftwaffe*, leaving the naval airmen to provide support for the ground forces. One pilot recalled having a good relationship with the US Army commanders who made good use of naval aerial reconnaissance.

The lessons of the Salerno landings had been learnt, with more aircraft carriers and adequate room to manoeuvre, while the carriers were able to retire to Corsica for replenishment and new aircraft, so there was none of the fuel shortages that had so nearly placed the Salerno operation in jeopardy. It was also fortunate that the weather conditions were ideal for carrier operations with a breeze and gentle swell offshore.

For many of the American carrier pilots, it was their first experience of operational flying, and much attention was paid to minimizing their casualties during the vital first sorties.

'We were very worried about the Americans, they were . . . unblooded,' George Baldwin recalled[3].

They had come straight from the United States and never seen any kind of action before. So they had been given a very considerable briefing by some of our air staff on the sort of things they needed to know about the German opposition . . . type of anti-aircraft fire and what not to do . . . The poor chaps, they flew a flight of four aircraft over Marseilles the first morning in formation in a straight line and the first salvo from the 88-mm guns knocked two of the four aircraft out of the sky. Sad loss . . .

The Americans had been warned that aircraft should never fly in formation or in a straight line, but instead be well spaced to allow weaving and never to fly between 9,000 and 11,000 feet when climbing or ascending, since the German 88-mm AA guns were very accurate between these heights. Sound advice, but it had either not been passed down to the squadrons or had been ignored.

113

The landings in the south of France were successful, putting additional pressure on German forces and providing yet another front on which German troops had to fight. They were followed soon afterwards in September and October by British naval forces, using nothing heavier than cruisers and escort carriers, cutting the German evacuation routes across the Aegean from Greece and destroying the remaining German naval units in the Aegean.

The Offensive against the *Tirpitz*

Having sunk the German battleship *Bismarck*, attention invariably had to turn to the fate of her sister ship, the *Tirpitz*. Having lost the pride of the German fleet in May 1941, the Germans were understandably reluctant to see *Tirpitz* share the same fate. They didn't need to risk the ship. The mere presence of the ship in a Norwegian fjord was enough to keep the British on their toes, and the mistaken belief that she was at sea caused the Admiralty to order that convoy PQ17 to Russia should scatter, with disastrous consequences. The ship also caused the Royal Navy and Royal Air Force to expend a considerable effort on attempts to sink her, with the Fleet Air Arm mounting no less than nine attacks on the ship and the Royal Air Force seven raids. This was difficult given the strong natural defences of her hiding place, but on 22 September 1943 an attack by British midget submarines damaged the *Tirpitz* so badly while she lay in the Altenfjord that she was out of action for six months.

Beyond the reach of the heavy guns of the fleet and situated where normal submarines could not get to her, attack from the air seemed to be the only course. On 3 April 1944, the Fleet Air Arm launched a major operation to sink the ship using no less than five aircraft carriers, including HMS *Victorious*, a sister ship of *Illustrious*, and the elderly *Furious*, as well as the three escort carriers, *Emperor*, *Pursuer* and *Searcher*. The larger carriers carried Fairey Barracudas for dive-bombing and torpedo-dropping, while the escorts carried a mixture of Grumman Wildcats and Hellcats and Vought Corsairs to provide fighter cover. A more effective aircraft than the Albacore, the Barracuda was another attempt to replace the Swordfish, and around 2,600 were built, even though it was described by some as a 'maintenance nightmare', and also had the unfortunate reputation of occasionally diving into the ground.

Given the difficult location, the raid needed to be conducted in daylight, and a dawn raid was decided upon to give the attackers at least the cover of darkness while on their way to the target. The aircrew were woken at 01.30, having been briefed that this was to be a very dangerous operation and that heavy casualties must be expected.

The first strike aircraft were flown off at 04.30, flying just above sea level to evade enemy radar, before climbing to 8,000 feet to cross the snow-covered mountains. They arrived over the ship at 05.30.

'As I looked at this hill, it fell below us slowly, and then with a sudden surge we were over the top,' recalled Sub Lieutenant John Herrald[4].

> There below us lay the *Tirpitz* in the exact place we had been told to look for her. Suddenly the leader shouted over the intercom: 'Attention fighters! Anti-flak! Over, over!' and as he said that he was slowly doing a half-roll and going down to the target. We peeled off and dived down behind him. While we were going down on our attack, the fighter squadrons were strafing the anti-aircraft positions and ships. They supported us with everything they had got, no risk seemed too great for them to take.
>
> I had the nose of my aircraft pointing just below the funnel of the *Tirpitz*. I could see the fighters raking her decks, and for a few seconds I lived in a world which just contained my aircraft and the *Tirpitz*. I kept her nose glued to that point of the ship. I gazed at my altimeter and saw that I had a thousand feet to go until I got to my bombing height. In the few seconds that followed I could see the details of the ship; the swastika painted on her funnel, the faces of the ack-ack crews glaring up at us, and, a great sight, the leader's bombs bursting on the turrets.

He dropped his bombs as he pulled out of his dive and started to weave to avoid enemy flak as he climbed away.

A second wave of aircraft appeared an hour later, fully expecting a hot welcome from the Germans, but they could still see the ship through a smoke screen produced by canisters placed around the fjord, while the smoke made it difficult for the AA gunners to see the attacking aircraft. The attack succeeded in inflicting further damage on the warship, with a large oil leak as evidence, ensuring that she was out of action for another three months.

One 1840 Squadron fighter pilot, Lieutenant Commander Ron Richardson, was flying one of the Grumman Hellcats that had strafed the *Tirpitz* and on his climb away from the ship spotted a German radar station on a hill top. Out of ammunition, he dropped his arrester hook hoping to catch the wire strung between two masts, and as he did so, he was caught by German AA fire and killed.

The Fleet Air Arm had done well to damage the ship for her position made it difficult to get low enough to launch a torpedo attack while the size of bombs used could only bounce off her armour plating. It was not until the advent of very heavy bombs that could be dropped alongside the ship that air attack presented a real threat. On 15 September 1944, Avro Lancaster heavy bombers from the RAF's famous 617 'Dam Busters' Squadron used 12,000-lb 'Tallboy' bombs, but again only caused damage, although this time it was serious enough for the ship to be moved south to Tromso for repairs. Here she was a far easier target, and on 12 November, operating without fighter protection, 617's Lancasters found her again, and this time their 'Tallboy' bombs scored three direct hits, causing her to capsize. The *Tirpitz* no longer presented a threat, but one Royal Navy officer had the bad grace to claim that she had still not been sunk as her hull was out of the water!

Notes
^{1–3} Imperial War Museum Sound Archive Accession No. 12038/3-6
⁴ Imperial War Museum Sound Archive Accession No. 2508/D/B

IX

TURNING BACK THE
JAPANESE TIDE

After their great success in the Battle of Midway, the Americans were in the position to take the initiative in the Pacific. It was American commanders who could decide where and when to strike on the offensive while Japanese forces were forced to be increasingly on the defensive. The construction by the Japanese of a naval base and airfield on the island of Guadalcanal, part of the Solomon Islands, posed a threat to sea communications between the United States and Australia. The Americans wanted to secure the sea lanes, having realized early on that isolating Australia from the United States would be a logical strategic move.

The still new Commander-in-Chief United States Navy, Fleet Admiral Ernest King, described this phase of the war as 'Offensive-Defensive', the earlier stage having been 'Defensive-Offensive'. This was a realistic assessment. In the earlier stage that had really ended at Midway, the Allies, meaning the Americans with Australian and British help, were primarily concerned with stopping Japanese expansion, and took the war to the enemy whenever they could and whenever their resources allowed. Midway had started as a defensive battle, as had the Coral Sea before it. Now, the Allies were increasingly well placed to attack the Japanese, but could still not neglect defensive measures. Officially, however, that is to King and to his Army counterpart, General George Marshall, the offensive-defensive started with the landing on the Solomon Islands on 7 August 1942. King's strategy was clear. Priority was to be given to holding Hawaii, followed by maintaining communications with Australia, the very line of communication that many Japanese strategists wanted to see broken. This line secured, King advocated a step-by-step general advance through the New Hebrides, Solomons and the Bismarck Archipelago. In fact, both aspects of the strategy were interdependent since Japanese forces would be drawn away from their attempts to isolate Australia from the United States to ward off the American advance. This step-by-step approach, creating a number of strong points along the way, also recognized that it was the only way of bringing substantial forces within reach of the Japanese home islands.

King's approach was cautious and never underestimated the enemy. There were to be no short cuts. A good example of his strategy unfolding was that he was brought under some pressure by General Douglas MacArthur, Supreme Commander of the South-West Pacific Area, to support the capture of Rabaul, for which MacArthur wanted a naval task force including two aircraft carriers, a division trained in amphibious warfare and a very substantial number of land-based heavy bombers. King and Marshall did not favour this plan, mainly because the balance of power was still at this early stage so finely balanced that Rabaul would be exposed to a strong enemy counter-attack, and indeed could prove to be more of a liability than an asset, taking forces that would be better used elsewhere. Another problem was that so early after American entry into the war, suitable transports for moving troops were not available.

The order of priorities in the Solomons was to be the capture of the Santa Cruz Islands and Tulagi, using a Task Force under the command of Admiral Chester Nimitz, followed by MacArthur taking Lae, Salamaua and the north-east coast of New Guinea, and only then was Rabaul to be taken, along with other positions in New Guinea. This would mean that when it was finally occupied, Rabaul would no longer be exposed and its defence would not tie down unnecessarily large forces.

Landings in the Solomons

Officially code-named Operation Watchtower, the landings on Guadalcanal and Tulagi on 7 August 1942 were under the overall command of Vice Admiral Ghormley, after heated disagreements between the United States Navy and United States Army over which service should take the lead in the war in the Pacific. Many cynics in the invasion force also called the landings 'Operation Shoestring' because too much haste and too many short cuts had been taken in its preparation, but Japanese plans lent an air of urgency to the exercise. Had the Japanese been able to establish themselves firmly on Guadalcanal, their presence would not only have posed a very real threat to the sea lanes between the United States and Australia, but once there with an operational airfield and naval base, they would have been very much more difficult to dislodge than while they were still working on these projects. Rear Admiral Turner commanded an assault force of nineteen transports carrying the 19,000 men of Major General Vandegrift's 1st Marine Division. Vice Admiral Fletcher provided support for the invasion with Task Force 61 comprising the three aircraft carriers USS *Enterprise*, *Saratoga* and *Wasp*, as well as the battleship *North Carolina*, six cruisers and sixteen destroyers, with Rear Admiral Crutchley commanding another eight cruisers and sixteen destroyers from the Royal Navy. The United States Navy had acted quickly to retire its Douglas Devastator torpedo-bombers after their poor showing at the Battle of Midway, but the nature of the operation also meant that the Dauntless dive-bomber was likely to be of far greater use.

The invasion started with a heavy bombardment at 09.00 on 7 August, and by evening all 11,000 men of the Guadalcanal invasion force were safely ashore, meeting little resistance as the Japanese had not anticipated an invasion and most of the manpower on the island were construction workers, most of whom disappeared into the jungle as the first bombs fell. The airfield itself was taken the following day and promptly renamed Henderson Field.

It was not until the night of 8–9 August that any response came from the Imperial Japanese Navy when at midnight Vice Admiral Mikawa attacked the Allied force of five cruisers and six destroyers lying to the west of Guadalcanal, off Savo Island, to protect the landing fleet, with the benefit of complete surprise from the direction of Rabaul with a hastily assembled force of seven cruisers and a destroyer. In the night action off Savo Island, a short but fierce clash, all five of the Allied cruisers were damaged, with two sinking the following morning and another two capsizing, while of the Japanese ships, only Mikawa's flagship *Chokhai* was hit. Having scored a brilliant success, for some reason Mikawa then failed to make the most of his advantage, ignoring the American landing fleet and rapidly withdrawing, only to have the cruiser *Kako* sunk by an American submarine.

A different situation arose on nearby Tulagi, where fierce resistance was met by the 6,000 men landed there and who only suppressed the 1,500 Japanese on the island after two days of heavy fighting. After the night action off Savo on the night of 8–9 August, they were cut off from their supplies until the Americans were able to start operating aircraft out of Henderson Field on 20 August.

Having taken Guadalcanal and Tulagi, the Americans had to defend their acquisitions, as the Japanese managed to land reinforcements on Guadalcanal on 18 August, and Henderson Field became the scene of intense fighting. The first batch of Japanese reinforcements with just 915 men showed that the Japanese had seriously underestimated the strength of the US forces, and was wiped out in a battle on 21 August. A steady war of attrition was then started by the Japanese, with reinforcements being landed under cover of darkness in an operation dubbed the 'Tokyo Express' by the Americans. A somewhat more determined effort to reinforce their troops on Guadalcanal came in late August when the Japanese sent four transports to reinforce their troops on the island, but the four transports were really just elderly destroyers and again the total number of troops to be landed totalled just 1,500 men, suggesting that the Japanese were still underestimating the size of the US forces.

The Japanese move found Vice Admiral Fletcher with TF61 still including the carriers *Enterprise* and *Saratoga*, with a total of 176 aircraft available, but with the *Wasp* away refuelling. His opponent was Vice Admiral Nagumo, who had survived the Battle of Midway and had retained his command. Nagumo, who was now responsible for ensuring the safe arrival of the transports, had three aircraft carriers, *Zuikaku* and *Shokaku*, with 131 aircraft between them, and the small *Ryujo*, with thirty-one aircraft which, with a cruiser and two destroyers, was to act as a diversionary force. Given the small size and number of the transports, Nagumo had a considerable number of surface vessels to protect these and his carriers, with three battleships, ten cruisers and twenty-one destroyers in addition to those with *Ryujo*, compared with Fletcher's single battleship, four cruisers and eleven destroyers.

The Americans were expecting increased Japanese activity and indeed spotted *Ryujo* early on, but had then lost track of the Japanese ships by 21 August. On 23 August, American reconnaissance aircraft once again found the Japanese transports, but a strike launched from the US carriers failed to find them. The next day, *Saratoga*'s aircraft found the *Ryujo* at 10.00 some 300 miles north of TF61, and this time the strike aircraft found her and promptly sunk her using bombs and torpedoes. Meanwhile, Japanese aircraft from *Shokaku* and *Zuikaku* found and attacked the USS *Enterprise*. The carrier's fighters and AA defences fought off the first wave of Japanese torpedo-bombers, but a second wave of dive-bombers managed to hit the *Enterprise* three times, starting fires, although these were soon extinguished and the ship remained capable of limited operations.

On 25 August, United States Marine Corps aircraft based ashore on Guadalcanal and Esperitu Sanctu attacked the Japanese troop transports, sinking the largest one and a destroyer escort, while a cruiser was also badly damaged. By this time, in addition to the ships lost, the Japanese had lost a total of ninety aircraft against just twenty US aircraft, and Nagumo decided to withdraw.

The United States had won yet another battle in the Pacific War, the Battle of the Eastern Solomon Islands. It is hard to see why the Japanese, having put so much effort into escorting such a pitiful reinforcement convoy, had not assumed a more aggressive role, and the only justification can be that the strategy was one of tying down US forces. Nor did the Japanese cut their losses and abandon the islands, as despite losing the battle, they continued to maintain the 'Tokyo Express', while the destroyers engaged on these runs also took the opportunity to shell Henderson Field. Had the Americans had airborne radar at the time, the night-time destroyer runs could have been stopped. On 31 August, a more substantial force of 3,500 Japanese troops were landed on Guadalcanal, building up their forces to a total of 6,000 men by early September, by which time the Americans had 19,000 men on the island. These Japanese troops were defeated in a night battle on 13–14 September. Vandegrift was given additional reinforcements on 18 September, bringing his troop strength up to 23,000 men, but it was at this stage that the Japanese Imperial Headquarters gave top priority to the re-conquest of Guadalcanal. The Japanese reinforcements arrived from Rabaul on 11 October, escorted by Yamamoto and the Combined Fleet, with the naval battle of Cape Esperance taking place that night, but this was inconclusive with few losses on either side, allowing the Japanese to land their reinforcements bringing their garrison on Guadalcanal up to 20,000 men, while Henderson Field was subjected to intensive bombing. Having failed to stop the Japanese, Ghormley was replaced by Vice Admiral Halsey.

The use of United States Marine Corps aircraft at Guadalcanal was at this stage by no means unusual, with a third of the ground attack aircraft being flown by Marine pilots. It was all the more surprising that the following year, Admiral Chester Nimitz, the commander of US forces in the Pacific, should decide to omit carrier training from the syllabus, especially as the new escort carriers were starting to become available and could have been designed 'Marine carriers'.

At the same time, the United States Marine Corp's flying had evolved from the original intent of providing an aerial observation post role for forces once ashore. The same process had happened to some extent in the United States Army some years earlier. During the Solomons campaign the United States Marine Corps had revived the AOP role, borrowing twenty-four Piper O-1 Cub high-wing monoplanes from the United States Army. The aircrew and maintenance personnel for this important task came not from the existing ranks of Marine Corps pilots but from those marines who had peacetime experience of private flying! Not only did it not denude the combat squadrons of experienced personnel, it also meant that the pilots of the AOP aircraft were often those who had the necessary experience of gunnery and so were well placed to help with artillery direction.

On the night of 11–12 October, in a surface fleet action using shipboard radar, the Americans managed to inflict a convincing victory on the Japanese. But, as we will see later, it was to take two major naval battles and much fighting ashore before the Japanese finally decided to abandon Guadalcanal. For the last time in the war they managed a successful evacuation of the 12,000 men left on the island during 1–7 February 1943, using destroyers at night and abandoning all of their heavy equipment. They lost 25,000 men during the six month campaign, more than a third of them through disease and starvation, compared with 1,592 US marines.

In the meantime, the Americans also lost the aircraft carrier *Wasp*, which had returned to TF61 and was attacked off Guadalcanal on 15 September by the submarine *I-19*, which put three torpedoes into the ship. The torpedoes caused serious fires to break out as aviation fuel lines ruptured and the *Wasp* had to be abandoned, finally being sunk by torpedoes from the destroyer

USS *Lansdowne*. The *Wasp* had served with the Atlantic Fleet before moving to the Pacific, and her loss was felt most in Malta, to which she had ferried almost 100 fighters on two trips into the Mediterranean. Her survival in a major battle was always suspect, as the carrier had been built to fit into total tonnage limitations imposed by the Washington Naval Treaty. The United States Navy had just 15,000 tons left under the Treaty provisions for aircraft carrier construction, and while a further vessel of the Yorktown-class would have been the preferred option, the General Board had no choice but to 'build down', incorporating as many features as possible from the larger carriers, and this, plus the desire to accommodate a full size carrier air group, produced a design with some potentially fatal flaws. Despite this, she was the first carrier to have a deck edge lift, something that has become very much a characteristic of American carriers since.

Battle of the Santa Cruz Islands

Throughout the war in the Pacific, Japanese intelligence seems to have been faulty, both at the macro and micro levels. At the latter, Japanese reconnaissance would frequently mistake a tanker for an aircraft carrier, at the former, it always seemed to under-estimate American strength or exaggerate Japanese successes, with any appreciation of the raid on Pearl Harbor being a good example. Yet another instance of Japanese over optimism came in October 1942, when the Imperial Japanese Navy received a report maintaining that Henderson Field had been recaptured, meaning that the Americans no longer had aerial superiority in the eastern Solomons. Unaware that the report was inaccurate, Admiral Yamamoto sent the Japanese Combined Fleet to complete the recapture of Guadalcanal, and in one sense, the balance of power was once again with the Japanese, since Admiral Halsey had just two aircraft carriers available following the loss of the *Wasp*.

The United States Navy's two aircraft carriers in the area were the *Enterprise*, recently repaired, in Vice Admiral Kinkaid's Task Force 16, with eighty-four aircraft, and the *Hornet* in Vice Admiral Murray's Task Force 17, with eighty-seven aircraft. Henderson Field had another sixty aircraft, mainly of the United States Marine Corps. The remainder of the US fleet was just one battleship, six cruisers and fourteen destroyers, many of which

123

were heavily engaged in blocking the 'Tokyo Express' operation.

The Japanese had no less than four aircraft carriers once again, with a total of 212 aircraft. Vice Admiral Kondo in the van of the fleet had *Junyo* with fifty-five aircraft, supported by two battleships, five cruisers and fourteen destroyers, while the main fleet under Vice Admiral Nagumo had the other three carriers, *Shokaku*, *Zuikaku* and *Zuiho*, with 157 aircraft, as well as two battleships, five cruisers and fifteen destroyers.

Aware of the approaching Japanese ships, the Americans launched their first strike on 25 October, but failed to find their opponent. Early the following morning, the Battle of the Santa Cruz Islands started in earnest, after US reconnaissance aircraft found the *Zuiho*, and at 07.30, the USS *Hornet* sent a strike of torpedo-bombers and dive-bombers, escorted by Grumman Wildcat fighters. Slightly before this, at 07.10, anticipating American action, Nagumo had sent a first wave of aircraft to attack the *Hornet*, with the aircraft reaching the ship shortly after 09.00. Fifteen dive-bombers and twelve torpedo-bombers fell on the *Hornet*, with one bomb hitting the flight deck before a bomber flew into the island, although it remains unclear whether this was an aircraft out of control, possibly with the pilot pulling out of his dive too late, or a pilot, perhaps frustrated by a bomb being 'hung up', attempting a suicide operation. Then two torpedoes hit the carrier on her starboard side, before three 500-lb bombs smashed their way through the wooden flight deck and into the hangar. Within ten minutes, the ship was ablaze and listing to starboard. Meanwhile, an American bomb had hit the *Zuiho*, causing serious damage.

At 09.30, the *Shokaku* was hit and seriously damaged by five bombs which, while they did not sink her, ensured that she was out of action for nine months. In what was an all-out battle between the two fleets, but conducted by carrier-borne aircraft, a second wave of Japanese aircraft found the *Enterprise* and managed to hit her with three bombs, but failed to put her out of action. In addition to putting up combat air patrols to provide fighter cover, the Americans mounted an extremely effective anti-aircraft fire, and it was this that accounted for most of the Japanese losses, with the battleship USS *South Dakota* alone claiming twenty-six enemy aircraft shot down.

That afternoon, a third wave of Japanese aircraft returned to attack the *Hornet*, which received a further torpedo and two bombs, eventually forcing the crew to abandon ship. The Americans then sent destroyers to sink the *Hornet* with torpedoes, but at this stage of the war American torpedoes were notoriously unreliable, with many not running straight and the nine that did hit failed to explode! The ship was finally sent to the bottom by torpedoes from a Japanese destroyer. All in all, it took four bombs and sixteen torpedoes, American as well as Japanese, to send *Hornet* to the bottom. She had been in service for just a year and seven days.

At this stage, it was clear to the Japanese that they had not recaptured Henderson Field and with their heavy aircraft losses, they were forced to withdraw. The loss of the *Hornet* was a major blow to the Americans, but in intense fighting, they had lost just seventy aircraft compared with the 100 lost by the Japanese.

Yet another Japanese attempt to land reinforcements came the following month, with a force of two battleships, two cruisers and fourteen destroyers under Vice Admiral Abe sent to Guadalcanal both to cover the landings and also to shell Henderson Field. This led to the naval Battle of Guadalcanal, one of the few in the Pacific War that did not include aircraft carriers. This started on 12 November when Rear Admiral Callaghan heard of the Japanese approach and took the two heavy cruisers *San Francisco* and *Portland*, with three light cruisers and eight destroyers. Callaghan had the advantage of radar, but not on his flagship, the *San Francisco*. His force had not trained together as a squadron and he decided to advance in a single line, but the coordination still necessary for this was found difficult to achieve. Approaching the Japanese as they shelled Henderson Field, in the darkness, at 01.40 on 13 November, the destroyer *Cushing* nearly collided with two Japanese destroyers, *Murasame* and *Yudachi*, and by this time confused as to which ships were which, the order to fire was not given until 01.45, but the Japanese managed to shell the light cruiser *Atlanta* and killed Rear Admiral Scott. The Japanese flagship *Hiei* sunk the *Cushing* and another destroyer, crippling a third. The two American heavy cruisers managed to hit the *Hiei* and also damaged two Japanese destroyers, but also crippled the light cruiser *Atlanta*. After Callaghan gave the order to cease firing at 01.55, the other Japanese battleship, *Kirishima*, hit the *San Francisco*, killing Callaghan. All in all, the first phase of the battle ended with the Japanese losing one destroyer, *Ataksuki*, which was sunk and having to abandon the *Yudachi*, while the

Americans lost two light cruisers, *Juneau* and *Atlanta*, the former damaged in the battle and sunk later by the submarine *I-26*, and five destroyers. During 13 November, aircraft from Henderson Field accompanied by carrier-borne aircraft from the *Enterprise* found the *Hiei* and sunk her.

Callaghan's difficulty in entering combat with a force not trained to fight as a squadron, and indeed one that found even steaming in line difficult, highlighted one problem facing the United States Navy having suddenly been thrown into a war by the Japanese attack on Pearl Harbor. The necessary training had not been taken, many commanders at all levels were inexperienced, and under the day-to-day pressures of fighting the war, there was neither the time or the opportunity, or indeed at first the ships, for training in many fleet manoeuvres. On the other hand, as the war developed, these became increasingly unnecessary as the burden of the aggressive war fell increasingly upon carrier-borne aircraft and submarines.

During the night of 13–14 November, the Japanese returned to bombard Henderson Field, destroying twenty aircraft. While a further surface vessel action did not materialize, after daylight aircraft from the *Enterprise* found the cruiser *Kinugasa* and sank her, after she had earlier been damaged, along with the *Izuso*, by aircraft from Henderson Field. *Enterprise*'s aircraft also damaged two Japanese destroyers. Aircraft from Henderson Field then sank seven out of the eleven transports under the command of Rear Admiral Tanaka taking troops to Guadalcanal, but the survivors continued to press on, expecting cover from a Japanese battle group.

Rear Admiral Lee, with the battleships *Washington* and *South Dakota* and four destroyers, was hastening to the area and was given the position of the Japanese battle group by the submarine *Trout*. Vice Admiral Kondo in the battleship *Kirishima* with three heavy and one light cruiser and nine destroyers started a further night bombardment of Henderson Field, and as the Americans arrived, a further night battle was started on 14–15 November. In the opening stages, in a gunnery duel, three American destroyers were crippled and later sunk, while the *South Dakota* suffered a complete electrical failure so that she was unable to use her guns, but was later fortunate to escape being hit in a Japanese torpedo attack. Unnoticed by the Japanese, the other American battleship, *Washington*, used her radar and in a surprise bombardment reduced the *Kirishima* to a wreck after which she sank. A Japanese destroyer also sank during the conflict. At 00.30 on the morning of 15 November, Kondo pulled his forces out of the battle, but Tanaka pressed on regardless, running his ships aground and landing a further 2,000 men, as well as 250 cases of ammunition and 1,500 bags of rice. The transports were destroyed by American aircraft later that morning.

Once again, the Japanese had shown themselves capable of putting a massive effort into an operation that could not justify the cost in personnel and warships. The Americans remained capable of keeping the Japanese under pressure both ashore and at sea, with a number of naval engagements, many of them involving just cruisers and destroyers. The one remaining success of the Japanese in the Solomons before they finally evacuated their troops from Guadalcanal was the sinking of the cruiser *Chicago* by a Japanese torpedo-bomber on 29 January 1943.

On 26 March 1943, a rare event in the Second World War, and especially so in the Pacific theatre, occurred when Rear Admiral McMorris with two cruisers and four destroyers attacked a Japanese convoy heading for the Aleutians, with Vice Admiral Hosagaya escorting the convoy with four cruisers and four destroyers. In a battle completely without aerial attack, the two forces fought an old fashioned naval engagement in the Battle of the Komandorski Islands, line against line, until their ammunition ran out. In the battle, the American cruiser *Salt Lake City* and a destroyer were damaged, as was the Japanese cruiser *Nachi*. Without ammunition and expecting an American aerial attack at any moment, Hosagaya turned back with the convoy.

As so often happens, once a major defeat is suffered, matters go from bad to worse. The Japanese soon saw that their luck had run out. They once again sent their carriers to Guadalcanal in April 1943, and suffered heavy losses from American aircraft based on the island. The Americans were not only in complete control of the air and the sea around the eastern Solomons by this stage, but they also had the advantage of knowing the Japanese codes. This was to pay a further dividend that same month, when they were able to intercept and decode the entire timetable for Admiral Yamamoto's planned inspection of the western Solomons. On 18 April, American fighters took off from Henderson Field and intercepted his aircraft, shooting it down. Admiral Koga was appointed in his place.

X

THE PUSH TOWARDS JAPAN

Having secured Guadalcanal at great cost to the Japanese and protected the sea lanes between the United States and Australia, the next move was to begin the advance towards Japan itself. This was easier said than done, for it literally meant island hopping across the Pacific until such time as bases were secured within reach of the Japanese home islands and the start of a bomber offensive that would see every Japanese city of more than 100,000 people razed to the ground, and culminate with the dropping of atomic bombs on Hiroshima and Nagasaki. In the meantime, one of the unsung successes of the Second World War was to be the American submarine campaign against Japanese shipping linking the furthest reaches of their new Asian empire, and its oil and rubber, with Japan itself. At the end, even the Inland Sea was not safe from American submariners.

After the Japanese withdrew from Guadalcanal, the Americans next moved to re-take Attu in the Aleutians on 11 May 1943, when Rear Admiral Kinkaid led a task force to land the US 7th Division, covering the landings with three battleships, an escort carrier, seven cruisers and twenty-one destroyers. By the end of May, Japanese resistance had ended and the 2,600 man garrison was either dead or captured. This was the first time that an escort carrier performed an offensive role, but it was not to be the last. Later, on 15 August, the Americans landed 34,000 men on Kiska, also in the Aleutians, after a heavy bombardment lasting two weeks, only to find that the Japanese had quietly evacuated the island before the bombardment started. This was one of the few instances of the Japanese sensibly making a strategic withdrawal, saving men and equipment. A planned contraction of the Japanese perimeter with improved convoy protection measures could well have made the war last longer.

Pressing Towards Rabaul

The Aleutians were important, being close to Alaska, that isolated state on the mainland of North America, but incidental to the main strategy, based on advances in Micronesia, which was initially to smash through the Bismarck Archipelago and capture the major Japanese base at Rabaul. A step-by-step approach was put in hand, anything else would have been risky and foolhardy. On 21 February 1943, the first step was taken when the US 43rd Infantry Division landed on the Russell Islands, finding that these were unoccupied.

Landing on an enemy shore has never been an easy business, and certainly not safe, but a major step forward came on 30 June 1943 with the American landings on Rendova Island, uncomfortably close to the Japanese air station on New Georgia. For the first time, purpose-designed landing craft were used, with three basic types introduced and making seaborne assaults much easier and faster. Rear Admiral R.K. Turner's landing fleet at Rendova included Landing Ship Tanks, or LSTs, each capable of carrying twenty tanks to the shore; Landing Craft Tank, LCT, each of which could carry three tanks; and Landing Craft Infantry, LCI, capable of carrying 400 men. Protecting this force were two aircraft carriers and three escort carriers, five battleships and supporting cruisers and destroyers, all in Task Force 31. A number of minor naval engagements took place as the landings and the resupply operations proceeded.

New Georgia was the obvious next step, and just two days after landing on Rendova, 2 July, American forces landed on the island. New Georgia proved to be an especially hard nut to crack. The Japanese garrison of 10,000 was ordered to hold the island for as long as possible, and the terrain favoured the defence, with tropical rain forest, wet climate and mountains, while there were reefs offshore on the north-east coast. Once again, the 'Tokyo Express' came into play, keeping the defenders resupplied under cover of darkness. At first, the Americans made little progress, but further landings followed, with an airfield being constructed by the Seabees, while heavy US bombing saw the destruction of all of the Japanese aircraft on the island, while eventually US naval forces in the Kula Gulf and Vella Gulf stopped the resupply operation for the Japanese forces. Even so, it was not until late October that New Georgia was secured, at a cost of around 1,000 American and Australian troops, many of whom died from tropical diseases, and 2,500 Japanese.

The same day that Kiska was taken, the Americans landed on Vella Lavella, bypassing the heavily fortified island of Kolombangara and tightening their grip on the Solomons. The following month, a new front opened with General MacArthur landing his VII Amphibious Force on Lae and Salamaua in New Guinea, with cover from a naval force led by Rear Admiral Barbey. Nevertheless, when Rear Admiral Wilkinson's III Amphibious Force landed the US 3rd Marine Division on the south coast of Bougainville, the most westerly of the Solomons and closest to Rabaul on New Britain, it proved impossible to end Japanese guerrilla resistance in the jungles until the end of the war.

On 5 November 1943, the Americans made their first big attack on Rabaul, where the Japanese had been reinforcing their naval units in anticipation of an American attack. Rear Admiral Sherman with the carriers *Saratoga* and *Princeton*, the latter a new light, or in British terms, light fleet carrier, sent ninety-seven aircraft in a surprise attack and damaged six Japanese cruisers for the loss of ten aircraft. Eight days later, on 11 November, Rear Admiral Montgomery sent 185 aircraft from the aircraft carriers *Essex*, *Bunker Hill* and *Independence*, damaging the cruiser *Agano*, already damaged in the earlier raid, and sinking a destroyer. A Japanese counter-attack from Rabaul was then successfully repulsed by the Americans without a single hit, as were further attacks on the US landing fleet at Bougainville, although two torpedoes hit American cruisers. Although not occupied by the Americans, Rabaul had been neutralized as an operational base.

By this time, the United States Navy was benefiting from the enormous strength of American industry, something that Yamamoto had feared even before the outbreak of war. The United States was capable of mass producing aircraft carriers on a scale never seen before or since. It could do the same with aircraft, all especially designed for carrier operation. Ships and aircraft are useless without trained manpower, and again, this was not a problem with the United States Navy churning out aircrew not only for itself, but for the Royal Navy as well. The Japanese could not replace their losses easily, the Americans could, and as the balance of power changed, American losses became less and less as airmen improved in experience, while the Japanese suffered correspondingly greater losses.

Essex was the lead ship of a new class of carriers, of which *Bunker Hill* was another. Laid down on 28 April 1941, she had been commissioned on 31 December 1942, despite displacing 27,200 tons. The Essex-class ships were intended to be an improvement over the last pre-war carrier, USS *Hornet*, with a ten per cent increase in aircraft capacity and more substantial protection, and, a sign of experience even this early in the war, a thirty-three per cent increase in aviation fuel. With the outbreak of war, all the old Washington Naval Treaty limits were immediately cast aside. The new ships were designed to carry ninety-one aircraft at the time of their construction. No less than twenty-four of these ships were built, some of them bearing the names of the United States Navy's early wartime losses, including both a new *Wasp* and a new *Hornet*, and later a namesake replacement for the light carrier *Princeton*, lost at Leyte Gulf. Within a year of the USS *Essex* being commissioned, another six ships had followed.

Features of the Essex-class included a much heavier anti-aircraft armament, but the changes went much deeper than this, with the machinery displaced so that the damage that could be done by a single torpedo strike was limited and the ship's survival was more likely. The Essex-class ships were easily identifiable by the 'pyramid' shape to the superstructure of the island. Despite lacking the heavy armour protection of the British fast armoured carriers, no Essex-class ships were actually lost during the war years, although a few were so badly damaged that they did not return to full operational duties. This might not have been a reflection of their condition so much as the inescapable fact that post-war the carrier fleet inevitably had to be reduced, and obviously the newest ships and those in the best condition were retained. Had hostilities continued, the badly damaged Essex-class vessels may well have had to return to service. It also seems that the Essex-class was much easier to repair than the heavily armoured British ships, even though, of course, they were also much easier to disable.

Of the other carriers mentioned, *Princeton* and *Independence* were both examples of the Independence-class. Realizing that more carriers were likely to be needed quickly, and that escort carriers, while cheap and easily produced, were not capable of keeping up with the fleet, the President of the United States proposed converting the hulls of the Cleveland-class light cruisers to aircraft carriers in an emergency carrier construction programme. Presidential intervention was not appreciated by the United States Navy which knew that the tight confines of a sleek cruiser hull was completely unsuitable for carrier construction, and in the event, the ships were unusual in appearance as the designers attempted to overcome the problems. The flight deck could not extend all the way to the bows because these were not wide enough to support it, and the curve to the bows, an attractive feature in a cruiser, so reduced headroom in the hangar that the forward lift had to be set slightly further back. The smallest island possible was designed and sponsored to starboard so that it did not impinge on the already limited width of the flight deck, while the four funnels were also offset to starboard and aft of the island for the same reason. The result was a fast light carrier of just 10,662 tons capable of carrying thirty aircraft. Nine ships were built, with another two as the Saipan-class with certain improvements in the light of experience. Despite the United States Navy's misgivings, the Independence-class was generally satisfactory and did much good work, except that the ships tended to be far more vulnerable to torpedo, bombing or kamikaze attack than the larger carriers, although it is debatable whether this was because of their smaller size and narrower beam, or because of design flaws. Although the Independence-class had two catapults forward for assisted take-offs, generally the United States Navy preferred to operate fighters and fighter bombers from these ships than the much heavier dive-bombers. Hangar space would also have been a consideration in this decision.

In considering the new carriers, it becomes obvious that British and American carrier design had diverged considerably in the years leading up to the outbreak of the Second World War. The Americans built their hangar and flight decks as part of the superstructure, while the British kept these features as part of the hull, so that the only superstructure on a British carrier was the island and smokestack. There were arguments in favour of either approach. The British design made it easier to have substantial armour protection on the flight deck and hangar deck and generally gave a far more streamlined approach. It was also easier to darken ship and yet continue working in the hangar. On the other hand, the American design made it easier to have side openings in the hangar, so that aircraft could be sent up to the flight deck with engines already running. On US carriers, testing engines in the hangar was much easier and safer than on the British carriers, although HMS *Unicorn* had features to help this. The design made repairs easier, although it was weaker than the British approach. Post-war, when the Admiralty decided to rebuild HMS *Victorious*, the costs, with successive design changes to incorporate new developments, were higher than the cost of a new carrier. The Americans, on the other hand, found it so much easier and cheaper to incorporate such features as the half-angled and then fully angled flight decks that so eased carrier operation and enhanced safety.

The one disadvantage of the superstructure hangar and flight deck was that it made it so much more difficult to make the ships light and weatherproof. Post-war, on refitting, many of the Essex-class ships received so-called 'hurricane bows', in which the bows of the ships were plated up to the flight deck, providing a smoother appearance similar to that of British carriers. While the forward AA armament tucked under the forward end of the flight deck was lost, this was obviously considered a minor inconvenience.

Taking the Gilbert Islands

Once the Solomon Islands were secured, American attention turned to the Gilbert Islands, also along the sea lanes between the United States and Australia and more than 1,000 miles to the north-east of the Solomons. This major move was delayed until late 1943, and in the meantime, the United States had used its carrier force sparingly, concentrating on building up its new carrier force and training the airmen, handlers and maintenance personnel. The Japanese had also been busy during the year; with just three carriers left operational, they had belatedly turned their attention to training and to rebuilding the much battered First Air Fleet.

The Americans now had redesignated their fleet for the Pacific, to be known alternatively as the US Fifth Fleet, under Vice Admiral Raymond Spruance, and the Third Fleet when under Vice Admiral 'Bull' Halsey. The exact composition of the two fleets could vary from time to time, but in essence the major fleet units were assigned to Halsey as the Third Fleet and Spruance as the Fifth Fleet, the concept being that while Halsey was at sea, Spruance was ashore planning his next campaign, and while

Spruance was at sea, Halsey would be ashore. The respective task forces within the fleets would also change their designation, so that TF38, for example, would become TF58 whenever Spruance was in command.

In preparing for the assault on the Gilbert Islands, the Americans not only had their two new classes of aircraft carrier, but they also had the escort carriers. The escort carriers were known informally to the British as 'Woolworth Carriers' because they were quick and cheap to build, while for the same reasons they were known in the United States Navy as 'Jeep Carriers'. The cynics took the official United States Navy designation of CVE, for carrier, escort, to mean 'combustible, vulnerable, expendable', since hasty construction – it was intended that they could be converted back to merchant ships after the war – and poor armour protection meant that they were vulnerable in battle. Known officially to the British as 'auxiliary aircraft carriers', by this time it was becoming clear that the British had a point as the Battle of the Atlantic had been virtually won by late 1943, and the so-called escort carriers, that had done so much in this and on the Arctic convoys, were now free for other tasks, acting as aircraft transports, maintenance carriers or providing additional flight decks, usually in support of forces ashore, as at Salerno, since their low speed made them unsuitable for fleet actions.

American tactics at this stage were also well defined. Before mounting any landings, considerable effort would be devoted to 'softening up' the target area using carrier-borne aircraft and the heavy guns of the battleships and heavy cruisers. This has become the standard since for any invasion, or indeed even any major assault across a front line. While such efforts obviously alert the enemy to the forthcoming attack, it not only wears him down, it also means that coastal artillery and fortifications, airfields, barracks and communications are all battered, hopefully reducing loss of life in the invasion force and enhancing the chances of success.

For the landings on the Gilbert Islands, Spruance had six large aircraft carriers, five light carriers, five battleships and six cruisers, as well as twenty-one destroyers. The carrier fleet, under Rear Admiral Pownall, consisted of *Yorktown, Lexington, Enterprise, Essex, Bunker Hill* and *Saratoga*, with the light carriers being *Independence, Princeton, Monterey, Belleau Wood* and *Cowpens*, accompanied by the battleships *South Dakota, Washington, Massachusetts, North Carolina* and *Indiana*.

The landings in the Gilbert Islands were preceded by a series of attacks by the 700 carrier aircraft of the Fifth Fleet, starting on 19 November. The main targets were all Japanese airfields within range of Makin and Tarawa, the two islands selected for the initial landings. It took just three days to put most of the aircraft, mainly belonging to the Japanese Navy Air Force, on the Gilbert Islands and the eastern Marshall Islands nearby, out of action. On 20 November, the landing fleet put ashore the US 2nd Marine Division and part of the US Army's 27th Infantry Division, with some 7,000 men landing on Makin and another 18,000 on Tarawa, which had the main Japanese garrison of some 5,000 troops. Makin was taken on the first day, despite fierce resistance by the Japanese garrison of 800 men. On Tarawa, despite the intensive softening up raids that continued, a third of the Marines making the initial assault were hit by enemy fire, and it took three days to suppress Japanese resistance which culminated in mass suicide attacks by infantry on the night of 22–23 November.

The landings were not without cost for the United States Navy, which saw the USS *Independence* crippled by a torpedo dropped by one of the few Japanese aircraft to get airborne on 20 November, putting the carrier out of service for six months. On 24 November, the USS *Lipscombe Bay*, an escort carrier, was torpedoed by the submarine *I-175*, and sank shortly afterwards.

Nevertheless, by 26 November, the US forces had overcome the fierce Japanese resistance and had occupied the Gilbert Islands.

After the Gilbert Islands were occupied, the carrier force was divided into four separate groups that could act independently or come together for major operations. On 4 December, two of the carrier groups mounted an attack on Kwajalein Atoll, a major Japanese air base and refuelling point in the Marshall Islands, and afterwards, as they withdrew, the new *Lexington* was struck by an air-dropped Japanese torpedo. Nevertheless, in the final month of the year, American forces landed on Arawe and on the south coast of New Britain, and on 26 December, at Cape Gloucester and on the western tip of New Britain, getting closer to Rabaul all of the time.

The Advance on Truk

The year 1944 started with further American landings in New Guinea, this time cutting off a substantial Japanese army, on 2 January. Between 29 January and 6 February, Vice Admiral Marc Mitscher took a substantial carrier force, Task Force 58, to attack Japanese airfields in the Marshall Islands, including Kwajalein Atoll, to cover landings by US forces. Mitscher's ships included the carriers *Essex, Enterprise, Yorktown, Intrepid, Bunker Hill* and *Saratoga*, as well as the light carriers *Belleau Wood, Princeton, Langley, Cowpens, Monterey* and *Cabot*, with a total of 730 aircraft, as well as the battleships *Washington, Massachusetts, North Carolina, Indiana, South Dakota, Alabama, New Jersey* and *Iowa*, escorted by three heavy and three light cruisers and thirty-six destroyers. This was entirely aimed at suppressing the Japanese defences, as the landing on Kwajalein Atoll by the US 4th Marine and 7th Infantry Divisions on 31 January was covered by Vice Admiral Raymond Spruance with eight escort carriers carrying 190 aircraft, and supported by the battleships *Pennsylvania, New Mexico, Mississippi, Tennessee, Idaho, Colorado* and *Maryland*, escorted by nine cruisers and forty-five destroyers. The landings were to take Kwajalein itself as well as the islands of Roi and Namur. A force of 8,800 Japanese troops put up yet another fanatical resistance, but within a week, the islands were in US hands, as was the unoccupied atoll of Majuru, seized to provide a good anchorage for the large American fleet.

Even in their most pessimistic moments, the Japanese planners cannot have conceived of being attacked, besieged even, by such substantial forces with a total of more than 900 aircraft between them.

If the Japanese forces had swept through southern Asia and across the Pacific in little more than a couple of months in the winter of 1941–42, the American advance was also impressive, given that they had to face fanatical Japanese resistance with often substantial bases. Much has been made of the deficiencies in the Japanese armoury, such as the absence of effective tanks, but this is largely irrelevant since the territory over which battles were being fought was not good tank country, being either mountainous or thick jungle, and sometimes managing to be both.

Any advance has to have a momentum, and mustn't be bogged down. An essential element in the planning is to be able to predict and forestall enemy counter-measures. For this reason, the next stage had to be an assault on the island of Truk, in the Caroline Islands and to the west of the Marshall Islands. Truk was home to substantial Japanese forces. This time it was Spruance's turn to lead the assault, taking the aircraft carriers *Essex*, *Enterprise*, *Yorktown*, *Intrepid* and *Bunker Hill*, as well as the light carriers *Belleau Wood*, *Cowpens*, *Monterey* and *Cabot*, with the battleships *New Jersey*, *Iowa*, *North Carolina*, *Massachusetts*, *South Dakota* and *Alabama*, escorted by ten cruisers and twenty-nine destroyers. Given the size of these forces, Spruance was disappointed to find that the harbour at Truk was occupied by only the lighter units of the Japanese fleet, although carrier aircraft found and sank the cruiser *Naka*. An auxiliary training cruiser, *Katori* and two destroyers were also sunk by the guns of the American battle-ships; the aircraft and guns accounted for twenty-six Japanese merchantmen. While the Japanese had been careful to keep their major surface units in the relative safety of the open ocean rather than penned up in harbour, they also lost 300 out of a total of 365 aircraft based on Truk. Combined, these losses meant that Truk had followed Rabaul in being neutralized. Inevitably, given the overwhelming superiority of the forces against them, the Japanese response was muted, and instead of the massed aerial attacks that the Americans had been dreading, just seven torpedo-bombers were able to mount an operation against the carrier USS *Intrepid*, which was hit by a single torpedo.

Such was the American success that they by now had an abundance of assets, and these were soon put to good use with the reserves earmarked for Kwajalein landed on Eniwetok, the most westerly atoll in the Marshall islands, on 17 February. After four days of intense fighting, the Japanese defenders were overcome. Meanwhile, two carrier groups were sent to attack Saipan, Tinian and Rota in the Marianas on 23 February. The Admiralty Islands, off the north coast of New Guinea, were taken next by MacArthur's troops on 29 February. After further landings on 20 March at Emirau in the Bismarck Archipelago, American forces had encircled the Japanese at Rabaul, leaving MacArthur free to bypass the remaining Japanese strongpoint in New Guinea.

XI

THE ROYAL NAVY RETURNS
TO THE EAST

The American successes in the Pacific War had been just that, with
the forces deployed overwhelmingly United States in origin,
although Australian and New Zealand forces were also involved,
and there were a number of Royal Navy units, usually cruisers and
destroyers. Now with the war in the Mediterranean going the way
of the Allies and with a growing number of land bases in Italy, and
the Battle of the Atlantic over, with the German submarine
menace neutralized, and the remaining major surface units stuck
in port, the Royal Navy could send its major fleet units to the East.
The operations of the Eastern Fleet had in any case been restricted
following the Japanese attacks against Ceylon because of the lack
of carrier air cover, and even had carriers been freed from
European waters earlier, there would still have been the question
of suitable fighters and even suitable bombers, as the Fairey
Barracuda was to prove ill-suited to operations in the tropics and
was soon withdrawn and replaced by Grumman Avengers.

The prospect of increased British involvement in the Pacific was
not welcomed by many senior officers in the United States Navy,
including Admirals Ernest King, despite his stated desire to see
greater use made of the Royal Navy, and Chester Nimitz. There
were many reasons for this, some good, some bad.

Many Americans felt that they could finish the job on their
own, and in some cases this was also a reflection of national rival-
ries and even animosity. Indeed, as has been shown already, there
was some justification for the American view that this was 'their'
war, and their successes by spring 1944 were evidence of success.
There was also the fact that combining the operations of two
fleets, and their aircraft, was in itself a major undertaking. Given
the success of the North Atlantic Treaty Organization in the post-
war world, it is hard to realize just how difficult combined

operations were, even with the forces of just one nation. International collaboration and exercises, including the creation of joint forces such as the naval standing forces in the Atlantic, English Channel and Mediterranean, had to await the creation of NATO. Had there been anything remotely like NATO combining and coordinating the British, French, Dutch and Belgian armed forces in 1940, the German advance westwards to the North Sea and the Atlantic could have been a very different story.

Even better reasons for American concern were that the British lacked bases in the area while those of the United States Navy were being operated at full stretch as the rapid massive expansion in the service, and the vast spread of ocean over which it was having to operate, had placed everything under considerable strain. The British also lacked experience of the kind of massed aerial attack by carrier aircraft that had become something of an American speciality. The Japanese attack on Pearl Harbor had almost twenty times the number of aircraft sent by the Royal Navy against the Italian fleet at Taranto: the operations being conducted by the United States from late 1943 onwards used more than twice the number of aircraft that had been seen at Pearl Harbor. In a very short time, the United States Navy had learnt how to operate large numbers of ships in modern fleet actions close together and do so safely and effectively. Even so, as we will see later, in the Battle of Leyte Gulf, different elements of the United States Navy were not where they were supposed to be. The Royal Navy, however, had rarely put to sea with a balanced fleet of adequate strength, and this had only happened briefly and relatively late in the war in the Mediterranean. Had this been done earlier in the war, *Glorious* might not have been lost for want of aerial reconnaissance and battleship or battlecruiser support, or *Prince of Wales* and *Repulse* for lack of air cover, or *Cornwall* and *Dorsetshire*, or *Hermes*, caught almost alone with nothing more than a destroyer for company and without fighter protection.

The British point of view was that they did not want to be seen to be leaving an ally on its own, especially given the growing American involvement in the war in Europe. While the continuation of the war in Europe meant that substantial British air and ground forces were heavily committed, the way it was moving also meant that substantial naval forces were effectively surplus and could be put to good use elsewhere. It was also a factor that both Australia and New Zealand had been promised

British support in the event of a Japanese attack before the outbreak of the Second World War, not realizing that such an eventuality might well find the British under pressure from Germany and Italy! Again, much of the territory overrun by the Japanese was British, and they wanted to make sure that when Japan was defeated, they would get it back. Most important of these territories in economic terms was Malaya with its rubber and tin, but there was also Singapore and Hong Kong, Britain's foothold on the coast of mainland China, and Burma as well.

Illustrious Returns

Prepared for war in the Pacific, the Royal Navy's Eastern Fleet had the USS *Saratoga* attached to it so that the Royal Navy could become familiar with American operating practices, but it was also intended that the British Eastern Fleet and the US Fifth Fleet would generally operate in different areas to avoid any problems of coordination and communication. It was to happen that crossover would occur from time to time, but the practice of giving each fleet different zones of responsibility eased operations considerably. There were many changes that had to take place, not the least of which was that the two navies used different carrier deck landing officer, or 'batsman' signals, to the extent that certain signals meant exactly the opposite to the other navy's airmen! In the end, the Royal Navy standardized on the American signals, recognizing that the United States Navy was now the larger navy.

It was decided that aircraft from *Illustrious* and *Saratoga* should combine for a raid on Sabang. This was to be the Fleet Air Arm's first experience of a massed air attack, and was comfortably away from the Fifth Fleet and its aircraft, but at the same time it was undeniably an important and worthwhile target, an island off the northern end of Sumatra with vital port installations and airfields.

For the operation, the Fleet Air Arm had at last what it had needed for years, a powerful fighter-bomber, the Vought F4U Corsair. During development, the Corsair had been the first American aircraft to exceed 400 mph in level flight, and in service it could carry two 500-lb bombs. The low-wing, crank-wing monoplane was not everyone's favourite however, since for every one who described it as 'the best fighter of World War II', someone else would describe it as 'the bent wing bastard from Connecticut'. The weaknesses of the Corsair were that it was big, so big that at first it was rejected for carrier service by the United States Navy, which was one reason why so many were available for the Royal Navy. To accommodate heavier armament as a result of lessons learnt in Europe, the cockpit was moved back three feet, restricting the pilot's view forward, especially in the crucial final moments before touch down on a carrier's deck. The long nose meant that, like the smaller Seafire, this was an aircraft that could bounce and topple forward on landing. On the other hand, it was strong with good protection for the pilot, and had fail-safe features, so that, for example, if the hydraulic system failed, the undercarriage and tailhook would drop down, making landing possible. In an emergency the undercarriage could be put down using a CO_2 bottle. The Royal Navy was also to find that the cockpit was well laid out, 'the cockpits of British contemporaries must have been designed by the office cleaner,' according to one British pilot. Maintenance was also simplified, not least because most US aircraft had the various components in the same place, reducing the amount of time maintainers spent scratching their heads and leafing through manuals!

'. . . They were damnably big fighters for their day,' recalled Norman Hanson, a wartime Royal Naval Volunteer Reserve pilot aboard *Illustrious*. 'They had a vast length of fuselage between the cockpit and the propeller which, together with a rather low sitting position and a not too clever hood (both of which were modified and greatly improved in the MkII version), made for very poor visibility when taxiing and landing.'

On the other hand, the aircraft had its advantages, not the least of which was an injection carburettor that meant the engine didn't cut out at the top of a loop, a weakness with many aircraft of the time fitted with normal carburettors, and something likely to undermine the confidence of a fighter pilot just at an awkward moment! A Corsair cruised using around sixty gallons of fuel per hour, but this rose to 100 gallons at operational speeds.

The first attack on Sabang was made early on 19 April 1944, with aircraft flying off *Illustrious* at 06.50. The carrier sent seventeen Fairey Barracudas escorted by thirteen Vought Corsairs. The war in the Pacific was to see the Corsair operate through to the end, but the Barracuda, only just satisfactory in the European theatre, was not to remain with the Eastern Fleet for long.

'My first sight of enemy territory was of a luscious green island, basking in the early morning sunshine,' Hanson remembers.

It was all so very beautiful that when red flashes burst from the deep, verdant green, I felt considerably put out . . . I was appalled that some vandal should set fire to Paradise. We dived down ahead of the Barracudas, firing enthusiastically at warehouses and quays and suddenly found ourselves at the far end of the harbour, unscathed. We were still green and hadn't yet learned about targets of opportunity. So we milled around like a lot of schoolgirls and left it to the Barracudas, who made a splendid attack on the harbour and oil installations . . . returned . . . with a feeling of a anti-climax. We had been to the enemy and had found no opportunity to cover ourselves with glory.

Indeed, had the Japanese put up a strong fighter defence, the Corsairs would have been embarrassed to be at low level having wasted their ammunition while the Barracudas would have been vulnerable. Tactics needed to be refined at this stage. Strategy was also weak, since Sabang only received occasional attention, giving the Japanese time to repair the damage. Limited resources and more pressing priorities elsewhere were doubtless to blame, but a single day's outing for two aircraft carriers was not enough. It was to take the arrival of additional ships before the Royal Navy was able to pull its weight in the Far East.

As it happened, several of the additional ships were delayed on their way to the Far East, and the Royal Navy in this theatre had a relatively quiet time of it during the second half of 1944. On 24 August, *Victorious* and *Indomitable* sent their aircraft to attack Padang, also on Sumatra, and then to attack the airfield at Sabang. The next major operation came during 17–19 October, when aircraft from *Illustrious*, *Indomitable* and *Victorious* attacked targets in the Nicobar Islands. Later, in December, there followed an attack on an oil refinery, this time at Pangkalan Brandan, in north-eastern Sumatra, about eight miles inland from the Malacca Straits, to which fifty-six aircraft were sent, twenty-eight Grumman Avengers, sixteen Grumman Hellcats and twelve Vought Corsairs, with the raid pressed home in poor weather.

It was decided that the main base for what became the British Pacific Fleet would be Sydney in Australia, with its fine natural harbour. There was also a Royal Australian Air Force base nearby at Nowra which became the air station for Fleet Air Arm aircraft when their carriers were at Sydney. Post-war, Nowra was to become the home base for the Royal Australian Navy's Fleet Air Arm.

Other changes also had to be made. British aircraft markings had already moved from the red, white and blue roundels that had evolved during the First World War to red surrounded by blue, which unlike the three coloured roundel did not contrast too sharply with camouflage. Unfortunately, the most obvious part of this marking was the bright orb of red, which looked very much like Japanese markings for ships' AA gunners, perhaps very twitchy after long hours under Japanese attack. The solution was to introduce a further modification to British markings for aircraft in the Far East, with roundels having an outer circle of dark blue with an orb of pale blue in the middle.

Palembang

The original plan was for the British Pacific Fleet to appear in force in Australian waters on New Year's Day 1945, but this was over-optimistic and the morale-boosting arrival of a large fleet was put back to the end of the month. Meanwhile, it was decided that en route to Sydney, *Illustrious* could attack Palembang, the large complex of oil refineries in the east of Sumatra. This was a decision only arrived at after some soul-searching at the Admiralty, as many senior naval officers felt that the target was beyond the resources and the experience of the Fleet Air Arm at the time.

Palembang was a difficult target as it entailed aircraft flying over 150 miles of enemy-held territory, across mountain ranges and dense tropical jungle, so that the crew of any aircraft in distress would have difficulty baling out, let alone trying to make a forced landing. The area was also home to substantial numbers of Japanese fighters, and a combat training ground for fighter pilots whose instructors included many veterans from the Japanese carrier fleet. On the other hand, Palembang was also a very important target, with two major oil refineries at Pladjoe and Soengei Gerong. Thanks to the actions of American submariners, oil was now becoming a major problem for the Japanese, and that made an attack on Palembang all the more tempting.

By November 1944, the Royal Navy had assembled four of its

fast armoured carriers at Ceylon, now Sri Lanka, with Rear Admiral Sir Philip Vian in command of the carrier force, in British terms, RAA, or Rear Admiral Aircraft Carriers.The four ships were *Illustrious, Victorious, Indefatigable* and Vian's flagship *Indomitable*. By this time, the aircraft available had changed, very much for the better. The poor performance of the Barracuda had seen it replaced by the potent Grumman Avenger, while another aircraft from the same stable, the Hellcat, was the fighter for the fleet. The Corsair stayed on as a fighter-bomber. A new arrival was the Fairey Firefly fighter-bomber, Fairey's latest offering to the Fleet Air Arm and a successor for the Fulmar that had been so outgunned and outpaced during the fighting in the Mediterranean.

Navigation in poor weather and radio discipline had proved to be problems with the Sumatra raid in December 1944, and before attacking Palembang, the Royal Navy decided to hold a dress rehearsal.

Before this, on 4 January 1945, aircraft from *Illustrious, Victorious, Indomitable* and *Indefatigable* were sent to attack oil refineries in north-eastern Sumatra, maintaining the pressure on Japanese oil supplies.

On 13 January, the day of the rehearsal for the raid on Palembang, the British carriers were sent to sea, steaming in the Indian Ocean to the east of Ceylon, and spent the day making attacks on the island. Both Colombo and Trincomalee, or 'Trinco' to British sailors, were subjected to repeated heavy attacks, while every airfield on the island was strafed by fighters in what became known as 'fighter ramrod' operations. The Royal Air Force and shore-based Fleet Air Arm units in Ceylon were fully up to strength and were sent up to intercept the carrier-borne aircraft. Every carrier pilot managed at least three sorties, some flew four, and despite the confusion in the air, there were no collisions, something which one naval pilot viewed as miraculous. Unfortunately, under such intensive operations and with pilots becoming tired, complete safety could not be guaranteed.

At 15.30 the four carriers turned for China Bay and by 16.30 the last aircraft were landing on. Hanson was amongst the last and as he waited, he watched in horror as one of his comrades, Sub Lieutenant Graham-Cann, 'normally a safe and dependable deck lander, he made a bit of a mess of this one and drifted up the deck, failing to catch a wire'. The aircraft hit the crash barrier strung across the deck full on, with the force of being so suddenly arrested, unhooked the aircraft's belly drop tank which swept forward to be cut in two by the propeller. A sheet of flame burst out and was swept aft by the wind over the carrier's flight deck. Unharmed, Graham-Cann jumped out of his cockpit, stood on the wing as if planning to jump forward, but changed his mind and jumped aft, slipped on oil, doubtless from a ruptured pipe on the stricken aircraft, and fell on his back into the flaming aviation fuel. Now burning fiercely, he got to his feet and staggered down the deck, to be caught by the deck party and wrapped in blankets before being taken to the sick bay. He was still alive but horribly burnt as the ship entered harbour, but died just as he was carried up the gangway of the hospital ship.

The impact of this on those still in the air can be imagined. There were at least nine of them, and unable to land until the fire on the flight deck was put out and the wreckage removed. They were now running low on fuel, so Hanson spoke to the ship's fighter direction officer and requested permission to take the remaining aircraft to the air station at China Bay, where they could refuel and await further instructions. Permission was granted. Their troubles were not over, as on landing they discovered that the monsoon rains had found their way into the station's fuel tanks, so refuelling had to be done through a chamois leather, a long and tedious process. As they lay on the grass well away from the aircraft and smoked, a dispatch rider came up with orders to return to *Illustrious*. Hanson sent away those aircraft that had already been refuelled, and finally it was his turn and that of another pilot, Sub Lieutenant Rogers. Rogers took off a quarter of an hour before Hanson. As he approached the ship, Hanson saw a splash off the ship's port quarter, but thought little of it, guessing that an Avenger had dropped a hooked-up depth charge. He landed and as he walked along the deck from his aircraft, Commander Flying leant over his bridge and beckoned to Hanson to come up to him.

'Hans, how many are there still to come?'

'None, sir. I'm the last.'

'What about Rogers?'

'Left just- well, ten or fifteen minutes – before me, sir.'

'Then he's the one.'

'One what, sir?'

'The one who's just crashed. Went in on his approach turn.'

The splash that Hanson had seen had been Rogers' aircraft after he had lost flying speed on his approach turn. The much-needed exercise had cost the Pacific Fleet two pilots within an hour.

The day of the attack on Palembang arrived. On 24 January 1945, at 06.00 on a dark and unpleasant morning with occasional squalls of rain, Hanson found himself strapped into his Corsair at the head of the aircraft ranged on the flight deck. He noticed a burst of black oily smoke as the engine room personnel flashed up additional burners to increase the carrier's speed. Commander Flying, 'Wings' to Fleet Air Arm personnel, called on the tannoy: 'Fighters start up!'

The Corsair pilots simply had to press their starter tits, and as the engines revved up in clouds of blue smoke, *Illustrious* turned to starboard into the wind. Then it was time to go. Within five minutes, fighters, fighter-bombers and bombers were in the air and milling around as they got into their formations.

This was the Royal Navy's second massed aerial attack after the raid on Sumatra on 4 January. The British Pacific Fleet was to the west of Sumatra off Engano Island. There were a small number of aircraft that didn't get into the air, mainly from *Victorious* and *Indefatigable*, but all in all there were forty-three Avenger bombers, each with a 2,000-lb bombload, with a top cover fighter escort of sixteen Corsairs and below them a middle cover of sixteen Hellcats and eight Corsairs, with another escort of twelve Fireflies ahead of the main force, and finally a stern escort of eight Corsairs, led by Norman Hanson. All in all, 103 aircraft, already a smallish force by the standards of the day.

As the aircraft climbed to cruising altitude, three Avengers suffered technical problems and had to return to HMS *Victorious*. Altitude was essential as the aircraft had to cross a 10,000 feet high mountain range on their way to the target. All in all, they had to fly some 200 miles. The Avengers with their heavy bombloads were slow in the climb, and the fighters had some trouble waiting for them, throttling back to 150 knots. Realizing that as they climbed, they could well appear on Japanese radar, Hanson took his eight Corsairs out of line to allow them to build up their speed so that if they encountered Japanese fighters, they would not be sitting ducks. As the Avengers reached the required altitude, Hanson was shocked to find that the Fireflies were missing and that his aircraft comprised the entire low cover for the bombers. He couldn't break radio silence to discover the

146

whereabouts of the Fireflies who were supposed to be providing forward or bow cover. In fact, a starter problem on the leading aircraft had held up everything behind it ranged on the deck, but the Fireflies were later to catch up.

Flying at 13,000 feet with the bombers, the aircraft flew over dense jungle broken only by the mountain ridges running down into the vegetation. The fighter pilots kept sweeping the sky with their eyes looking for Japanese fighters. Then, suddenly, they could see the massive oil refinery, the size of a town, straight ahead.

The radio silence was broken by top cover warning of fighters: 'Rats! Eleven o'clock up!'

The Avengers were by this time getting into position for their bombing runs as the fighters wheeled round to tackle the oncoming Japanese fighters. Hanson turned towards a Japanese fighter and fired, although he was never sure whether or not he had hit the enemy aircraft. Then there was a further warning of 'Rats, three o-clock up!' This time two Japanese fighters came streaking in, and one flight of four Corsairs turned on one of them while Hanson led his flight towards the other, and was pleased to see bits falling off the Japanese aircraft before it fell downwards. The loss of the Fireflies was being felt by this time, for not only did this place extra pressure on the other fighters, but part of their role was to race in ahead of the Avengers and shoot down the barrage balloons tethered over the target area. They did arrive, nevertheless, to take part in the air battle that was soon in full flood.

The Corsair pilots were kept busy, mainly by 'Oscar' and 'Tojo' fighters – Nakajima Ki43 and Ki44 – of the Japanese Army Air Force, but their efforts were not in vain as they kept most of the fighters from the bomber formation. The defences would have put up even more fighters, but a fighter ramrod attack by Corsairs across an airfield destroyed thirty-four Japanese aircraft on the ground. As the fighters turned to regroup for the flight back to the carriers, heavy black smoke was starting to obscure the target – the bombers had done their work well. The Japanese fighters continued to press home attacks as the attack force withdrew, but the constant harrying fell away as the formation reached the sea. There was relief all round as they came upon the fleet, with the four carriers in a square formation around the two battleships, and already turned into the wind waiting to receive the returning aircraft. This was another hazardous operation as two aircraft could easily approach the ship from different directions and, while turning as they started their approach, fail to see each other as they banked.

Of the aircraft that reached Palembang, six Corsairs, two Avengers and a Hellcat were lost. This was not bad for a target that had been well defended.

The original plan had been to make a second strike at Palembang on the following day, but bad weather once again intervened and delayed the operation. Each morning the tannoy would burst into life at 01.00 and announce that the operation had been postponed for another twenty-four hours. It was not until 29 January that the aircraft were once again climbing away towards the mountains. The intervening period had not been wasted, as the squadron commanders carried out a post mortem on the first operation. Once of the main complaints was that the fighters in middle cover should have given better protection to the bombers instead of looking for fighters to engage in combat. This was also a criticism made of the *Luftwaffe*'s fighters by bomber crews in the Battle of Britain – the temptation to look for a duel rather than simply warding off fighters and stopping them from breaking up the bomber formation. Once again, it was stressed that it was vital that the barrage balloons be shot down before the attack developed. Poor radio discipline once silence was broke was yet another point. Even so, on the second raid, two Avengers were lost when their wings caught barrage balloon cables.

Overall, during the two strikes on Palembang, the Fleet Air Arm lost a total of forty-one aircraft, of which sixteen were lost in air-to-air combat, another eleven ditched near the fleet, including Hanson's aircraft returning from the first strike and as a result of which he was judged medically unfit for the second strike, while another fourteen aircraft were lost in deck landing crashes. Against this, it was estimated that thirty-eight enemy aircraft had been destroyed on the ground and another thirty had been shot down. Most important, while Palembang was not completely destroyed, production was seriously affected for some months.

XII

THE GREAT MARIANAS TURKEY SHOOT

Meanwhile, the United States Navy had been continuing its advance towards Japan, indeed, it was gaining momentum. On 30 and 31 March 1944, Vice Admiral Marc Mitscher sent carrier aircraft to attack Japanese airfields in the Palau Islands, inflicting further heavy losses on the enemy for the cost of twenty-five US aircraft. When the actual landings at Hollandia in New Guinea took place on 22 April, Mitscher then provided air cover for the invasion force and there were further attacks on Japanese airfields. The landings themselves were covered by Vice Admiral Kinkaid with the Seventh Fleet, with eight escort carriers and five cruisers, while the 24th and 41st Infantry Divisions were put ashore. A week later, the carriers made a further attack on Truk, losing twenty-six aircraft to the Japanese ninety losses. Further landings took place on 17 May at Wakde, a small island off the north coast of New Guinea, and on which the Americans established an airfield after overcoming light resistance. Ten days later, Biak, another island further west, was also invaded by the 41st Infantry Division, although this time resistance was more determined and it took a month to subdue the island.

Preparing to attack the Marianas, Mitscher divided his carrier fleet, now known as TF58, into four groups to destroy Japanese shore-based aircraft over 11–17 June, while Japanese attempts at a counter-attack were unsuccessful. During this period, on 15–16 June, two carrier combat groups were sent to attack the Bonin Islands, half-way to Japan, to ensure that further reinforcements could not be sent to the Marianas, and succeeded in destroying 300 Japanese aircraft for the loss of just twenty-two American aircraft.

On 15 June, TF52 under Vice Admiral Turner, landed V Amphibious Corps under Lieutenant General H.M. Smith on

Saipan at the southern end of the Marianas chain. Smith had the US 2nd and 4th Marine Divisions with the 27th Infantry Division in reserve, using a landing fleet of 550 ships, while cover was provided by eight escort carriers with 170 aircraft while another four escort carriers carried reserve aircraft. The battleships *Tennessee, California, Maryland, Colorado, Pennsylvania, New Mexico* and *Idaho* were escorted by eleven cruisers and fifty destroyers. Believing that there would be underwater obstacles to prevent an invasion, the Americans sent in frogmen, but no obstacles were found. Nevertheless, resistance by 22,700 Japanese soldiers and 6,700 sailors was especially intense as the defenders expected the Imperial Japanese Navy to intervene, as indeed it did, so that on 19 and 20 June, the Battle of the Philippine Sea, known to the Americans as the 'Great Marianas Turkey Shoot', took place.

The Fleets Clash

Opposing each other were the US Fifth Fleet under Admiral Raymond Spruance and the Japanese Combined Fleet under Vice Admiral Jisaburo Ozawa. Spruance had 890 aircraft in his carrier fleet commanded by Mitscher, with ships including *Hornet, Yorktown, Bunker Hill, Enterprise, Wasp, Lexington* and *Essex* and the light carriers *Cabot, Cowpens, Bealleau Wood, San Jacinto, Langley, Bataan, Monterey* and *Princeton*, supported by the battleships *Iowa, New Jersey, Washington, North Carolina, South Dakota* and *Indiana*, as well as eight heavy and thirteen light cruisers and sixty-seven destroyers. At this stage in the war, the Japanese could no longer compete with the United States, even though Ozawa had a far stronger carrier force than had been sent to Pearl Harbor with *Taiho, Shokaku, Zuikaku, Junyo* and *Hiyo*, and the light carriers *Ryuho, Chitose, Chiyoda* and *Zuiho*, albeit with a total of just 430 aircraft, supported by the battleships *Yamato, Musashi, Haruna, Kongo* and *Nagato*, with eleven heavy and two light cruisers and twenty-eight destroyers.

Possibly the best measure of the increasingly desperate state of the Imperial Japanese Navy was that in April 1944, the Japanese Navy Air Force had fewer than 100 experienced pilots available for duty in the central Pacific, not simply because of the predations of American fighters but also due to sickness, especially malaria. When 500 new pilots and 500 radio operators graduated from the training school at Kasumigaura, their training was still incomplete and, of course, they lacked combat experience. The new airmen were sent to Admiral Ozawa to continue their training, but he was running short of airfields and his carriers, based at Tawi Tawi in the Sulu Islands, seldom went to sea for fear of attack by US submarines. While there were still nine Japanese carriers left following the completion of the new *Taiho* on 7 March, both *Shokaku* and *Zuikaku* were badly battered and in need of a refit. Most of what remained were best described as light carriers, although some approximated more to escort carriers.

Nevertheless, those ashore defending the Marianas were right in believing that the Imperial Japanese Navy would be coming to their aid, as the Japanese planned a strong counter-attack using both carrier and shore-based aircraft.

In the days before battle was joined, Ozawa moved his fleet to a position east of the Philippines, ready to relieve Saipan, while the Americans were positioned west of the Marianas in order to cover the landing fleet. Ozawa's plan was to get the US Fifth Fleet between his carriers and the Japanese Army Air Force bases in the Marianas, so that the Americans could be attacked from both sides. He anticipated his aircraft striking at the Americans and then continuing to land at Guam and Rota to refuel and re-arm, so that they could then mount a second strike on the Fifth Fleet on their return to the carriers – in effect what became known in the later stages of the air campaign in Europe as 'shuttle bombing'. Ozawa divided his carrier force into three, with Force A, under himself, including the new *Taiho, Shokaku* and *Zuikaku*, with 207 aircraft, Force B had *Junyo, Hiyo* and *Ryuho* with 135 aircraft, while Kurita had a van force with *Chitose, Chiyoda* and *Zuiho*.

Both navies sent submarines into the Philippine Sea, although only the American submarines saw action, engaging Japanese warships and also providing additional reconnaissance.

Japanese reconnaissance aircraft first sighted the American carriers during the afternoon of 18 June, but at this stage Mitscher was still unaware of the exact position of the Japanese carriers.

The following morning, realizing that he was vulnerable to Japanese attack, Mitscher had most of his fighters prepared and either in the air on combat air patrols or ranged on deck ready for take-off at an early hour. It was not until 10.00 that the first Japanese attacks came, but these were shore-based aircraft from Guam. Additional aircraft were launched from the carriers to reinforce the combat air patrols and in the fierce dog fights that ensued, just twenty-four out of the sixty-nine Japanese aircraft sent against the Fifth Fleet survived. The next wave consisted of 130 aircraft, of which ninety-eight were shot down. These attacks were followed by the first of four waves of carrier-borne aircraft, but anticipating an attack, Mitscher had positioned his fighters fifty miles ahead of the fleet, and once again the Japanese suffered heavy losses, with those aircraft that managed to evade the fighters being caught by the intense anti-aircraft fire put up by the ships. Just twenty or so aircraft managed to press home their attack, and hits were scored on the battleship *South Dakota* and the carriers *Wasp* and *Bunker Hill*, but no ship was badly damaged and all continued in action. There were also near misses on a number of other ships, including the *Indiana* and a cruiser. These strikes continued for five hours, but most of the aircraft in each successive wave were successfully repulsed by the fleet's fighters before they could reach the ships. Even those aircraft that managed to reach the shore bases in Guam were attacked and destroyed by American fighters as they landed. Ozawa had viewed Guam as an unsinkable aircraft carrier; unsinkable perhaps, but it lacked the manoeuvrability of a ship at sea!

American Submarines find the Carriers

While the American aircraft were attacking the airfields in Guam, the Japanese carriers were themselves under attack, but from below the waves. At 09.11, just after the Japanese aircraft had taken off, the submarine *Albacore* torpedoed the *Taiho*, Ozawa's flagship but which enjoyed a very brief operational career, as aviation fuel fumes from a fractured pipe filled the whole vessel and, after six hours, a gigantic aviation fuel explosion destroyed the ship and killed half her crew. Just over three hours later, at 12.20, another submarine, the *Cavalla*, put three torpedoes into *Shokaku*, at one time with *Zuikaku*, pride of the Imperial Japanese Navy, and three hours later, she also blew up as aviation fumes ignited and sank. To make their misery complete, during the afternoon just 100 aircraft returned to the Japanese carriers. Ozawa meanwhile had moved his flag to the cruiser *Naguro*.

The Americans had successfully deployed their carrier fighters using 300 Hellcats in rotation to provide constant air cover and remaining capable of sending up reinforcements when required.

At one time, alerted by the radar aboard the battleship *Alabama* of an incoming Japanese attack, Mitscher managed to get 200 aircraft into the air.

'So, we got word that a great number of Japanese planes were being staged into Guam,' recalled Butch Voris, an American fighter-bomber pilot[1]

> We immediately launched half of our ready strike force for Guam, to intercept them and try to destroy them there before they could get to our fleet. So we sent the first wave out . . . that first wave caught the aeroplanes both landing and on the ground re-arming and refuelling. I happened to be in . . . the second strike . . . I guess that we were about 225 miles from Guam.

Butch took off and climbed to 20,000 feet, but suddenly the aircraft in his wave had an emergency recall, implying that the fleet was about to come under attack.

> It was a major wave and I would think that it would be somewhere around two to three hundred Japanese fighters and dive-bombers and torpedo planes. A major strike against our carrier force. And they were at high altitude . . . somewhere between 25 and 30 thousand feet. Now that's way above our normal operating altitude in those days, and so as we climbed up to intercept them . . . we saw them coming . . . they had already started their run in . . . and were heading downhill picking up speed. And I remember the fighters criss-crossing over the dive-bombers, and the attack, and the torpedo planes, and we just went full throttle and came right on top of 'em . . . right on down . . . we were able to work the attack force for a period of about a hundred miles and we just started as you will, one at a time, dibbling them away and by the time they had traversed that last hundred miles I don't think more than a dozen . . . ever reached our task force.

Japanese tactics when attacking ships at sea differed little from those of the Americans, which was not surprising since the nature of the aircraft dictated how the mission should be flown. Torpedo aircraft attacked low, at no more than 200 feet, while the dive-bombers remained at medium altitude ready to start their dive onto the selected target. Above it all remained the fighters. Voris recalls having to go for the fighters and yet not forget to destroy the strike aircraft.

> We had to get a fighter on the way through and then keep going after . . . main body of the striking force . . . I couldn't get through the fighters . . . I got tied up with a fighter immediately and I couldn't disengage . . . in fact we got right into anti-aircraft range of our own forces before we got the last ones[2].

Having lost three-quarters of his aircraft and two of his largest carriers, Ozawa had little option but to withdraw, and after darkness fell started to steam slowly to the north-west. Mitscher realized that this could be a major opportunity. By this time, many of his carriers were low on fuel, but he made the most of this problem by leaving these behind to neutralize enemy air power on Guam. Mitscher sent three carriers under Rear Admiral Clark in pursuit of Ozawa's fleet.

Chasing the Enemy

Reconnaissance aircraft from TF58 were launched starting at 05.30 on 20 June. Despite reports from American submarines that had spotted the Japanese fleet, looking for even ships as large as aircraft carriers in the vast reaches of the Pacific was akin to searching for a needle in a haystack, and it was not until 15.00 that an American aircraft located the retreating Japanese. At this stage, Ozawa's ships were at extreme range from the pursuing American carriers.

Butch Voris was amongst those sent looking for the Japanese, taking part in the first search that had involved him flying 350 miles from his ship, the USS *Hornet*, and then flying fifty miles on a cross leg before returning to his ship. His day had started at 02.30 and at 15.00 he was dozing in his bunk, convinced that the Japanese were out of reach and had escaped. He was awakened by the sounding of an emergency flight point, the signal that every aviator had to man his flight quarter stations immediately. He checked the teletype and saw that it contained a contact report of the Japanese fleet on a bearing of 330 degrees at a distance of

225 miles. The distance was wrong; the Japanese were much further away.

This was Mitscher's opportunity. He immediately ordered an attack on the fleeing Japanese. Butch in his Hellcat was among 200 aircraft that were sent that afternoon to attack the Japanese ships, but as he sat in his aircraft, its engine roaring, waiting to take-off, he happened to see the 'talker' holding the blackboard standing in the wind, with the message that the new enemy position was 350 miles away! It was his turn to take-off, but as he raced down the deck and into the air, his thought was 'how can we do this?' Nevertheless, Voris and everyone else knew that this was a great opportunity to inflict major damage to Japan's ambitions.

The American aircraft struggled to use as little fuel as possible, with their pilots flying them on as lean a mixture as possible and taking a full two hours to reach the Japanese fleet. They had plenty of time to think about the difficulty of operating at full pressure over the combat zone and then returning to their ships, and if they didn't manage to conserve enough fuel, in all probability having to ditch in the sea at night, hoping to be rescued by the advancing fleet. This prospect dominated their thinking far more than the reception that they could expect from the Japanese. The pilots and navigators on the torpedo-planes believed that they could not hope to return to their carriers, while their comrades in the dive-bombers considered that it would be touch and go. The fighter pilots thought that they could do it, if only they didn't use too much fuel in a dogfight or find themselves forced to operate at full power for too long. Part of the problem was that even the fighters were carrying bombs, increasing their weight and spoiling their performance with their drag, because everyone was expected to take a shot at a Japanese ship, even if they had little or no bombing experience. Then, of course, there was the unspoken question mark hanging over the position of the enemy ships: would they be exactly where they were expected to be, or would fuel be wasted searching for them?

Flying at 18,000 feet, the strike force was in bright sunshine, although most reckoned that down on the surface, it would be sunset. Looking ahead, Voris could see a large cumulus cloud, and beneath it he spotted ships that seemed to be turning. It was the Japanese carriers turning into the wind to launch their fighters.

Seeing that the Japanese were aware of their presence, the leader of the strike broke radio silence and started to issue instructions.

> We held our altitude in case we ran into Japanese Zeros, recalls Voris. Then just rolled over and just came straight down because that increases your accuracy . . . don't have to compute for slant range and angle of attack . . . I just remember saying 'boy, that's an awful small target when you're that altitude' . . . you see the flight deck get larger . . . I could see an anti-aircraft screen . . . magnificent . . . bursts of purple, and green and lavender . . . and then coming back real quickly to realize that if I end up in one of those it's all over . . .[3]

Unlike the Allies, the Japanese used different colour powder in their ammunition, something that distracted many of the American pilots and perhaps reduced the sense of threat from enemy AA fire. For those who hadn't bombed a Japanese ship before, there were also the different deck markings, another distraction! The Japanese were heavily dependent on AA fire for their survival as Ozawa had just thirty-five fighters left to protect his fleet.

One problem with dive bombing was that pilots could not see whether or not their bombs had hit the target as they would have to pull back the control column as they released the bombs, allowing themselves enough height above the target for the aircraft to bring its nose up – the steeper the dive, the more room needed to pull up and climb away – this was another danger for the inexperienced, especially in the fading light.

After the attack, the aircraft had to reassemble for the long flight back to the carriers. The fighters needed the navigators carried by the torpedo and dive-bombers. As he prepared to rejoin the main force, Voris was nearly caught by a Zero, but as he turned to attack it, his flight commander ordered him to get into formation before he could shoot it down. Certainly, the small number of Japanese fighters was another memory the American pilots had of this operation, while one also recalled that the Japanese fighter defence showed little organization.

Down below, the carrier *Hiyo* was so badly damaged that she sank within two hours in yet another fuel vapour explosion. Two of the fleet's precious tankers were also sunk. Of the other carriers, *Zuikaku*, *Junyo*, *Ryuho* and *Chiyoda* were all badly damaged, as was the battleship *Haruna* and a cruiser. Just twenty American aircraft had been shot down in the attack.

The attackers turned for home, flying at 7,000 feet to conserve fuel. Flying in the darkness, the steady drone of the aircraft engines was interrupted from time to time as one pilot after another called that they were running out of fuel and would have to ditch. Eventually, all of the torpedo bombers were in the water, then it was the turn of the dive-bombers as they flew the last 100 miles to the carriers, coming at full speed towards them. Homing beacons guided the aircraft towards the carriers, but the ships themselves were blacked out and the pilots could not see them until Clark ordered searchlights to be shone onto the sea.

> I saw the three lights of the landing signal platform, Voris remembers. I made my left turn and started in towards the 180 degree turn to the . . . stern of the ship and as I got right in and the landing signal officers used two great wands, that all you could see about three foot long and at first I remember a high and then an Okay and then a frantic wave off, the ship wasn't right into the wind yet, it was still 40 degrees turning . . . had I gone straight on I'd have run right into the island so I made an emergency turn away . . . the next time . . . I landed and I stopped right behind a number of four five-inch turrets, and had I missed a wire I'd have been killed[4].

His wingman was next down, missing all of the wires in the dark and then hitting the barriers, destroying all five of them and wrecking his aircraft, which was immediately pushed over the side so that nothing would delay the following aircraft, all desperately short of fuel. There was no time to replace the wrecked barriers and everything depended on *Hornet*'s remaining aircraft catching the arrestor wires. Inevitably, another aircraft missed all of the wires and hit the AA guns on the port side of the flight deck.

Eighty aircraft had been lost on the return flight after running out of fuel. Mitscher wanted the pursuit to continue, but on hearing of the losses, Spruance forbade it. In any case, even though the fighters could carry small bombs, it was the torpedo-bombers and dive-bombers that would be needed to inflict real damage on the Japanese, and almost all of these had been lost. Combined, the attack and the homeward run saw forty-nine American aviators killed, with most of those ditching being rescued (bearing in mind that most of the aircraft were torpedo and dive-bombers with a two-man crew). Nagumo, whose career seems to have been marked with missed opportunities and failures, finally committed hara kiri ashore on Saipan when he learnt of the defeat. Kakuta and some of his staff officers also seem to have committed suicide, although there is some doubt about this as it may have been an accident.

Japanese aircraft losses were so high that the Americans promptly described the Battle of the Philippine Sea as the 'Marianas Turkey Shoot'. Ozawa had lost three aircraft carriers and 400 carrier-borne aircraft, as well as another fifty aircraft based ashore. American losses overall were 130 aircraft and seventy-six aircrew.

On 24 June, Mitscher took three of his four carrier groups to Eniwetok for refuelling and replenishment, while Clark took the fourth group to attack Iwo Jima and the Pagan Islands. It was not until 9 July that Japanese resistance on Saipan ended, and on 21 July, the Americans landed on Guam with Task Force 53 under Rear Admiral Conolly putting III Amphibious Corps ashore with the support of many of the battleships and escort carriers involved in the landings on Saipan, while Mitscher's carriers sent their aircraft to attack Japanese bases within range of the Marianas to prevent them from harassing the invading troops. The escort carriers involved in the Guam landing for the first time sent their aircraft on close air support sorties to support the troops ashore. It took several weeks for Japanese resistance on Guam to be broken, but the island then became the major US base in the western Pacific.

Landings on Tinian followed next, on 24 July, when Task Force 52 put V Amphibious Corps ashore, with US Army heavy artillery ashore on Saipan joining the battleships in providing heavy fire support.

Meanwhile, on 15 September, landings were made on Morotai when General MacArthur's VII Amphibious Force landed the 31st Infantry Division, finding the island to be lightly defended. The capture of Morotai finally brought the US Army Air Force into the war in the Pacific after a period when their main effort had been attacking Japanese forces in Burma, using

Consolidated B-24 Liberators, an aircraft known for its long range. The eastern islands in the Sundra Group were now within US Army Air Force range.

Between 15 and 23 September, Rear Admiral Wilkinson took Task Force 31 to land III Amphibious Corps on the Palau Islands, an important stepping stone between Guam and Saipan, and the Philippines. No less than twelve escort carriers were used on this operation, as well as the battleships *Pennsylvania*, *Tennessee*, *Maryland*, *West Virginia* and *Mississippi*, with eight cruisers and twenty-seven destroyers. The undefended Ulithi Atoll was also seized and a forward naval base constructed. At the same time, on 21 and 22 September, TF38 attacked Manila Harbour, sinking three destroyers and twenty merchantmen, as well as causing extensive damage to harbour installations and to airfields ashore. This was followed by attacks on Japanese shipping and airfields in the central Philippines on 24 September, destroying 1,200 Japanese aircraft, many of them on the ground, and a further thirteen ships, all for the loss of seventy-two United States Navy aircraft. The attacks showed that the defence of the Philippines was far weaker than the Americans had expected, and led them to advance the date for the first landings from December to October. General MacArthur, who had been in command of the defence of the Philippines when the Japanese invaded, had pressed to be given command of the liberation force, and the ships and landing craft of the newly-formed Central Pacific Command under Admiral Nimitz were placed under MacArthur's overall command, leaving Halsey's Third Fleet to operate independently.

But first the Americans wanted to take the vital island of Formosa, close to the coast of China and also within easy range for heavy bombers heading for the Philippines and for the Japanese island of Okinawa as well as Japan itself. Formosa also sat comfortably close to the shipping lanes between Japan and its empire, or, more importantly, the resources that the empire could send home to Japan.

Notes
[1-4] Imperial War Museum Sound Archive, Accession No. 3021/3).

XIII

FIGHTING FOR FORMOSA
AND THE PHILIPPINES

Leaving the Philippines after the Japanese invasion, General Douglas MacArthur promised that 'I shall return'. It was a promise that he intended to keep even while he struggled to push the Japanese out of New Guinea. Because of this promise, the Americans found themselves pushed to retake the Philippines first, rather than invade Formosa, closer to Japan and off the coast of China.

As with the other major landings during 1944, the invasion of the Philippines was preceded not just by a heavy aerial assault on the islands themselves, but by heavy attacks on those Japanese airfields within range of the landing forces, including those on Formosa. The Battle of Formosa started on 10 October with Halsey sending 340 aircraft to attack Okinawa, and followed this with a diversionary attack on Luzon, the main island in the Philippines, before attacking Formosa itself. While most of the Japanese air power in the Philippines had been neutralized, it was known that Formosa would not be an easy action, with very heavy Japanese forces occupying the island and with the Japanese Navy Air Force's powerful 2nd Air Fleet, under Vice Admiral Fukudoma, based ashore.

Recognizing the growing threat to Japan's communications posed by the American advances, Imperial Japanese Headquarters had ordered a series of war games so that the best strategy could evolve. It was decided that the best strategy would be for all available aircraft to be evacuated to Kyushu so that they would remain available for the later defence of the home islands. Not for the last time, the plan was wrecked by the failure of the commander in the field to follow his orders as Fukudoma gave battle. A persistent weakness amongst even such senior Japanese officers throughout the war seems to have been a failure to appreciate broader strategic considerations.

Once again, Mitscher's Task Force, by now TF38 with seventeen aircraft carriers, was divided into four carrier task groups, each with supporting battleships, cruisers and destroyers. Vice Admiral McCain commanded TG38.1, with the *Wasp* and *Hornet* and the light carriers *Monterey*, *Cabot* and *Cowpens*, while TG38.2 was led by Rear Admiral Bogan, with *Bunker Hill*, *Hancock* and *Intrepid*, and the light carrier *Independence*. Rear Admiral Sherman had Mitscher's flagship *Lexington* as well as the *Essex* and the light carriers *Langley* and *Princeton*, while Rear Admiral Davison had *Enterprise* and *Franklin*, and the light carriers *Belleau Wood* and *San Jacinto*.

On 12 October, aircraft from all seventeen carriers attacked Formosa and an intense air battle developed, with the Japanese losing 160 aircraft to the United States Navy's forty-three. The next day, the emphasis of the American attack switched to the airfields and port facilities on Formosa, while the Japanese attempted a counter-attack against TF38, but succeeded only in putting a single torpedo into the heavy cruiser USS *Canberra*, the only US warship to be named after a foreign city and a compliment to HMAS *Canberra*, lost in the night battle off Savo Island. On 14 October, the pattern of attacks was repeated, although on this day operations were also mounted against targets in northern Luzon, and again the Japanese counter-attacked, putting a torpedo into the heavy cruiser *Houston*. The heavy air battles resumed on 15 October as the Third Fleet attempted to withdraw, with the unfortunate *Houston* suffering yet another torpedo, but still the Japanese failed to sink the ship. By this time, during the period beginning 10 October, the Japanese had lost 600 aircraft in Formosa, Luzon and Okinawa compared with the ninety lost by the Americans. The Japanese estimates of their losses were lower than those of the United States, at 312 aircraft.

Japan's propaganda machine remained undamaged by the losses with yet another great victory proclaimed. The *Asahi* newspaper was able to publish on 19 October a list of enemy warships lost: 'sunk, eleven carriers, two battleships, three cruisers and one destroyer; damaged, eight carriers, two battleships, four cruisers and thirteen unidentified ships . . .'

The Search for a Classical Naval Engagement –Leyte Gulf

Following their success over Formosa, the United States was ready to retake the Philippines. The operation called for one of the biggest efforts so far. On 20 October, General MacArthur's forces went ashore for the first time, with Vice Admiral Kinkaid's Seventh Fleet of 300 landing ships and transports landing Lieutenant General Krueger's Sixth Army at Tacloban on Leyte, one of the smaller islands in the Philippines. As on previous landings, heavy fire support was given by six battleships and nine heavy and light cruisers, supported by fifty-one destroyers and with no less than eighteen escort carriers, with aircraft to provide close air support and fighter protection, all under the command of Rear Admiral Oldendorf. The eighteen escort carriers were commanded by Rear Admiral Sprague, and were divided into three groups known as 'Taffy One', led by Sprague himself, with subordinate commanders leading 'Taffy Two' and 'Taffy Three'. Japanese airfields on Luzon and in the central Philippines were kept under constant attack by aircraft from Halsey's Third Fleet, with Mitscher still in command of TF38 with its four carrier groups with eight fleet carriers, *Lexington*, *Wasp*, *Hornet*, *Hancock*, *Intrepid*, *Essex*, *Enterprise* and *Franklin*, and another eight light carriers, *Monterey*, *Cabot*, *Cowpens*, *Independence*, *Langley*, *Princeton*, *Belleau Wood* and *San Jacinto*, supported by six battleships, fifteen cruisers and sixty destroyers. The Third Fleet's carriers had 1,000 aircraft between them.

Even so, despite the earlier heavy raids on airfields in northern Luzon, the Japanese managed to counter-attack and a torpedo was put into the cruiser *Honolulu* and a bomb found the cruiser HMAS *Australia*.

Japanese desperation now reached its peak with a desperate plan calling for four aircraft carriers, the recently repaired *Zuikaku* and the light carriers *Zuiho*, *Chitose* and *Chiyoda*, with just 116 aircraft, still commanded by Vice Admiral Ozawa, and a total force of nine battleships, nineteen cruisers and thirty-five destroyers. The primary objective was to finally bring the Japanese battleships, which had enjoyed a quiet war as fleet clashes had become the preserve of carrier-borne aircraft, into action. The result was to be what many have described as the greatest battle in naval history. It was to be in four parts, with an air-sea battle in the

162

Sibuyan Sea on 24 October followed by a night battle in the Surigao Straits on 24–25 October, with a battle off Samar and an air-sea battle off Cape Engano that same day. Every Japanese ship in the area was put into the battle with the fleet divided into four, with Ozawa having the carriers, two battleships, the hybrid *Ise* and *Hyuga*, with a flight deck in place of the after armament but with no aircraft, three cruisers and nine destroyers, with the task of luring the Third Fleet to the north, away from Leyte. To the west of Luzon, Vice Admiral Shima was to head south from Japan with three cruisers and seven destroyers, while from the west would come Vice Admiral Kurita's First Striking Force with five battleships, including the giants *Yamato* and *Musashi*, twelve cruisers and fifteen destroyers, and, to the south of Kurita, Vice Admiral Nishimura with two battleships, four cruisers and four destroyers. These force dispositions show just how depleted the Imperial Japanese Navy had become, with limited air power available and none at all to the west of the Philippines.

Japanese desperation did not stop ambitious and increasingly unrealistic plans being prepared, with even more ridiculous names being coined for these strategies. The grand design was called Operation Sho-Go, meaning 'to conquer'. Whatever impact this might have had on the hot heads, the more realistic amongst Japan's planners and senior officers knew that the best that could be managed would be to inflict such unacceptable casualties amongst the Americans and their Allies that some form of compromise could be negotiated between Japan and the Allies. Belatedly, the Japanese had come to realize that they could no longer look for and expect to win any air-to-air combat, and that a classic ship-to-ship naval engagement was not to be expected, but that the only hope of success lay in attacking American troop transports before they reached the landing areas, while they were still at sea and where the loss of life would be greatest.

Throughout the long chain of defeats, the Japanese had managed to maintain a strong propaganda effort aimed at convincing their own people that all was well. This went beyond censorship of correspondence from those in the front line, with the survivors from the worst defeats detained in barracks on their return to their home ports, and kept there until they could be posted abroad or to their next ship. At higher levels, including the upper echelons of the armed forces, there was an incredible inability to face the facts as they presented themselves and instead

163

refuge was taken in self-delusion. For these people, Sho-Go was not a plan to stave off defeat, but instead a plan to defeat the Allies and give Japan the victory that she had anticipated from the outset of the war.

Part of the problem was that from the Doolittle raid onwards, there was no bombing of the Japanese home islands until after the American conquest of the Marianas in June 1944 had brought the United States Army Air Force bases within reach of Japan. The air raids on Japan started that autumn. Minelaying operations and submarine warfare also had a tremendous impact, so that between March 1944 and August 1945, the volume of shipping through the Shimonoseki Straits fell from more than half a million tons to just 5,000 tons. By August 1945, the daily ration could provide just 1,400 calories, and many believe that had the war continued for another year, as many as eight million Japanese could have died from malnutrition. The initial US Army Air Force bombing sorties from the Marianas concentrated on Iwo Jima, and it was not until November 1944 that the Japanese began to suffer the start of a heavy bomber campaign against their cities.

The emerging American threat to the Philippines should have concentrated Japanese minds wonderfully because the loss of the islands would sever the route between the vital oil supplies of Sumatra and the rubber of Malaya, and Japan itself. In fact, a few minds were so concentrated, but not enough, even though the Americans were expected to invade through Leyte.

The Imperial Japanese Navy organized war games in anticipation of a major battle, while the remaining carriers were hidden and camouflaged in the Inland Sea. There were six carriers left, *Zuikaku*, *Zuiho*, the converted submarine tenders *Chitose* and *Chiyoda*, and the new sisters, *Unryu* and *Amagi*, little enough to counter the ever-stronger US Third Fleet, but there were few aircraft left and even fewer well-trained and experienced pilots. A strategic decision was taken to keep most of the available shore-based aircraft in Formosa, ready to counter the expected invasion there, but there would be 300 Japanese aircraft on Luzon drawn from both Japanese Navy Air Force and Army Air Force units.

The action that the Japanese were anticipating was known to them as the Second Battle of the Philippine Sea, and to the Americans as the Battle of Leyte Gulf. At the outset, Kurita was pessimistic.

. . . the enemy transports would have to be destroyed completely. My opinion at the time was that, in view of the difference in strength of the opposing forces, our chance for a victory after the sorties would be about fifty-fifty. I had also thought that the aerial support would fall short of our expectations.

The Fleets Clash

The Japanese effort got off to a bad start when, on 23 October 1944, two American submarines, *Dace* and *Darter* discovered the First Striking Force and torpedoed three heavy cruisers including Kurita's flagship *Atago*, which sank almost immediately as did the *Maya*. Kurita's orders were to be off Leyte on 25 October, but fighting had started the previous day when aircraft based on Leyte attacked the most northerly of the American carrier groups in the Battle of the Sibuyan Sea. This attack was intended to involve Ozawa's carrier-borne aircraft, so that the US Third Fleet would be drawn away and leave Kurita with a clear run at the transports, but the aircraft failed to find the American ships and, running short of fuel, attempted to fly to bases on Luzon. Many of them were intercepted by American fighters on the way.

Aboard the USS *Langley*, Lieutenant John Monsarrat, the fighter direction officer, had spotted Japanese aircraft on his radar screen and ordered four of the ship's Grumman Hellcats to intercept and immediately asked *Essex* to send reinforcements. The larger carrier promptly ordered eight patrolling Hellcats to join those from *Langley*. Very unhappy at sending four fighters to intercept what seemed to be sixty Japanese aircraft, Monsarrat then called to his fighters, 'Help is on the way, coming up close behind you'. The Hellcats for the *Essex* were indeed close behind, and between them the twelve fighters accounted for half the Japanese aircraft. The American pilots noticed the tailhooks on the Japanese aircraft, and took this to mean that they had come from a carrier.

Meanwhile, the shore-based aircraft managed to hit just one of the American carriers, the USS *Princeton*. It was to be a lucky shot for the Japanese. A single 550-lb armour-piercing bomb shot straight through the flight deck just forward of the aft elevator, punching a neat hole in the flight deck as it continued down into the ship, eventually reaching the ship's bakery, where it exploded and killed everyone present.

The explosion reached up into the hangar deck where six aircraft were being refuelled and re-armed, setting them alight and the heat caused their torpedo heads to explode. This was the result of what had at first seemed a minor matter to the ship's commanding officer, Captain William Buracker: 'I saw the hole, which was small, and visualised slapping on a patch and resuming operations'.

A rather more realistic assessment of the situation soon came from the flight deck, where Ensign Paul Drury was standing by his Grumman Hellcat of the carrier's fighter squadron VF-27. He felt the shock of the explosions below, and later recalled that: 'I knew that there was no way we were going to get airborne under those circumstances'.

The bomb had struck the ship at 09.35, and at 10.10, it was no longer a case of damage control but Salvage Control Phase 1, as the fire threatened the aviation fuel. Two-thirds of the ship's company of 1,570 were ordered to abandon the ship, leaving behind firefighters and AA gunners, but the latter were also ordered to leave once the ship's AA ammunition started to explode in the heat. A destroyer came alongside and took the men away. Despite the damage with burning aircraft and exploding ordnance, the fires were slowly brought under control and the ship remained on an even keel without any hull damage. It looked as if she was going to be saved. By 13.30, the only part of the ship still ablaze was that near to the aft magazine. The light cruiser USS *Birmingham* was ordered alongside to provide further firefighting assistance and then to provide a tow, but this was delayed until 15.30 by alerts over attacks by enemy aircraft and as a Japanese submarine was also reported in the vicinity. The cruiser drew alongside with many of her crew on her decks, either helping the firefighters or simply watching, and it was then, without any indication of what was about to happen, that the aft magazine exploded, tearing off the carrier's stern.

'There was a terrible staccato of metal on metal as shrapnel of all shapes and sizes – pieces of *Princeton* – raked across *Birmingham*'s exposed decks like the deadly grapeshot canisters fired from the cannons of yesterday's sailing ships,' recalled one eyewitness. 'The effect was the same. Hundreds of men instantly fell dead or horribly wounded. Within seconds, the ship's scuppers ran red with blood as it poured forth from thousands of grotesque wounds, and severed limbs lay about the blood-smeared deck like the casual droppings on a slaughterhouse floor'.

Princeton was lost, although the *coup de grâce* had to be delivered by a destroyer's torpedoes, but the *Birmingham* survived, but the casualty list told a different story. On the cruiser, 233 men were killed and 211 were seriously wounded, with just twenty-five having minor injuries. Aboard the carrier, 108 were killed, mainly firefighters and 190 wounded. One of the seriously wounded was the carrier's next commanding officer, Captain John Hoskins, who lost a foot but had the presence of mind to use a length of rope to quickly tie a tourniquet. Later, when a new *Princeton* was built, an Essex-class carrier, Hoskins managed to persuade the United States Navy to allow him to become her first commanding officer.

While the *Princeton*'s tragedy was being played out, two of the other US carrier groups had found Japanese warships steaming through the Sibuyan Sea. The carriers sent four waves of aircraft throughout the day and the giant battleship *Musashi*, with *Yamato* one of the two largest warships in the world at that time with the heaviest main armament, 18.1-inch guns, was hit by eleven torpedoes and nineteen bombs, so badly damaged that she eventually sank, slipping beneath the waves as she steamed slowly in circles, her steering gear jammed. Her fate had been sealed once her commanding officer, Rear Admiral Toshihira Inoguchi, refused permission for her gunnery officer to use her 18.1-inch guns to fire large anti-aircraft rounds, similar in concept to large shotgun cartridges, because these had been found to damage the gun barrels which had to be kept for the expected battles off Leyte. Permission was finally given as the repeated torpedo attacks flooded an engine room, and when all nine 18.1-inch guns fired at once, those aboard thought that the ship had been hit again so great was the recoil. It was too late. Shrapnel flew through the sky, but not one American aircraft was damaged, while one of the gun barrels was later found to have been damaged.

Damage on a battleship from a direct hit by a bomb tended to be rare, as bombs usually bounced off armour plating, but even in this, *Musashi* was ill-starred.

'One bomb detonated directly on the pagoda-like tower housing the command bridges,' recalls an eyewitness.

The damage was extensive and for a brief time it appeared that no one was in command of the ship. Then Inoguchi's voice emanated from a speaking tube, saying that all personnel on the main bridge had been killed and that he was shifting to the secondary bridge. Moments later, another series of explosions rained heavy shrapnel on *Musashi's* command tower. This time Inoguchi was not so fortunate. His weakened voice echoed in the brass speaking tube, saying, 'Captain is wounded. Executive Officer, take command.'

Other Japanese ships were badly damaged, with the heavy cruiser *Myoko* forced to turn back. The other giant battleship, *Yamato*, was also hit as was another battleship, *Nagato*, but both managed to remain operational. Vice Admiral Nishimura's force to the south of Palawan Island was also found by American carrier aircraft and attacked, but while several ships were damaged, none was sunk.

Facing with such an onslaught, Kurita reversed course, a tactical manoeuvre that Halsey misread as a victory, and while carrier group 38.1 refuelled, he took the other three groups and gave chase. This was a mistake and against the plans prepared by the Americans before the battle, which called for the Third Fleet to guard the San Benardino Straits while the Seventh Fleet guarded the Surigao Straits against the Japanese Southern Force. With the San Benardino Straits open, Kurita was able to reverse course yet again and pass his ships through them under cover of darkness.

During the night of 24–25 October, Nishimura's Southern Force was attacked by American motor torpedo-boats, although only one ship, the light cruiser *Abukuma*, was damaged. At 02.00, the US Seventh Fleet mounted a torpedo attack by destroyers, sinking the battleship *Fuso* and three Japanese destroyers. It was not until 04.20 that a classic naval gunnery engagement got under way, with Nishimura's flagship, the battleship *Yamashiro*, suddenly blowing up, with the two halves of the ship burning furiously and no survivors, and the cruiser *Mogami* damaged. United States Army Air Force aircraft attacked shortly after daybreak, sinking the crippled *Abukuma*, and this was followed by an attack by aircraft from the Seventh Fleet's escort carriers, which sank the *Mogami* and the remaining destroyers. Two heavy cruisers managed to escape.

At 06.45 on 25 October, American reconnaissance aircraft discovered Kurita's battle fleet east of Samar, a large island to the north-east of Leyte. Just thirteen minutes later, the Battle of Samar began, with Kurita's Centre Force battleships discovering and starting to shell Sprague's 'Taffy One' group of escort carriers, the most northerly of the force. The escort carriers, with only AA armament, were unable to respond, so Sprague ordered all of the aircraft to be flown off and withdrew his ships to the south. A number of the escort carriers were able to put up smoke, while the remainder attempted to improvise a smokescreen by changing the fuel-air mixture for their boiler fires, but this was a dated tactic as the Japanese flagship *Yamato* now had radar, as did some of the other ships. In desperation, the Americans mounted another destroyer torpedo attack, damaging the cruiser *Kumano* and causing her to withdraw, but at the cost of three US destroyers.

'That morning I had a duty on the flight deck,' recalls George Smith[1] who was a maintainer aboard an escort carrier.

> . . . yelled at me and said you'd better get your helmet on and your Mae West – your life belt – because here comes the Japs and about that time I heard an explosion on the fantail. First I thought it was one of our own planes exploding back there and I looked up and saw all this tin foil falling, this tin foil to jam our radar and of course GQ (General Quarters) and everybody manned GQ stations and then they started shooting . . . trying to get our range, our skipper turned the ship . . . zig-zagged it, as we were trying to escape from the Japanese . . . Then we started laying down smoke . . . trying to blind the Japanese . . . and they pulled pretty fast on us, they caught one of our carriers back there and they sank it . . . they got so close we could even see the Japanese flags flying . . . of course we were opening up with everything we had . . . this was running battle of about two hours . . . we were going between these two islands and the Japanese decided that it was leading to a trap . . . so they broke off the engagement.

The escort carriers were like sitting ducks and this was the best opportunity the Japanese ever had of destroying part of the American carrier fleet. Aboard the ships, those without any role were left trying to take what shelter they could. The aircraft that had been flown off, attempted to attack the Japanese ships, but this had little effect as they were either loaded with fragmentation bombs for use against Japanese ground troops or simply had their guns, with which they attempted to strafe the warships hoping to catch crew members in exposed positions such as the flying bridges. Inevitably, there were some without any ammunition who could only hope to distract the Japanese, and many were short of fuel having been scrambled with whatever was in their tanks, often just the remains of the previous day's final sortie. Some of the aircraft did run out of fuel and their pilots ditched close to the fleeing carriers, hoping to be picked up, but no one dared stop.

The escort carrier sunk was the USS *Gambier Bay*, but another three, *Fenshaw Bay*, *Kalinin Bay* and *White Plains*, were damaged. Then, it all ended as the Japanese broke off the one-sided engagement and turned away.

Kurita was convinced that he was heading into a trap, but once again, Japanese naval intelligence was lacking, as instead of escort carriers, he was convinced that he was attacking standard fleet carriers which, with their much higher speed, would take some time to overtake. This conclusion was strange indeed, since it meant that Kurita, an experienced senior naval officer, thought that the escort carriers were withdrawing at 30 knots or more, double their maximum speed! A second group of escort carriers ahead of him was also mistaken for further fleet carriers. Expecting further American carriers to approach from the north, Halsey's Third Fleet, he decided that it was safer to do battle in the open sea rather than in the confined waters of Leyte Gulf.

'Taffy Two', the second group of six escort carriers, was next to receive the unwanted attentions of the Japanese, as the first properly planned Kamikaze attacks started. Four aircraft from shore bases dived on to the Second Escort Carrier Group, hitting both *Suwanee* and *Santee*, with the second ship also being hit by a torpedo from a Japanese submarine. As Kurita returned to the east of Samar, there were further Kamikaze attacks, blowing up the escort carrier *St Lo* and damaging both *Kalinin Bay* and *Kitkun Bay* in 'Taffy One'. Kurita was unaware of the Kamikaze attacks, and certainly knew nothing about their successes. This was the man who had signalled to his ships the previous day: 'Braving any loss and damage we may suffer, the First Striking Force will break into Leyte Gulf and fight to the last man.' Yet, at noon, he ordered a withdrawal, having failed completely in his mission to destroy the American transports, scuttling three of his heavy cruisers, while another two, although badly damaged, were considered to be capable of returning safely to Japan.

It was not until later that the Americans realized that they were the targets for suicide attacks. The first few aircraft were seen either as having crashed out of control or having been deliberately flown into the ships by pilots who were frustrated after their aircraft had been badly damaged. After all, in the days before ejection seats, escape from a fast, low flying aircraft was well nigh impossible.

'We thought they was (sic) dropping bombs on us because one of the carriers off the port side took a direct hit from a Kamikaze,' George Smith explained.

> They hit this carrier just dead centre and as we went by men were abandoning ship . . . and as we got beyond it the whole ship just seemed to explode . . . there was nothing there. And about that time on our ship a Kamikaze came in on us . . . just like regular landing I guess he was trying to sneak in on us like one of our own planes . . . And he started to drop in and of course the skipper seen what was going on so he turned the ship hard port . . . the men on the starboard side were banged against there, they swung our guns round and shot across the flight deck hitting the Kamikaze and the Kamikaze he winged over and dropped on the other side . . . into the water and exploded.[2]

The senior officers in both navies were confused and unaware of the true situation. Both Nimitz and Kinkaid believed that Halsey was working to plan and safeguarding the San Bernardino Strait, and then had to send signals demanding to know his true position once they realized that he had left the Strait open to the Japanese. Halsey was then ordered to return south. Had he sent part of his force northwards, Halsey could have covered the Strait with his remaining force.

Meanwhile, Mitscher's reconnaissance, using an aircraft from the light carrier *Independence*, had located the Japanese Northern Force at 02.08, and later discovered that this had divided into two. Halsey sent TF34 forward, with the battleships and cruisers ahead of the carriers.

'The Commander Third Fleet's plan for pushing strong surface forces ahead of his carrier groups and toward the enemy was a logical piece of tactics . . . ,' explained the official US Navy report on the battle.

> Our expectation, based on past achievements, is that in an exchange of carrier attacks between fleets, it will be our enemy's fleet that takes the worst of it, and starts retiring while still at a distance many times greater than gun range. The only possibility then of closing and capitalizing on our gun power is to overtake cripples or ships of naturally low speed.

In short, as with the Japanese plans for the battle, Halsey wanted to use his battleships and cruisers.

At 08.00 Mitscher sent the first of six waves with a total of 527 aircraft to attack Ozawa's Northern Force with its four aircraft carriers to the east of Luzon. This was to become the Battle of Cape Engano. Against the overwhelming American attack, Ozawa had just twenty fighters left, and these were shot down almost as soon as the attackers arrived. The light carrier *Chitose* was sunk quickly, slipping beneath the waves at 09.37, with *Zuikaku*, *Zuiho* and *Chiyoda* and a light cruiser all damaged, and Ozawa moving his flag from *Zuikaku*. The three remaining carriers, now with no fighter defence at all, inevitably fell victim to the succeeding waves, with *Zuikaku* on fire and burning out of control after the third wave of 200 aircraft had attacked. By the afternoon, she too had sunk. Another light cruiser was crippled, and finished off by an American submarine, while three destroyers and a tanker were also sunk.

Halsey then turned his attentions to Kurita's Centre Force, which he should have encountered earlier. Taking his flagship, the battleship *New Jersey*, at first he was unlucky, but later that day and on 26 October, carrier aircraft from the Third and Seventh Fleets found the Centre Force and attacked, sinking two cruisers, including one that was not one of Kurita's ships but was instead escorting a Japanese transport to Leyte.

Overall, the Japanese had lost three battleships, four aircraft carriers, six heavy and four light cruisers, eleven destroyers, a destroyer transport and four submarines, while the Americans had lost a light carrier and two escort carriers as well as three

172

destroyers. The Japanese had lost 150 aircraft, both shore-based and carrier-borne, compared with 100 US aircraft. Some 10,000 Japanese had lost their lives compared with 1,500 Americans.

Obviously, this was another American victory and yet another Japanese defeat. Kurita had failed to make the most of his opportunities, but Ozawa's strategy had worked, drawing Halsey northward and giving Kurita an opportunity, except, of course, that Ozawa did not have sufficient aircraft even at the outset to ward off a determined American attack.

The big failing at Leyte went far beyond the question of who won the naval battles. The objective had been to catch the American transports at sea and inflict such heavy losses amongst them that the United States would be forced to think again. Yet, the battle did not develop until several days after the first landings on 20 October, and even had Kurita followed his plan to the letter and finally found himself amongst the transports, it would have been far too late. The transports had done their work unchallenged. The day for the attack should have been 19 October as the transports neared the Philippines with their troops. Once again, it was a case of too little, too late. The Americans were now setting the agenda.

Halsey does not come out of this without criticism. His belief in not dividing his forces was a nonsense given the overwhelming strength at his disposal, and in disobeying orders and leaving the San Bernardino Strait unguarded, he had left the vulnerable escort carriers and transports at the mercy of Kurita's force, and it was only the Japanese officer's bungling that saved the situation. If he had been determined to give chase, he could have at least communicated his decision to the Seventh Fleet and given Kinkaid the opportunity to take the necessary measures to safeguard his flank. Of course, the reason for not letting Kinkaid know was simply that Halsey realized that Nimitz in turn would have got to know and would have ordered him to return to his position. Halsey was simply fortunate that his luck remained good and that Kurita failed, for all of his bravado before the battle, to press home his attack. Believing that he was heading into an American trap does not come out as a good excuse for withdrawal, as even a quick glance at a map beforehand would have shown the dangers. The irony is that had Halsey stayed in position, Kurita would have found the naval battle that so many Second World War admirals on both sides were looking for, but it would have been even more conclusive as without air power, Kurita's major surface units would have been at a disadvantage. If Kurita had really believed that he was facing the full might of the US Third Fleet, he should have withdrawn promptly.

The Imperial Japanese Navy was by now a spent force. It had lost its aircraft in the First Battle of the Philippine Sea and its ships in the Second Battle of the Philippine Sea. The fact that Japan had decided to resort of suicide attacks on American warships spoke volumes about the course of the war, and about the outcome.

There is a nagging suspicion that during the war in the Pacific, the Japanese were let down by their commanders, both afloat and ashore. There were repeated failures of army commanders to adhere to carefully prepared plans for the defence of territory. The best justification for disobeying orders is success, indeed, it is the *only* justification, but the generals concerned did not enjoy success. Nagumo's failure to send a third and even a fourth wave of attackers to Pearl Harbor was an early example of poor leadership. He may have been concerned at being found by the American carriers, but good reconnaissance would have reduced the risk. The failure to listen to the experienced carrier officers before Midway was yet another example, as was the poor reconnaissance pattern mounted beforehand, or the indecision that led to aircraft being re-armed and disarmed, and the failure to keep one of the four available flight decks free to launch fighters, all showed poor leadership. Yet, this was a navy with an uninterrupted control of its own aviation.

Yet again, attacking the American carriers may well have been a worthy objective, but the real priority was to attack the transports *before* they could land troops and equipment. Looking for a traditional naval engagement so that the wasted assets of the battle and cruiser fleets could justify their existence, was another example of commanders failing to have any strategic sense and being unable to comprehend just how naval warfare had moved on, when the two roles that these heavy ships could undertake were ignored. These roles were, of course, operating close enough to the Japanese aircraft carriers to provide additional and desperately needed anti-aircraft fire, and heavy bombardment of Allied forces ashore, including transports, especially those on the re-supply operation.

On 15 December 1944, US forces landed on Mindoro, a small

island to the south of Manila, with three battleships, six escort carriers and seven cruisers providing support. At this time of year, the Pacific was not nearly as calm as its name suggests, and three days later Halsey's Third Fleet was struck by a typhoon, often referred as 'Halsey's Typhoon', while still providing support for the landings on Mindoro by mounting heavy air attacks on airfields on Luzon. The typhoon sank three destroyers and damaged three of the light carriers, and caused serious damage to the forward end of the wooden flight decks on two of the Essex-class fleet carriers, while also destroying 146 aircraft that were either washed overboard or smashed in their hangar decks.

Luzon itself was finally invaded on 9 January 1945, again with support from the US Third Fleet that allowed MacArthur's I and XIV Army Corps on the island, once again with close support by Kinkaid's Seventh Fleet. As at Leyte, there were eighteen escort carriers providing close support, as well as the battleships *Mississippi, West Virginia, New Mexico, California, Pennsylvania* and *Colorado*, in addition to eleven cruisers. Once again, Kamikaze attacks were launched at the invaders, with damage to several ships and the loss of an escort carrier, as we will see in the next chapter, but by 12 January, the US Third Fleet's carrier-borne aircraft had destroyed all Japanese air power on Luzon.

Close air support of an invasion fleet had seemed to be the natural role of the United States Marine Corps' air squadrons. But when Nimitz decided to omit carrier training from the syllabus for aspiring US Marine Corps pilots in 1943, the Corps found itself increasingly on the sidelines in the major campaigns of 1943 and 1944. This was an unaccountable decision since the Marines had become proficient at ground-attack operations, and when required were able to mount strafing, bombing and rocket attacks on enemy positions as close as seventy-five yards away from friendly troops. Early 1945 was to see the US Marine Corp's welcome return to these operations.

Notes
[1-2] Imperial War Museum Sound Archive, Accession No. 3060/1(B)

XIV

KAMIKAZE!

'Because Japan is an Imperial Domain,' wrote Lieutenant Yukio Seki to his parents, 'I shall carry out a ramming attack against a carrier to repay the Imperial Benevolence. I am resigned to this.'

Seki was writing at the start of the Battle of Leyte Gulf which had seen the first Kamikaze attacks. Kamikaze, or 'Divine Wind' had its origins in the storm that had sprung up in 1274 and which wrecked the Mongol Emperor Kublai Khan's fleet as it was poised to invade Japan. It did not necessarily mean suicide, as it had even been adopted as the name for a distance record setting aircraft of the 1930s. Nor indeed did Kamikaze necessarily involve aircraft as, lacking effective anti-tank weapons, Japanese soldiers with satchels of explosive had thrown themselves under American tanks during some of the fiercest land battles of the Pacific War. There had even been Kamikaze commando raids.

Part of the problem was that Japan, today seen as a leading exploiter of technology, lagged behind the other industrial powers at the time. The highly acclaimed Zero fighter was described in a post-war evaluation by one American officer as a 'sport plane', meaning that it depended on its success for the fact that it carried a pilot of small stature and low weight rather than any technical merit, and being smaller it was also more manoeuvrable. Its early successes were due to the poor quality of the fighter aircraft deployed in the Far East by the British and the Dutch, and their limited numbers. Whereas the Germans countered heavy anti-aircraft fire with remote controlled glider bombs, used for the first time against the Allies at Salerno, the Japanese used suicide aircraft. As American bombers flew ever higher, the Germans invented the rocket-powered Messerschmitt Me163 interceptor, but the Japanese simply stripped everything out of their fighters to save weight and sent their pilots to fly head on into the American bombers in another manifestation of the Kamikaze concept. That Japan and Germany were allied as

176

fellow members of the Axis amounted to not very much in practice, as little technology was transferred and there was no military collaboration and coordination. Even if there had been a liaison process, by late 1944 Germany was also broken and heading for defeat, the only question was when, and to some extent, how, the Third Reich would fall. Hitler had indeed hastened his own downfall by declaring war on the United States when that country declared war on Japan in response to the attack at Pearl Harbor – but it could be said that Hitler had simply provided the Americans with an excuse as, given the growing United States support for the British war effort, it is doubtful whether the USA would have stayed out of the war with Germany for much longer. American neutrality had been heavily biased towards the democracies, not simply providing equipment under the Lend-Lease Scheme, but providing training at American bases and refitting badly damaged British ships, such as HMS *Illustrious* after her savaging off Malta in January 1941, and allowing her own nationals to volunteer for service with the British armed forces, especially the Royal Air Force.

Kamikaze or Hornet?

Suicide attacks mean exactly that, a strategy in which those involved are sent on an operation with the deliberate aim of killing themselves to ensure that the attack is pressed home. In many armed forces, there have been instances of men being sent on a mission with scant chances of survival, or of those who have been badly wounded crashing their aircraft onto a target, but in none of these cases was suicide part of the strategy. The attack by the destroyers *Ardent* and *Acasta* on the German battlecruisers *Scharnhorst* and *Gneisenau* was hopeless and risky in the extreme, and indeed both destroyers were sunk, but it was not a suicide attack and many of those aboard were alive to abandon ship afterwards. Much the same could be said about a further attack on these two battlecruisers, when six Fairey Swordfish had made their desperate attack on the two ships with the cruiser *Prinz Eugen*, during the celebrated 'Channel Dash' in February 1942.

Even the Japanese were reluctant to resort to Kamikaze attacks at first when these were suggested by Admiral Arima. The proposals were rejected and Arima informed that his superiors were only interested in attacks in which the pilot returned alive.

Arima refused to be discouraged by official rejection and raised the idea anew each time the Americans inflicted a further defeat. Much further down the Japanese officer class, Ensign Shoichi Ota of the Naval Air Technical Depot began the design of a human bomb following the American invasion of the Marianas. The human bomb was designated the 'Okha', one of the Japanese terms for cherry blossom, because cherry blossom falls at the height of its beauty and to the Japanese symbolized the young warrior dying in battle.

The Okha first appeared in September 1944, and was intended to allow the Japanese to mass produce a disposable aircraft for Kamikaze use rather than waste standard aircraft. It also had the advantage that once in the Okha, the pilot was committed to carrying out his attack and could not return. Powered by five rockets and of flimsy construction, the single-seat Okha had to be carried to within range of its target by a land-based bomber, and after being released it could fly under power for up to eleven miles before diving or gliding onto its target with its 2,600-lbs of explosive. Usually, the pilot would fly in the mother aircraft and then climb down into the Okha before release, but occasionally the hapless pilot had to spend the entire flight in the aircraft. The big weakness of the concept, apart from the flimsy construction and poor manoeuvrability of the Okha, was that the mother aircraft had to get close to the target, well within range of Allied radar and fighters, and as fighters increased in numbers and their pilots in experience, the mother aircraft was extremely vulnerable.

Of necessity, the Okha had to be launched from a land-based bomber, but oddly enough, there were fifty of these aircraft aboard the new aircraft carrier *Shinano*, converted from the uncompleted third battleship of the Yamato-class, when she was sunk by six torpedoes from the submarine USS *Archerfish* on 29 November 1944, just ten days after being launched. Possibly the ship, the largest aircraft carrier ever built outside the United States, was acting as a transport or was intended to launch twin-engined 'Betty' bombers in a repeat of the Doolittle raid. The ship sank seven hours after being torpedoed, partly due to poor damage control and her crew still being unfamiliar with her, as much as to the torpedo attack. It was not until much later that the Americans believed the commander of the submarine!

Another Japanese officer to advocate Kamikaze attacks was

Captain Eichiro Jo, who put the idea to his commander, Admiral Jisaburo Ozawa, who had so conspicuously failed at the Battle of Leyte Gulf, and who passed it on with his recommendation to Admiral Toyada, the new commander-in-chief of the Combined Fleet. Toyada in turn passed the idea to Mitsuo Fuchida for comment. Fuchida was by this time a staff officer with the rank of captain. He was unenthusiastic about the idea, not from any humanitarian principles, but because he doubted whether inexperienced pilots could handle the project effectively as they would have no strategic sense. Indeed, many of the Kamikaze pilots were not simply inexperienced, but as the pressure on Japan grew, often their training was limited to the bare essentials that would enable them to get the aircraft or flying bomb to the target.

At this early stage, the name 'Kamikaze' had still to be chosen, and one alternative name was that of a specially trained and selected 'Hornet' Corps; the rationale being that when a hornet attacks, both the insect and the victim dies. Eventually the name 'Kamikaze' was chosen by Vice Admiral Takijiro Onishi.

Fuchida was also concerned that relatively small numbers of aircraft would not be able to inflict sufficient damage on the enemy. He had seen enough to realize that the American strength had been in massed attacks that caused the defences to divide their fire and which swept aside all resistance. It was not to be until the massive air battle off Okinawa that the first massed Kamikaze attacks were to occur, at a time when the Japanese were finding it difficult to mount any other form of massed air attack of their own. Had Kamikazes been used in massed attacks against American troop transports, they might indeed have inflicted the terrible casualties that many Japanese senior officers believed would force the United States to seek a compromise solution.

Certainly, most Kamikaze pilots were senior ratings or very junior officers, and strategic sense was lacking. Usually, Kamikaze pilots would aim for a destroyer or escort carrier and only one at a time. Their preferred spot when attacking a carrier was the join between the island and the flight deck, which often caused considerable loss of life, but the lifts, even on the armoured British carriers, would have been more vulnerable, not only putting ships out of action but with the very real possibility of setting aircraft in the hangar below on fire, and starting a chain of events that could end in the loss of a carrier.

Pressure to introduce Kamikaze attacks grew, and soon Fuchida was on the receiving end of a considerable correspondence and increasing pressure to support the idea. In what seems to have been the typical Japanese fashion by this stage of the war, it was left to Takijiro Onishi to introduce the concept on his own initiative after he became commander of the Fifth Base Air Force in the Philippines on 19 November 1944, so once again a local commander ignored the wishes of his superiors and pressed ahead, regardless of the waste of life or equipment. Onishi started the Kamikaze attacks using Zero fighters, which were manoeuvrable indeed, but could only carry a bomb of 550-lbs, (250-kg), and were completely wasted on vessels with armoured decks.

Later, when the concept received official backing, it became known as Operation Sho.

Meanwhile, in an attempt both to prove the concept and to force the pace of decision-making, Rear Admiral Arima himself flew the first officially-recorded Kamikaze mission on 13 October 1944, crashing his aircraft into the carrier USS *Franklin*. It was also at this time that volunteers were called for from 201st Air Group based in the Philippines at the base known to the Americans as Clarke Airfield. In calling for volunteers, the Japanese commanders made it clear that they were looking for men without family commitments, but nevertheless the entire unit volunteered, becoming the 1st Special Attack Force or '*Tokhai Tai*'.

The Divine Wind of Desperation

Lieutenant Yukio Seki was given command of the first group of twenty-three petty officer pilots. At first, the aim was that every attack should secure a hit, but Seki himself had to fly four missions before finding a suitable target. This was an option open only to those flying modified aircraft as the pilots of the Okha flying bombs had no chance of turning back. In fact, those around him noticed that Seki's enthusiasm waned with each unsuccessful sortie.

Tactics varied. Provided that the Kamikaze managed to evade the increasingly experienced and effective fighter defences, the pilot could either opt for an attack from high altitude, around 20,000 feet, or make a lower approach at around 3,000 feet. The high altitude attack meant that the aircraft could not dive at a very steep angle for fear of losing control, making accuracy difficult, but from 3,000 feet a steep dive was possible. Either way, the final stages were through heavy and accurate AA fire. Manned suicide aircraft were never as accurate as one might imagine.

The general idea has always been that a weakness of suicide missions was the absence of any feedback, on the grounds that it is impossible to debrief a dead pilot, but this was not the case. The anti-ship Kamikaze missions were usually escorted by fighters, who as well as fighting off the Allied fighters were also expected to report back on the success of the mission. Unfortunately, there was a consistent tendency to report back that the missions were far more successful than was in fact the case. This tendency to exaggerate may have been because the fighter pilots had indeed been so preoccupied with US and British fighters, or it may have been a subconscious desire to laud the performance of those who had died; a sense of guilt or failure that they had not volunteered for a Kamikaze mission perhaps? On the other hand, once again this could have been because of poor intelligence and poor ship recognition, with tankers often mistaken for escort carriers and destroyers for cruisers. To be fair, the fighters would probably have been caught at some distance from the target.

The more cynical historians believe that one duty of the escorts was to discourage any Kamikaze pilot who had second thoughts and wished to return. There could be some truth in this as not all of the 'volunteers' seem to have been genuine and others seem to have signed up under peer pressure, as when entire units 'volunteered', and those who were reluctant to volunteer were sometimes found dead after an air raid. On the other hand, many Kamikazes did turn back, either because they couldn't find a suitable target or because of technical difficulties with their aircraft.

While the Kamikaze pilots maintained that they were fighting in the tradition of the 'Bushido spirit', there were many other Japanese who maintained that they were mad men. Even Christian Japanese airmen volunteered for kamikaze missions, maintaining that it was their duty to die for the Emperor.

Japanese propaganda, able to put a gloss on the worst defeat if not distort it completely out of all recognition, naturally enough claimed that every Kamikaze sank a ship, but this was a gross distortion of the truth. Even so, at Leyte Onishi's men were successful enough to cause the United States Navy great concern. At the outset, one senior US naval officer, Admiral Morison, thought that the Japanese had 'sprung a tactical surprise that might prolong the war another year'. At Leyte, four escort carriers were damaged by Kamikaze attack and a fifth, USS *St Lo*, sunk. It seems that one in four Kamikaze inflicted damage while one in thirty-three sank a ship. Even so, the United States imposed tight censorship on reports of Kamikaze attacks so that the Japanese could not discover how much damage they were doing, while it was also important not to place too much stress on the attacks because of their impact on American morale.

Certainly, the Kamikaze attacks gave the Americans serious concern, despite the very heavy volume of anti-aircraft fire that American warships could put up at this stage of the war.

'We didn't see him until he was about 8,000 yards away,' recalled Lieutenant Harry Stanley, a gunnery officer aboard one of the American warships. 'He came in low and fast, how he missed all the stuff we threw up at him, I don't know.'

The frustration and feeling of helplessness that the Americans felt at this new type of warfare was almost beyond description.

'Every time one country gets something, another country soon gets it,' commented one senior officer. 'Whether it is a new kind of engine, or a new plane, another country soon gets it, but the Japanese had the Kamikaze and no one else is built like that.'

On the other hand, another American officer maintained that: 'If that son of a bitch has the nerve to die in here, then we've the guts to fight back.'

In November 1944, the second month of Kamikaze attack, while the US Third Fleet was operating east of the Philippines, suicide attacks sank a destroyer and damaged the aircraft carriers *Essex*, *Franklin*, *Hancock*, *Intrepid* and *Lexington*, as well as the two light carriers, *Belleau Wood* and *Cabot*. The attacks reached a peak on 25 November. By this time, on Japanese-held airfields, aircraft were having to be scattered around and hidden under trees to avoid detection and destruction by the United States Navy, which enjoyed complete aerial supremacy. Five bases each contributed five aircraft, suggesting that ordinary squadron pilots had been expected to 'volunteer', but this time bombers rather than the lightweight Zero fighters, including some of the new Nakajima B6N Jill bombers, while seventeen Zero fighters were sent along to escort and observe.

The Kamikaze force found the Third Fleet at sea, 150 miles off Manila. Leaving the escorts to tackle the American fighters, the suicide pilots selected their targets ready to dive on to them. *Hancock* was the first target, but the Kamikaze was shot down by intensive AA fire. Even so, as the aircraft broke up, burning debris struck the deck and started fires while a single large item knocked out an AA position.

Worse was to follow as the Kamikaze aiming for *Intrepid* managed to avoid the protecting curtain of AA fire and crash into one of the AA gun positions and then through the carrier's deck into the hangar, before exploding and bending the deck upwards. Then a second Kamikaze hit the ship, once again crashing through the flight deck and into the hangar, where it too exploded. The large carrier was out of action and her crew busy fighting fires while her aircraft had to be recovered by other ships.

Cabot was also the target for two Kamikaze, with the first scoring a direct hit on the flight deck. The second Kamikaze was shot down and crashed into the sea, but still caused some damage as the aircraft exploded close to the ship. *Essex* was luckier, for although the Kamikaze struck her flight deck, its bomb failed to explode.

The attacks on *Intrepid* and *Cabot* were amongst the most successful Kamikaze attacks on major warships and suggests that the pilots had been more experienced aircrew than was usual for such operations, not only managing to dodge the AA fire but also selecting a part of the ship where the most damage could be inflicted. It is also noteworthy that more than one aircraft attacked the same ship in each case, for another problem with many Kamikaze attacks was that they did not concentrate their efforts on a single ship but instead tended to look for individual targets, and so were unlikely to cause enough damage to put a ship out of action let alone sink her. Even so, sending twenty-five aircraft was hardly enough to cause severe damage on such a large fleet so well defended and was, in fact, akin to a series of pinpricks by the demanding standards at this stage of the war, when massed aerial attacks to overwhelm the defences had become the order of the day. As it was, out of the combined total of forty-two fighters and Kamikaze aircraft sent against the Third Fleet that day, sixteen returned to their bases despite some of the fighters having been shot down, indicating that some at least were Kamikaze. Even when large numbers of US ships were at sea,

Kamikaze pilots did return claiming that they hadn't been able to find a target, while others returned because of technical problems with their aircraft.

The bomb that didn't explode on the *Essex* was to prove to be a far more commonplace incident than might have been expected. The Kamikaze pilots flying aircraft rather than flying bombs were under orders not to prime their bomb until after they had selected their target. This was because the early Kamikaze pilots had often primed their bomb early and if they couldn't find a target either had to waste their bomb by dropping it into the sea, or even crashing into the sea themselves, or risk landing with a live bomb under the aircraft. In the stress of pressing home the attack, many pilots forgot to arm their bombs and so any damage was left to the speed of the aircraft and the impact, as well as any fuel left in their tanks.

By late November, it was clear that the original attacks at Leyte had not been a one-off, possibly an expression of the frustration and despair felt by the pilots of a single unit, but that instead it had been the start of a concerted campaign. It was also clear that the larger carriers were vulnerable as well as the lightly built escort carriers. It soon became clear that the different structures of American carriers with their superstructure flight decks made them more vulnerable than the armoured British ships. Several large American carriers had to be taken out of service for heavy repairs after receiving Kamikaze attacks. There were many casualties amongst those working on carrier flight decks or in the hangars, and amongst those manning the AA defences.

While the aircraft carriers seem to have been prime targets for the Kamikaze attacks, they were far from the only targets. Cruisers and destroyers could be very vulnerable, especially in confined waters with little room for manoeuvre. As in any other type of attack, most vulnerable of all were merchant vessels, especially ammunition ships. On 28 December 1944, a Kamikaze hit the ammunition ship USS *John Burke*, which blew up with every man aboard.

Following the American landings on Luzon, one of the largest of the Philippine Islands, on 9 January, Kamikaze attacks built up to a new peak. The escort carrier *Ommaney Bay* was sunk and three others damaged, as were two battleships, *New Mexico* and *California*, and four cruisers. All in all, around 100 American warships were damaged or sunk, with 4,000 casualties. Vice

Admiral Onishi's First Air Fleet also supported the Kamikaze attacks with their own raids from airfields in Luzon. When all seemed lost in the Philippines, Onishi evacuated the remaining Kamikaze pilots, but left the ground crewmen to fight to the end as infantry.

A fresh Kamikaze unit was formed on 18 January 1945 ready for action against US warships off Formosa (now Taiwan). The Essex-class aircraft carrier USS *Ticonderoga*, which had commenced her service in the Pacific only the previous November, was hit twice. The first hit penetrated the flight deck and started serious fires which were soon burning out of control in the hangar, while the second, about an hour later, severely damaged the island. Skilful damage control, helped by the commanding officer manoeuvring the ship to minimize the effects of the prevailing wind on the fires and ordering the port side of the ship to be flooded, put out the fires and protected the magazines. Despite the damage, '*Tico*', as she was known to her crew, was repaired and back in service during April, able to take part in the attacks on the Japanese home islands. Her aircraft took part in the sinking of the battleships *Haruna*, *Hyuga* and *Ise*, as well as the new carrier *Kaiyo*.

Off Iwo Jima on 21 February 1945, Kamikaze aircraft sank the escort carrier *Bismarck Sea*, which was hit by two Kamikazes, and the *Saratoga* was hit no less than six times, although she was not the only American carrier to be hit this often, and the ship's company had to struggle to save her. Later, the prolonged Kamikaze offensive off Iwo Jima that started on 6 April is covered in detail.

Ticonderoga was not to be the last American carrier to suffer grievously from the pressure of Kamikaze attack. The attacks on 21 February 1945, caused considerable damage to the USS *Saratoga*, one of the former battlecruisers converted to an aircraft carrier as a result of the conditions imposed on the United States Navy by the 1922 Washington Naval Treaty and commissioned in her new form in 1927. '*Sara*' was hit six times, but four of the aircraft inflicted the real damage. The first aircraft went into the hangar deck, causing a violent explosion, while the second struck the ship on the starboard below the waterline. Two more Kamikazes added to the earlier damage. The fifth, nearly missed her altogether, although heading for the island, but managed to carry away the signal antennae, while the sixth, the last to hit the ship, struck her on the starboard side. In addition to this, a number of bombs also struck '*Sara*'. Badly crippled by this onslaught, the elderly carrier withdrew and headed for Puget Sound, where she was repaired at Bremerton, a yard which had earlier repaired the carrier following a torpedo strike from the submarine *I-6* off Pearl Harbor in January 1942. *Saratoga* seems to have been unlucky, as a further attack by the Japanese submarine *I-26* on 31 August 1942 had seen three boiler rooms flooded and other damage that left her immobilized, having to be taken in tow for urgent temporary repairs before she could steam to Pearl Harbor for permanent repairs. On the other hand, while she was unlucky, she was not so unlucky as to be sunk!

It was in March 1945 that the first serious attacks by the Okha piloted bombs began. The initial operations were mounted by a so-called 'Thunderbird' unit, although the aircraft was known to many Japanese, doubtless the more cynical and realistic of the Emperor's men, as the *Bako*, or 'Fool's Plane'. Foolish indeed, for in the first attacks, all of the Mitsubishi 'Betty' bombers were shot down. The aircraft would have been a relatively easy target for the American fighters at the best of times, but lumbered with the Okha flying bombs, the aircraft were vulnerable.

At all times, the Kamikaze attacks were just one aspect of the increasing desperation with which the Japanese were fighting the war. Following the invasion of Iwo Jima, just 200 out of the 22,000 Japanese troops ashore survived. The fanaticism of the Japanese took its toll on US forces ashore, with 6,000 Americans killed on Iwo Jima and another 17,000 wounded.

Life under Attack

By spring 1945, the carriers of the British Pacific Fleet were working alongside the American fast carrier force as Task Force 57, indicating that the US force had been re-titled the Fifth Fleet. Although operating with the Americans, the British carriers were still set their own targets, which were the three islands of the Sakishima Gunto, Miyako, Ishigaki and Iriomote. TF57 had to neutralize the airfields on these islands to prevent the Japanese from flying reinforcements and replacement aircraft for the defence of Okinawa.

The routine aboard these four ships was that aircrew, hangar and flight deck parties were awakened at 03.30, and the ship closed up to action stations at 05.00, prepared for Kamikaze attacks. The ships had three states of readiness, of which the lowest was yellow, with fighters on standby; blue, meaning fighters at readiness, and red, meaning that fighters had to scramble.

On 1 April, HMS *Victorious* was attacked by a Kamikaze that had passed over the ship before going into a near vertical dive. Once he was committed to his dive the Kamikaze pilot was unable to manoeuvre, the ship's commanding officer turned her to port leaving the Kamikaze to crash into the sea just off the carrier's starboard bow.

The armoured deck of the fast British carriers was now to show its worth.

'There was a scream of a diving aircraft passing over us,' recalled Norman Hanson, who was still aboard *Illustrious*.

> The hell of a bang followed as a suicider slammed into *Indefatigable*, sailing parallel to us about 300 yards on our starboard side. She took the blow in the worst possible place – in the angle between flight-deck and island – and casualties in dead, wounded and missing were heavy. The armour-plated deck protected the hangar from damage, but itself suffered a dent from the sheer impact . . . Quick drying cement was poured into the depression and levelled off. Within a few hours *Indeft* was operating her aircraft as though she had experienced nothing more than a slight hiccup.

Later that day, it was the turn of *Illustrious*, although the aircraft missed the ship after being shot down by her AA gunners, one of whom was Lieutenant Bob Finlay, the Captain's secretary.

'The wind was from the starboard side and we were immediately inundated with a shower of crankshafts, pistons, sections of fuselage and assorted pieces of Mitsubishi manufacture,' Hanson remembers.

> The pilot's dinghy, a gaudy red and yellow affair, flew lazily across the deck, inflating itself in transit, and fetched up on the port aerial mast. The pilot's own skull was the first object to land on the deck, to be gathered up quickly by the medical profession.

Bob opened up again, but had to cease fire momentarily to flick away, somewhat petulantly, something which partially obscured the ring-sight. He didn't feel very well two minutes later when he realised that what he had removed so peremptorily was a slender strip of Japanese flesh, about half a rasher . . .

At the start of the attack, the carrier had had two Corsairs ranged on the flight deck, ready to take off. One of the pilots forgot to switch off his engine as he left the aircraft, and when the Kamikaze crashed into the sea, exploding with such force that at first some of those aboard thought it had been a torpedo attack, the chocks holding the aircraft were dislodged, and with the vibration from the heavy AA fire, which on these ships also included sixteen 4.5-inch guns in eight turrets, the aircraft started to move. As the Corsair rolled towards the side of the flight deck, with great courage and considerable presence of mind, one of the ship's electricians ran from the island, jumped into the cockpit and hit the foot brakes before switching the engine off. Then, despite the battle raging all around him, sat in the cockpit until two of the flight deck crew ran across with a set of chocks. Despite his courage, the young rating was simply mentioned in dispatches, a disappointment for Hanson who tried to get him the Distinguished Service Medal, DSM.

In such tense conditions, aircraft returning to their carriers were liable to be fired at by their own anti-aircraft gunners, keyed up after a long period at readiness and having endured repeated enemy attacks.

The End of the Kamikaze

While many Japanese regarded the surrender following the use of atomic bombs against Hiroshima and Nagasaki in August 1945 as a national humiliation, so much so that some considered a *coup d'état*, few found it harder to accept than the men of the Kamikaze units. These men had been prepared to make the supreme sacrifice and treated even the very concept of surrender with contempt: it was not for Japanese warriors. In fact, scarce fuel had been set aside for a mass Kamikaze attack of 5,000 aircraft against the expected Allied invasion fleet, although how effective this would have been is open to doubt since many of the aircraft were unsuitable, often elderly trainers, and many of the pilots had only enough training to get into the air.

The commander of the remaining Kamikaze units was Admiral Ugaki, who took off in the leading aircraft of a formation of eleven bombers intending to make a final attack against US forces in Okinawa. Four hours later he sent a final message:

> I alone am to blame for our failure to defend the homeland and destroy the arrogant enemy. The valiant efforts of all officers and men of my command during the past six months has been greatly appreciated.
>
> I am going to make an attack on Okinawa where my men have fallen like cherry blossoms. There I will crash into and destroy the conceited enemy in the true spirit of Bushido, with firm conviction and faith in the eternity of Imperial Japan.
>
> I trust that members of all units under my command will understand my motives, will overcome all hardships of the future, and will strive for the reconstruction of our great homeland that it may survive forever.
>
> Tenno heika. Banzai!

This was denial at its best – ignoring the fact that Japan had started the war and invaded a whole string of territories across the Pacific and Asia and accusing the Americans of arrogance and conceit! In fact, four of the eleven aircraft returned claiming mechanical difficulties. This might sound like a happy coincidence, but it is possible, given the shortage of spares and trained mechanics, for these too had been lost when the carrier fleet had been destroyed, that the aircraft were none too reliable as the war ended.

That night, Admiral Onishi, who had effectively started the Kamikaze campaign, committed hara kiri, the Japanese means of committing suicide. Having made the ritual cut across his abdomen with his short sword and then brought the weapon up, he then tried to cut his own throat, but failed. Weakening from loss of blood, he lay back and waited for the end. He was found the following morning by a servant lying in a pool of blood, weak but still conscious. Onishi refused offers of medical assistance and asked to be left alone to die – but it took him until 18.00 that evening.

XV

THE NET CLOSES:
IWO JIMA AND OKINAWA

With Japanese air power in the Philippines finally defeated, Halsey took the Third Fleet into the South China Sea, attacking harbours and shipping over an area of sea stretching from Saigon in French Indo-China, now Vietnam, to Formosa, now Taiwan, over the period 10–21 January 1945. The carriers' aircraft met little resistance and 200,000 tons of enemy shipping was sunk. The Kamikaze re-emerged, however, and both *Ticonderoga* and *Langley* were hit. Nevertheless, by the spring most of the southern Philippines were controlled by American forces.

The Japanese were left in no doubt now that the net was tightening around them. On 16 and 17 February, with the fleet redesignated the Fifth Fleet once more and under the command of Admiral Raymond Spruance, Mitscher took the sixteen carriers of what was now Task Force 58, with nine battleships, fourteen cruisers and seventy-seven destroyers, to launch the first large-scale attack by the United States Navy on the Japanese home islands. The primary targets were Japanese airfields, against which the Navy's fighters and fighter-bombers could be more effective than the US Army Air Force's heavy bombers, which were concentrating on the cities. In the operation, more than 500 Japanese aircraft were destroyed, against eighty-eight of the strike force and its fighter cover.

The attacks by the long-range bombers on Japan from their bases in the Marianas were thought to be vulnerable to Japanese fighters, although this problem was to ease considerably with the introduction of the Boeing B-29 Superfortress. Meanwhile, to provide fighter cover for the bombing raids, bases were needed for the fighters much closer to Japan itself, and the island of Iwo Jima was seen as ideal. On 19 February, the first American forces landed on Iwo Jima, covered by the Fifth Fleet with TF58's carriers. The actual landing saw Vice Admiral Turner's TF51 with 500 ships put Lieutenant General Smith's V Amphibious Corps ashore, with direct support provided by seven battleships, eleven escort carriers and five cruisers. Ashore, there were 20,000 Japanese troops in well defended positions. The Kamikaze attacks on 21 February against the *Bismarck Sea* and *Saratoga* have already been mentioned in the previous chapter. It took a month and 23,000 American dead and wounded for Japanese resistance to be broken.

Having established a strategy of attacking Japanese airfields within reach of the next landing objective, it was necessary for TF58 to attack Japan once again before the landings on Okinawa, a measure of the island's proximity to the home islands. On 18 and 19 March, carrier aircraft once again struck at airfields and naval bases in Japan itself, using 1,200 aircraft from the carriers *Hornet, Bennington, Enterprise, Franklin, Essex, Bunker Hill, Hancock, Yorktown, Intrepid* and *Wasp*, as well as the light carriers *Belleau Wood, Bataan, San Jacinto, Langley, Independence* and *Cabot*. The carriers were supported by the battleships *Massachusetts, Indiana, North Carolina, Washington, South Dakota, Wisconsin, New Jersey* and *Missouri*, as well as the battlecruisers *Alaska* and *Guam*, and sixteen cruisers and sixty-four destroyers.

Ashore in Japan, Vice Admiral Ugaki organized a counter-attack, including his own Kamikaze force, with hits on the aircraft carriers *Franklin, Enterprise, Intrepid, Yorktown* and *Wasp*. Of these, the *Franklin* suffered most, with 1,000 casualties amongst her ship's company after just two 550-lb bombs had penetrated her flight deck, smashing their way into the hangar and exploding amongst armed and fully fuelled Avengers, Helldivers, Hellcats and Corsairs waiting to be taken up to the flight deck for a further strike. The carrier was put completely out of action by the chain of explosions and the holocaust that followed, and was the only Essex-class carrier to come near to being lost. Nevertheless, in an outstanding feat of damage control, the ship was saved and was taken to Pearl Harbor for major repairs. The fact that she never returned to service and after rebuilding and recommissioning was eventually scrapped was largely due to the normal peacetime reduction in post-war naval strength.

The Battle of Okinawa

At the end of March 1945, the US 77th Infantry Division was landed on the Kerama Islands, finding them lightly defended, and a forward naval base was quickly built ready to support the forces that would be tackling the toughest objective encountered so far, Okinawa. Battling through heavy seas and high winds on their way to the beachheads, US forces landed on Okinawa on 1 April 1945 to find Lieutenant General Ushijima and almost 80,000 troops, as well as a further 10,000 naval personnel based on the island who were also pressed into service. The defenders had well-prepared positions, especially on the south of the island. The landings were once again covered by the US Fifth Fleet under Admiral Spruance, and within this force was both Mitscher's TF58 with its ten large and six light carriers, and TF57, the British Pacific Fleet under Vice Admiral Sir Henry Rawlings, with its force of 220 aircraft aboard four carriers under Rear Admiral Sir Philip Vian. The British also had the battleships *King George V* and *Howe*, five cruisers and escorting destroyers. While TF58 was to suppress Japanese air power on Okinawa, TF57, as already mentioned, was to protect the left flank of the US Fifth Fleet and stop the Japanese moving aircraft across the islands of the Sakashima Gunto. There was also TF51 under Vice Admiral Turner with 430 transports and large landing ships, with close cover provided by the battleships *New Mexico*, *Maryland*, *New York*, *Arkansas*, *Colorado*, *Tennessee*, *Nevada*, *Idaho*, *West Virginia* and *Texas*, eighteen escort carriers with 540 aircraft, and thirteen cruisers. These ships were only the spearhead of the assault, as the Fifth Fleet also included tankers, aircraft transports (escort carriers with replacement aircraft), vessels that were floating workshops and ocean-going tugs.

The initial landings were by the US Tenth Army, under Lieutenant General Buckner, on the west coast of the island, and resistance was very light. In fact, yet again the Japanese response seems to have been slow in coming, and it was not until 6 April that a battle group consisting of the giant battleship *Yamato*, sister of the ill-fated *Musashi*, put to sea heading for Okinawa escorted by a cruiser and eight destroyers while, at the same time, a fresh Kamikaze offensive began. The following day, Mitscher sent 280 United States Navy aircraft to find and attack *Yamato*, sinking the battleship and the cruiser as well as four of the destroyers, leaving just four to escape. Nevertheless, the Kamikaze attacks proved to be the most concentrated of the war with 2,000 pilots sacrificed by the Japanese, with the campaign lasting for six weeks, and no less than twenty-six Allied ships were sunk, although none of them larger than a destroyer, while another 164 ships were damaged. Those ships damaged included the aircraft carriers *Intrepid, Enterprise, Franklin* and *Bunker Hill* as well as the British *Formidable, Indefatigable* and *Victorious*, and the battleships *Maryland, Tennessee* and *New Mexico. Enterprise* was hit by a suicide aircraft on 11 April, and was forced to suspend flying operations for forty-eight hours.

'When a Kamikaze hits a US carrier, it's six months repair at Pearl,' commented an American liaison officer surveying the after effects of a Kamikaze attack aboard a British carrier. 'In a Limey carrier, it's a case of "Sweepers, man your brooms!"'

This might have been an over-generous appraisal of the situation, but it was certainly true that the Royal Navy's six fast armoured carriers proved the value of their armoured flight decks and hangar sides and decks during the kamikaze campaign.

Command of the Japanese air counter-attack was in the hands of Admiral Soemi Toyoda, and his air offensive was timed to coincide with the start of the sustained Kamikaze attacks on 6 April. Out of the 900 aircraft that attacked the US Fifth Fleet on that day, 355 were Kamikaze. TF58 claimed to have shot down 249 aircraft and of the 182 estimated to have struggled through the fighter cordon, 108 were shot down. The terms 'claimed' and 'estimated' have to be used since sometimes more than one fighter pilot or AA gunner would claim to have shot down an aircraft, and despite rigorous checking by intelligence officers afterwards, completely accurate figures can be difficult to find. It is conceivable, for example, that a fighter pilot having seen an aircraft heading downwards in flames, would claim it as one of his score, while if the aircraft continued towards a ship and was then caught in its AA fire, that would also claim it as part of its score.

This was by now a war of attrition. Between 6 April and 29 May, 1,465 aircraft from one of the Japanese home islands, Kyushu, were used in ten massed Kamikaze attacks. Of these aircraft, 860 came from the Japanese Navy Air Force's Fifth Air Fleet and the remainder were from the Japanese Army Air Force's Sixth Air Army. Another 250 aircraft appeared from Formosa, now Taiwan, with around eighty per cent of these being from the Japanese Navy Air Force. In addition, they mounted a further

3,700 conventional sorties and the Japanese Army Air Force another 1,100.

The operations of the Fifth Fleet demonstrated considerable flexibility. On 9 April, with the need for additional sorties over Okinawa, TF57 was called upon to attack airfields in the north of the island, while its role of keeping the airfields on the Sakashima Gunto under constant attack was taken over by the escort carriers of TF51. The Admiralty Naval Staff History of the campaign referred to TF51 as having to do all of the odd jobs, describing as: '. . . the backbone of the attacks against the defence installations, and provided the close support for the assault of the western islands . . . It was apparent that this force realised what was required of it far better than did the fast carrier force, and its pilots were far more assiduous in engaging concealed defences.'

After Okinawa fell, the Allies were able to examine the Okha flying bombs for the first time, including the later versions, the Okha III, powered by three rockets and with a 4,500-lbs explosive charge which, had it hit a carrier, even an armoured British carrier, would have almost certainly inflicted fatal damage.

Aboard TF57

TF57 was back on duty off the Sakashima Gunto later in April, and after being rotated out of the battle area for replenishment, by 4 May was off Miyako, one of the islands in the group. The carriers were especially vulnerable on this day as the battleships, capable of mounting such an intense AA barrage around them, were away shelling coastal targets on Okinawa following a request from the forces ashore. It was not long before a Kamikaze attacked HMS *Formidable*. It was witnessed by Geoffrey Brooke, the ship's fire and crash officer.

> It was a grim sight. I thought at first that the Kamikaze had hit the island and those on the bridge must be killed. Fires were blazing around several piles of wreckage on deck and a lift aft of the island and clouds of dense black smoke billowed far above the ship. Much of the smoke came from fires on deck, but as much seemed to be issuing from the funnel, which gave the impression of damage deep below decks. (John Winton. *The Forgotten Fleet*, Coward McGann, London, 1970)

The carrier had been hit at 11.31 by a Kamikaze that managed to put a two foot dent in the flight deck, although without bursting through into the hangar. The flight deck had been crowded at the time, as aircraft were being ranged ready for launching, so eight men were killed and forty-seven wounded, many of them with severe burns. It could have been even worse. The ship's medical officer had decided to move the flight deck sick bay from the Air Intelligence Office at the base of the island where the Kamikaze had struck. As it was, two officers were killed in the AIO and the others with them all horribly burned.

Five later, on 9 May, *Formidable* was hit yet again, and this time the Kamikaze hit the after end of the flight deck and ploughed into aircraft ranged there. This was made even worse than it might have been as a rivet was blown out of the deck and burning aviation fuel poured into the hangar, where the fire could only be extinguished by spraying, causing damage even to those aircraft not on fire. Seven aircraft were lost on deck, and another twelve in the hangar, leaving the ship with just four bombers and eleven fighters.

Worse was to come, with the nautical equivalent of an 'own goal' on 18 May. After having refuelled and taken on board replacement aircraft, in the hangar an armourer working on a Corsair failed to notice that the aircraft's guns were still armed. He accidentally fired the guns into a parked Avenger, which blew up and set off another fierce fire, this time destroying thirty aircraft. Yet, the ship was operational again by that evening.

American misgivings about the Royal Navy's state of preparedness for intensive operations in the Pacific have been mentioned earlier. The concerns were not without foundation.

Before leaving Sydney for Okinawa to replace *Illustrious*, many of *Formidable*'s ship's company had seen a film, *Fighting Lady*, about an American aircraft carrier in the Pacific.

'I came to the unpalatable conclusion that our fire-fighting equipment was totally inadequate and was shocked to discover that there was no more left in the dockyard store,' recalls Geoffrey Brooke.

In some trepidation I went and bearded Captain Rocke-Keene, who, hardly looking up from his papers, said 'Are you sure? Then buy some!' Knowing better than to ask how, I took myself off to the largest store in Sydney and asked for

195

the fire-fighting department. To my surprise there was an excellent one, full of the latest American gear, I ordered a variety on approval, and had a field day testing them on the flight deck and invited the skipper to a demonstration of the choicest items. On completion, he said, 'Come ashore with me in half-an-hour,' and I found myself the rather embarrassed third party to a verbal meal, with much table thumping, of the Captain of the Dockyard. By the end of it he was only too glad to get rid of us by underwriting the expenditure of many thousands of pounds.

This was not the only example of the problems faced. The concept of extended operations some distance from a convenient shore base was new to a service that had enjoyed the frequent refuelling and replenishment afforded by a vast empire. A large chunk of this empire was now in Japanese hands. At the outset, there were just three tankers for fleet replenishment, although this later rose to five. While the Americans used the now widely accepted method of replenishing with the ships abeam, the British used the much slower method of refuelling astern, which also affected station keeping and only allowed one ship to be refuelled at a time.

'I had just come from the USS *Lexington*, the second *Lexington*,' reported David Devine, who was a war correspondent for Kemsley Newspapers and transferred to a British ship.

I'd been living in her for a long time. *Lexington* would fuel willingly in a wind of Force 6 provided the sea wasn't up to the wind yet. The American tankers could take a ship on either side in that kind of weather. They would have every-thing aboard, three lines pumping, in twenty minutes . . . *KGV* (the battleship *King George V*) went up astern of one rusty old tanker, which appeared to be run by two Geordie mates and twenty consumptive Chinamen and it took us, I think, an hour and a half to pick up a single buoyed pipeline, fiddling around under our bows.

The pressures of the Pacific War did have a beneficial impact on operations. At one stage HMS *Implacable* was able to land aircraft on with an average interval between aircraft of 31.8 seconds, which required great confidence in the deck landing officer, the 'batsman', excellent airmanship, and well-trained and energetic deck parties, including someone who was a dab hand at raising and lowering the barrier so that aircraft that had hooked on could taxi forward to the deck park and leave the after end of the flight deck free for the next aircraft.

At the end of the Okinawa campaign, Operation Iceberg, the British Pacific Fleet, aka TF57, had been at sea for sixty-two days apart from an eight-day replenishment at Leyte. Strikes had been flown from the carriers on twenty-three days, giving a total of 4,691 sorties, dropping 927 tons of bombs and firing 950 rocket projectiles. The number of Japanese aircraft destroyed has been estimated at between 75 and 100, while airfields and shore installations also received attention. While twenty-six aircraft had been shot down by the enemy, another seventy-two were lost in accidents, including no less than sixty-one while landing on. Another thirty-two aircraft had been accounted for during the Kamikaze attacks, as well as the thirty lost in the wholly unnecessary fire.

Over the Sakishima Gunto

The wartime Royal Navy had an especially heavy New Zealand presence in its Fleet Air Arm, due entirely to the fact that the Royal Navy had a recruitment office in New Zealand, while the Royal Air Force did not. Any Kiwi wishing to fly, therefore, had the choice of signing on for the Fleet Air Arm, or of making his way to the UK to join the RAF, which was not an easy task in wartime. The Royal New Zealand Air Force was relatively slow at building up its strength at first, due largely to the country's very small population and also the lack of an aircraft industry, which meant that new equipment for expansion had to come a long way. One of these New Zealand fliers was Lieutenant Donald Cameron, who joined as a volunteer reservist although later switching to become a regular officer in the post-war Royal Navy. Cameron was serving in HMS *Victorious* during the attacks on the Sakashima Gunto, and he was involved in one especially unlucky operation.

During the afternoon of 9 May 1945, Cameron was due to lead a flight of four Corsairs to escort a raid by a squadron of Avengers against airfields on the island of Miyako. If no enemy fighters were encountered, after the raid the Corsair pilots were encouraged to look for targets of opportunity.

The fighter flight was dogged by ill-luck from the start. When it took off at 15.30, it left behind one of the aircraft with engine trouble, and as they escorted the Avengers, another aircraft had to return to *Victorious* because of low oil pressure, leaving just Cameron and his wingman. No fighters were encountered and the Avengers carried out their raid successfully and started to return to the carrier. The airfield at Ishigaki appeared busy, and Cameron and his wingman, who had a 500-lb bomb under each wing, decided to attack. Cameron suggested that his wingman, No.4, choose a target and let him know when he was prepared to dive so that he could accompany him and force the airfield's AA fire to be divided between the two aircraft.

'"Going in now, 501," my No.4 called, and we both winged over together,' recalled Cameron. 'At about 2,000-ft I pulled up to port in a skidding climbing turn and see-sawed my way back to 15,000-ft. No sign of No.4. I called again, but no reply. Slowly circling I saw a large fire burning amongst the hangars of the airfield. That had to be No.4 . . .'

He looked around the airfield, still hoping to see No.4 flying around below. He saw what appeared to be a large aircraft at the corner of two hangars. Cameron dived down once again, at more than 400 mph and reached the airfield at about 45 degrees to the main east-west runway, and at low altitude raced across the airfield as the hangars rushed towards him. He had a fleeting glimpse of men running and jumping down from an aircraft outside a hangar, before he was climbing again and over the sea. He decided to repeat the exercise, despite the fact that this was definitely not recommended as not only were AA defences alerted by the first pass, but the gunners would also have adjusted to the high speed low level run across the airfield.

I streaked up the runway at nought feet and as I passed the hangars at the far end there was a terrible bang and the aircraft seemed to jump sideways. Bits of cowling shot over the hood and the cockpit filled with smoke.

Keeping low I shot the hood back with my left hand and the airflow enabled me to see ahead. I was by this time out to sea . . . the aircraft still handled normally apart from the burning smell . . . no oil pressure at all . . . cylinder head temperature was off the clock.

I eased the throttle back, eased the nose up a little and tried to get what height I could. At about 2,500 feet I called 'Mayday, Mayday, 501 ditching 20 miles west of Ishigaki.'

He repeated the call, held the hood back and prepared to ditch, with the aircraft splashing down tail first into the sea.

Off harness, out on wing, reach in and tear dinghy off bottom of parachute, turn on a small CO2 bottle, the dinghy inflates, and I jump into the sea with it.

Now comes the hard part, trying to get in the small dinghy. I had to let the air out of my Mae West and after repeatedly tipping the dinghy over onto myself managed to hold one end under water while I got the top of my body on top by kicking my legs, raising my behind, and pulling towards my knees with both hands, I finally flopped into the bottom of the dinghy . . .

Cameron was unlucky, as the Japanese found him before his own ships could, and he spent the rest of the war in a POW camp, suffering barbaric treatment from his captors. In some ways, he could count himself lucky as he did survive, while many Allied airmen were shot on discovery by the Japanese.

After Okinawa

It took until June before Okinawa could be regarded as occupied after much bloody fighting, and at a cost of 48,000 US servicemen dead and wounded. There were few major objectives left ahead of the US Fifth Fleet, apart from Japan itself. Meanwhile, some of the tidying-up and infilling saw Amphibious Group 8 landing the 24th and 31st Infantry Divisions on the west coast of Mindanao on 17 April.

Further west, the British Eastern Fleet had sent the battleships *Queen Elizabeth* and *Richelieu*, the latter a Free French ship, to bombard Sabang once again, with just two escort carriers, two cruisers and five destroyers, as the main force had moved further east in the creation of the British Pacific Fleet. On the night of 15–16 May, British destroyers torpedoed the Japanese heavy cruiser *Haguro* as she steamed through the Malacca Straits.

On 27 May, Halsey took over the Fifth Fleet from Spruance and the designation changed back to Third Fleet once more, with the same adjustment to the numbers of the task forces. Command of the American carriers also changed, with Vice Admiral McCain taking over from Mitscher as commander of what now became TF38.

With Okinawa secured, between 14 and 18 July, the Third Fleet returned to heavy aerial attacks on the Japanese home islands. While the airmen attacked airfields and harbours, and coastal shipping, the battleships were sent to bombard industrial targets along the coast for the first time. After refuelling and replenishment, Halsey took the Third Fleet back to Japan to resume its attacks between 24 and 30 July, this time giving priority to bases on the Inland Sea. The new aircraft carrier *Amagi* was sunk, along with three battleships, *Ise*, *Hyuga* and *Haruna*. The dropping of the atomic bombs on Hiroshima on 6 August and on Nagasaki on 9 August did not produce an immediate Japanese surrender, so again the Third Fleet returned to the attack between 8 and 14 August. During these attacks, the British Pacific Fleet also operated against targets in Japan. On 9 August, Lieutenant Robert Hampton Gray, a Royal Canadian Navy Volunteer Reservist, was leading a strike of Corsairs of 1841 and 1842 Naval Air Squadrons from HMS *Formidable*, when he came under heavy AA fire from five warships as he attacked a destroyer in the Onagawa Wan. He pressed home his attack despite his aircraft being badly damaged, and succeeded in sinking the destroyer before his aircraft crashed into the harbour. He was awarded a posthumous Victoria Cross, the VC, Britain's highest decoration.

Although hostilities ceased on 15 August, it was not until 2 September that the war with Japan was formally over.

XVI

THE AXIS CARRIERS

Two of the Axis powers had gone through the war years without aircraft carriers, although both had ships on the slipways and never completed. With the benefit of hindsight, this seems to have been a strange omission. At the time, however, both Germany and Italy suffered even more than the Allies from inter-service infighting. Germany's naval leaders may well have given an aircraft carrier a lower priority than the ship deserved pre-war as many of them believed that war with the United Kingdom would not come before 1945, by which time a very large balanced fleet was envisaged.

Even before Hitler assumed absolute power in 1933, it was recognized that the future *Kriegsmarine*, should have some form of air power other than the inclusion of reconnaissance aircraft aboard its battleships and cruisers. The problems faced by the German Navy were in fact immense, lacking any experience of carrier design or operations, and without any airmen who had flown off, or even more difficult, onto a ship. Even at this early stage, the Germans were unable to take advantage of British and American experience, and had not established strong links with the Japanese, while French experience had little to offer. The best that they could do was look at the British Courageous-class, then the latest European design, and attempt to copy it, although this involved making a number of assumptions. As the Anglo-German Naval Treaty of 1935 allowed Germany a theoretical total aircraft carrier tonnage of 42,750 tons, it was decided to build two carriers, and since the actual tonnage was slightly less since the agreement was based not on the Washington figures but instead thirty-five per cent of the actual carrier tonnage of the Royal Navy, these were intended to be of 19,250 tons apiece.

Laid down at the end of 1936, the first ship, the *Graf Zeppelin* (not as strange as it sounds, since Zeppelin, famous for his airships, also designed heavier-than-air aircraft), was launched on 8 December 1938. The design was modified several times even before she was laid down, with the result that her displacement increased from 19,250 tons to 28,090 tons. Like the *Courageous* and *Glorious*, the *Graf Zeppelin* was originally intended to have a lower flying-off deck and she was completed with two hangar decks, but as she neared completion, increased emphasis was placed on defensive armament, not only a heavy AA armament for use against attack by land-based aircraft, but also a strong battery of sixteen 5.9-inch guns for defence against destroyer attack. Powerful machinery was fitted with the intention of being able to outrun any battleship or aircraft carrier she was likely to meet. There were three centre line hangar lifts and two catapults forward. The island was relatively low, and there was a single large funnel, later fitted with a raked cap that raised its height.

A unit with Junkers Ju87A Stuka dive-bombers and Messerschmitt Bf109B fighters was established for training and evaluation, and these were later succeeded by navalized versions of both aircraft with catapult points, arrester hooks and manual wing-folding; the Bf109T, based on the Bf109E, and Ju87C, based on the Ju87B.

In mid-1940, as completion drew close, work was suspended on both the *Graf Zeppelin* and her sister, *Peter Strasser*, still on the slipway, to concentrate resources on the U-boat programme, although planning continued, with the original idea of thirty fighters and twelve dive-bombers switched around, and work started on a torpedo-bomber variant of the Stuka. By the time that completion of an aircraft carrier re-emerged as a priority, shortages of materials affected further work. *Peter Strasser* was scrapped on the slipway, and although torpedo bulges were added to the leadship, she was never completely ready for service and was scuttled by the Germans shortly before the end of the war. She was refloated by the invading Soviet forces, loaded with looted materials and taken under tow to Leningrad in late summer 1947, but capsized, possibly due to overloading, and sank.

During the early years of the war, the Germans continued building major warships, including a Hipper-class heavy cruiser, the *Seyditz*, and in 1942, as work resumed on the *Graf Zeppelin*, this ship had her superstructure removed and work started on conversion to a flush-decked carrier, but the following year, work was abandoned and the ship, which had been launched in early

1939, was scuttled. The Germans also considered conversion of three liners to carriers.

Had the Germans been able to send one or more of these ships to sea, the outcome of the war, especially in the North Atlantic, would have been very much different. Whether or not they could have staved off final defeat, especially given the growing shortages of fuel and rubber, under the pressures of the Allied bombing campaign and the reverses suffered in the Soviet Union, is open to question. On the other hand, possession of such ships could have made the Battle of the Atlantic immeasurably more difficult for the Allies, while the Arctic convoys could have become impossible. Convoys to Gibraltar and the Cape would also have suffered. With air cover, *Tirpitz* could well have enjoyed an operational existence outside of her Norwegian fjords, while better use would have been made of *Scharnhorst* and *Gneisenau*, and *Bismarck's* fate might not have been sealed on her first operational mission.

At the same time, and there always seems to be a 'but' in such considerations, would the aircraft have measured up to the task? Would the naval commanders?

The Ju87 would probably have adapted very well to carrier life, being a robust design, but could the same have been said of the Bf109, renowned for its relatively weak tailplane? Would such an aircraft have adapted well to the rough house of carrier operations, or would it, like its opponent ashore, the Spitfire, have been too genteel just as the Seafire proved to be? The Focke Wulf Fw190 might have been a different question altogether, if the *Luftwaffe* had allowed this precious aircraft to be deployed away from defending German cities.

As for the naval commanders, with even less experience of naval airpower and its potential than their British counterparts, could they have made good use of a carrier? Would the importance of a carrier operating as part of a balanced fleet have been fully appreciated? After all, the British failed to protect *Courageous* or *Glorious* adequately, and tiny *Hermes* hardly at all. They also sent their capital ships into harm's way without air cover, as happened first with *Repulse* and *Prince of Wales*, and then with the heavy cruisers *Cornwall* and *Dorsetshire*. Would the Germans have done better, would they have ensured adequate refuelling facilities, would they have taken the extreme weather conditions of the North Atlantic into account, especially off Iceland and

Norway? After all, they sent their armies into the Russian winter insufficiently well equipped. The truth is, we shall never know.

What is certain is that the provision of good safe bases for the German carriers would have been difficult. Unlike the heavy surface units, these would have been vulnerable to heavy air attack once in port, and the French ports may well have been too vulnerable for them, as would the Norwegian fjords, while access to German ports would have been difficult. The British, after all, depended heavily on bases outside the reach of German bombers, or at extreme range.

Italy also planned to have aircraft carriers, but instead of building from the keel upwards, conversion of the liner *Roma*, launched in 1926, was decided upon. Initially the plans were for a basic conversion, so that she would have been almost a large escort carrier, although much faster, but as work progressed, a more thorough conversion was put in hand, with the hull lengthened and fitted with bulges to improve stability and protection for her machinery spaces. Two lifts and catapults were provided from Germany. The ship, renamed *Aquila*, would have been smaller than the German carriers, at 23,350 tons, and was planned to operate thirty-six aircraft which, with the single hangar, could have been a tight squeeze as the Reggiane Re2001 fighters planned for the ship were to have non-folding wings, although it was hoped that a version with folding wings would be developed. This single aircraft type was also to act as a light bomber and torpedo plane.

Conversion started in mid-1941 and was almost complete at the time of the Italian surrender in September 1943, when she was taken over by the Germans to prevent her being taken to an Allied port. Realizing the menace posed by the ship, the Allies targeted the ship, first in a raid by heavy bombers and then by using human torpedoes, possibly with Italian volunteers, which left her so badly damaged that she was scuttled. She was refloated postwar and taken for refitting, but was eventually scrapped in early 1952 before work started.

Another passenger liner, the *Augustus*, 30,418 tons, launched in 1927, was also seen as suitable for conversion to an aircraft carrier, and the original idea was that this should also be a limited conversion of the kind proposed for the *Aquila*. This would also have had a single hangar with two lifts, although a separate flying-off deck was also envisaged at one stage. Unlike the *Aquila*, there was to be no island superstructure, but instead the diesel engines had exhausts that protruded to port and starboard amidships. The ship was first renamed *Falco* and then *Sparviero*. Conversion was not started until September 1942 at Genoa, but the only part of the work completed at the time of the Armistice with Italy the following September was the removal of the liner superstructure, and the ship was almost immediately requisitioned as the Germans occupied northern Italy, and suffered the ignominy of being scuttled to block the entrance to Genoa harbour. While *Aquila* would have had a decent turn of speed, as much as 30 knots, *Sparviero* would have had a more pedestrian 18 knots which, with just one catapult, would have inhibited operations to some extent.

The role of the Italian carrier has to be questioned. The strategic position of Italy and the way in which the country almost cuts the Mediterranean Sea in two meant that the need for a carrier was far less than for the British. Clearly, the presence of a carrier with its own air group at the Battle of Matapan would have been beneficial, but like the British carriers in 1941, any Italian carrier would have found the Mediterranean uncongenial, with ships easily spotted and targeted by shore-based aircraft. While carrier-borne aircraft could have helped in the disastrous Italian attempts to invade Yugoslavia and then Greece, land bases were available in both cases. With bases ashore in both Sicily and North Africa, carrier-borne aircraft would not have been needed to protect the convoys carrying reinforcements and supplies between Italy and North Africa. Not the least of the Italian carriers' problems would have been that of suitable aircraft, although the *Regia Aeronautica* was supplied with a small number of Ju87 Stuka dive-bombers and these would have been far better suited to the strike role than the Re2000, yet another Second World War fighter that suffered from structural weaknesses. Indeed, it is hard to conceive of the Re2000 being an effective fighter-bomber let alone a torpedo-dropper!

Both the Italians' and the Germans' attempts at naval aviation would also have been inhibited by the retention of all aircraft and their personnel by the respective air forces, the *Regia Aeronautica* and the *Luftwaffe*. This would have inhibited tactical and strategic development of naval air power, not simply because of the 'air force' mentality of the aviators, but also because of the lack of any transfer of experience from the pilots' cockpits to the bridges of the carriers: with a few notable exceptions, the best carrier commanding officers were ex-naval aviators or people working closely with them, such as air direction officers. This may also have explained another weakness of the German and Italian carrier plans – the lack of any aircraft dedicated to anti-submarine patrols, always an important aspect of the Royal Navy's operations. A failure to provide anti-submarine and anti-shipping reconnaissance, backed up by an aircraft capable of loitering around the fleet or around a convoy *à la* Swordfish and an effective anti-submarine screen of destroyers, could have proved to be the Achilles' heel of these ships.

XVII

THE COMMANDERS

No consideration of the way in which the war progressed can be complete without an assessment of the Allied and Axis commanders, since inevitably these were in a position to influence events. The outcome of the war in the Mediterranean would undoubtedly have been different if Iachino had had the characteristics of Cunningham and Cunningham had those of his Italian opponent. The same can be said about the war in the Pacific if the natures of Nagumo and Nimitz had exchanged sides!

Not every naval commander in the Second World War had the opportunity to influence strategy. The Royal Navy's Rear Admiral Sir Philip Vian, for example, did an excellent job in commanding the British Pacific Fleet's squadron of aircraft carriers in the closing stages of the war against Japan, but he did not influence strategy, and his ships and their aircraft provided an important supporting role on the flanks of the US Third and Fifth Fleets – in reality one and the same fleet – as the war was taken ever closer to the Japanese home islands and it became imperative to stop Japanese reinforcements getting through. On the other hand, Pound as commander of the British Mediterranean Fleet, and his successor in both this post and then as First Sea Lord, Cunningham, had much to contribute. Cunningham's opposite number at the German *Kriegsmarine*, *Grossadmiral* Karl Dönitz, played no part at all in carrier strategy, having none to deploy, but instead seems to have managed to escape the notoriety for masterminding the German U-boat campaign, being highly regarded by many British naval officers, and if ostracized at all, it seems to be for having been Hitler's successor as Führer! He does not seem to have been blamed for the actions of the field police, who dealt brutally with deserters even when all was lost, as Germany crumbled with the Red Army in the suburbs of Berlin. In today's terms, despite spending time as a convicted Nazi war criminal in Spandau prison, Dönitz was 'Teflon man'.

The different atmosphere in which these senior officers lived and worked cannot be ignored. The Japanese lived in a country with a maritime tradition, as did the British, and despite being a continental power, much the same could be said of the United States. After all, the Americans had conducted a naval war with Britain in 1812, and then often forgotten, joined the British and Dutch in clearing the Mediterranean of Barbary pirates in 1816, the country's first overseas venture. Paradoxically, it was the United States that opened Japan up to the west. The first major naval battle of the twentieth century was between the Japanese and the Russians at Tsushima in 1905 – the Japanese won an overwhelming victory against Russian incompetence. It took the First World War for the United States to finally appreciate beyond all doubt the importance of being a major naval power, and at the resulting Washington Naval Conference, the United States Navy was given parity with the Royal Navy, and during the Second World War became and remained the world's greatest naval power.

Italy's Missed Opportunities

Despite the history of exploration and the importance of Genoa and Venice in pre-unification Italy, Italy was not a true maritime power. It didn't need to be, with few colonial possessions and those relatively close at hand. In Italy as well as in Germany, the air force was the favoured service. The Italian Navy, or *Regia Navale*, was not consulted over Italy's entry into the Second World War, despite the Chief of the Italian Naval Staff, Admiral Domenico Cavagnari, also holding the political post of Under Secretary of State for the Navy, which meant that he should have had great influence. Cavagnari wrote to Mussolini, highlighting the folly of entering a war belatedly, when all chance of surprise was lost. The admiral felt that Italy was in a weak position, as the United Kingdom and France could block the Mediterranean at both ends, cutting off the supplies of fuel and raw materials needed for Italy to continue to fight, while in any conflict, both sides could expect heavy losses.

His pessimism would have been justified had France not fallen, but with Britain and her empire fighting alone for a period of eighteen months, the threat to Italy was much diminished. True, supplies could not pass through the Straits of

Gibraltar or the Suez Canal, but at first Germany was able to ensure supplies of fuel and raw materials, and even went so far as to provide vital components for Italian industry. It was not until after the failure of Operation Barbarossa and the advance of the Red Army that supplies to Italy became a problem, as the Germans gave priority to their own forces. Had the Italians ensured better coordination between the *Regia Aeronautica*, or air force, and the navy, Cunningham would have had a much more difficult time in the Mediterranean. Nevertheless, the major problem was that the Italian Navy was ill-prepared for warfare, with Cunningham coming to the conclusion, following a pre-war courtesy visit by the Italians to the British Mediterranean Fleet in Malta, that his future foe was not very much further forward than the British had been during the First World War. Technically, the Italians were far behind, even lacking radar and giving the Royal Navy a massive advantage. Even when convoys had to be prepared to protect the movement of reinforcements and supplies to North Africa, the absence of preparation was obvious, with just one or two small warships to protect several merchantmen. Here again, air-naval coordination could have done much to reduce the losses suffered and which directly impinged on the campaign being fought by the Italians, and then the Italians and Germans together, in North Africa.

Again, better coordination could have made the Royal Navy's great success at Taranto much more difficult, even without Italian radar. Incredibly, the Italians had their air force flying with German units against the south of England on the night that the Fleet Air Arm struck, not meeting a single Italian fighter on their way to or from the target. Lacking radar that would have made night fighters a realistic possibility, one should not be too surprised at this, but there was no serious attempt to attack the Mediterranean Fleet as it withdrew to Alexandria. Of course, the operation against Taranto would not have been as successful as it was had the torpedo nets been put back after the morning exercise had been cancelled, and the training of the Italian anti-aircraft gunners also fell far short of what might have been achieved in, admittedly, difficult conditions.

This was just the final failure in a series of failures and missed opportunities. On Italy's entry into the Second World War, the Italians should have had their battleships and heavy cruisers bombarding either Malta or the south of France, where Italian troops were fighting French Alpine troops in an attempt to gain some French territory before an armistice. Once France had fallen, due entirely to German efforts, the battleships and cruisers should have been redirected to Malta if not already there, but at no time did Malta come under Italian naval shell fire, although there was an unsuccessful but brave, almost to the point of fool-hardiness, attack by light naval vessels filled with explosives and the inevitable air raids, although again, these were never pressed home with great determination and never mounted with substantial numbers of aircraft at any one time, until the *Luftwaffe* became involved in January 1941.

On a small island, with nowhere far from the sea, heavy naval bombardment could have made Malta impossible to defend within weeks of the fall of France, while the British convoys could have been stopped, but as it was, convoys continued to get through until 1941, and Malta remained a base for offensive operations for most of the time. The Royal Air Force and the British Army both believed that Malta could not be defended, Cavagnari could have proved them right.

The Italians had plans for aircraft carriers, but there was no real role for them. They could have been useful at Matapan, but radar would have been even better. They could have helped in the Balkans, but the Royal Navy and in particular British submarines would have been an ever-present hazard. A 'Taranto' style raid against the Royal Navy at Gibraltar, especially when Force H was present, perhaps with a convoy, would have been one possibility for a carrier, but this would have had to be almost a one-off operation before the carrier was hunted down. Important though it was, Gibraltar was not a base on a par with Taranto, while the Italians had no aircraft suitable for offensive strikes from a carrier and would have had to depend entirely on Germany providing dive-bombers. Given Italy's commanding geographical position in the Mediterranean, reinforced by bases in North Africa, a carrier was not a priority.

Far more important to the role of the aircraft carrier during the war were the British, United States and Japanese admirals.

The British

No one admiral takes the credit for the attack on Taranto. That the operation was conceived at all could even be regarded as a happy accident or a stroke of luck, since the loss of more than 55,000 naval aviators and their support teams into the Royal Air Force in 1918 deprived the Royal Navy of an entire generation of senior officers with first hand experience of naval aviation. By the time war broke out, these were holding senior positions in the Royal Air Force, and their number included Air Officer Commanding Middle East, Air Chief Marshal Sir Arthur Longmore, who had made the first drop of a torpedo from an aircraft as a young officer in the Royal Naval Air Service.

The history of the operation dates some years before the outbreak of the Second World War in Europe. In 1935, Italy invaded Abyssinia, and the then commander-in-chief of the Mediterranean Fleet, Admiral Sir William Wordsworth Fisher, expecting his country to declare war on Italy immediately, was prepared for any eventuality. Disappointed when told to apply peaceful sanctions, including checking Italian ships, this was made even worse by being forbidden to close the Suez Canal to Italian shipping, even though the ships were carrying troops and supplies to support the invasion of Abyssinia. Worse still were strict orders not to interrupt Italian oil supplies! Closing the Suez Canal to Italian supply ships immediately would have brought the invasion to a standstill and resolved the crisis.

In addition to barring the Suez Canal to Italian shipping, Fisher had tentative plans prepared for aircraft from the Mediterranean Fleet's carrier at the time, HMS *Glorious*, to attack the Italian fleet in its harbour at Taranto. Tension arose again just three years later, in March 1938, when Adolf Hitler annexed Austria. By this time, the Mediterranean Fleet was commanded by Admiral Sir Dudley Pound, although *Glorious* remained. Her commanding officer was Captain Lumley St George Lyster, not a naval aviator but still one of the few senior officers with a strong belief in the potential of aviation. As the threat of war with Germany and Italy loomed, Pound asked Lyster to consider a plan for the ship's aircraft to carry out an attack on the Italian fleet at Taranto: this was the first occasion when serious planning was put in hand. No mention of the plan was passed on to the Admiralty in London.

Pound realized that the balance of naval power was in Italy's favour, unless his fleet was substantially augmented by units from the Home Fleet and the Far East Fleet. As it turned out, he was to be proved correct in his belief that with Malta less than twenty minutes flying time for bombers based in Sicily, the

211

Mediterranean Fleet's aircraft carrier would not survive long, but at least she could have one strike at the enemy before either being sunk or, hopefully, withdrawn to safety.

He recognized that the lumbering aircraft of the time would be vulnerable in daylight and ensured that the squadrons aboard *Glorious* became highly proficient in night flying. Asked by the Admiralty which of his squadrons was the ship's night flying squadron, he responded proudly, 'All of them!'

Pound was called away at short notice to the Admiralty in London to become First Sea Lord, as his predecessor, Sir Roger Backhouse, was seriously ill. He too was to have a short tenure of office as his health also failed, whether under the relentless pressures of the job, or the strain of working alongside Britain's wartime Prime Minister, Winston Churchill, or both, has never been clear.

On a wider assessment, Pound's influence on naval aviation is less clear. He was seriously ill even by the time he took up his post as First Sea Lord. General Sir Alan Brooke, later Field Marshal Lord Alanbrooke, the Chief of the Imperial General Staff, records him frequently nodding off at meetings. Running any of the armed services, especially in wartime, requires high levels of stamina, which means good health. Pound certainly was unable to stand up to Churchill, a man of many ideas, but inevitably, not all of which were good. It is impossible to forget that it was during Pound's tenure of office that the costly and completely useless, strategically and tactically, raids on Petsamo and Kirkenes were mounted.

Pound's successor in the Mediterranean and afterwards also as First Sea Lord, was Admiral Sir Andrew Browne Cunningham. Cunningham's support for naval aviation has always been open to question. In command of the Mediterranean Fleet's cruisers during the late 1930s, he showed impatience with an officer wearing his pilot's 'wings' on his sleeve above the curl, despite this being the correct form. Most British naval aviators at the time were limited to flying reconnaissance aircraft off battleships and cruisers, although a few managed to find their way into carrier squadrons, whose aircraft were normally flown and maintained by members of the Royal Air Force. At this time, the cruiser squadron included the fleet's aircraft carrier.

This may have simply been Cunningham's strict and gruff approach to his subordinates. He certainly never wasted any sympathy on them. Even staff officers never came close to the man, with one recalling that the staff consisted of just eight officers who were driven very hard indeed.

'I've never heard of a staff officer dying of overwork,' Cunningham is supposed to have said on one occasion. 'And if he does I can easily get another one.' (*Daily Telegraph* 11 November 1999).

It is true that keeping a senior officer's staff small improves coordination, but this particular officer had to be returned home on sick leave because of the stress of working for Cunningham.

On the other hand, after HMS *Illustrious* entered the Mediterranean, Cunningham visited the ship and told the crews of her Fairey Fulmar fighters that 'they had changed the course of the war in the Mediterranean'. He also showed great concern over the need for better aerial reconnaissance. His failure to appreciate just what had been achieved at Taranto can be put down to his failure to appreciate just how successful the operation had been, something to which he only admitted in later years. Cunningham's relief when Lyster, formerly CO of *Glorious* and by this time a rear admiral, took over as Rear Admiral Carriers may simply have been due to the easing of his own workload rather than any desire to get rid of naval aviation. At one stage, Cunningham also had the foresight to propose to his opposite number in the RAF in Egypt, Air Chief Marshal Sir Arthur Longmore, that there should be joint RAF and Fleet Air Arm exercises, a request that Longmore had to decline because of his own shortage of squadrons. Certainly, when Lyster eventually did leave to go to the Admiralty, Cunningham, according to his biography, *A Sailor's Odyssey*, 'let him go with great regret'.

As First Sea Lord, Cunningham presided over the continued massive expansion of the Fleet Air Arm, with the carrier fleet boosted by the steady stream of escort carriers supplied from the United States. His initial reluctance to accept naval aviation may well have been due to his fondness for the 'big gun' navy, while he also firmly believed that officers who conducted themselves with heroism were simply doing their duty. Certainly, while with the Mediterranean Fleet, he expended much effort attempting to bring the Italian Fleet to a traditional naval engagement between capital ships. While his own flagship *Warspite*, a much modernized veteran of the First World War was certainly up to it, he could have had problems with the older British battleships in the Mediterranean, such as *Barham* and *Malaya*.

Admiral Lumley St George Lyster also deserves a mention, since he had left Cunningham to become Fifth Sea Lord on the Board of Admiralty. This post was one created for the senior officer with responsibility for naval aviation – actual command was left with the various fleet commanders. Perhaps Lyster's greatest achievement was in his work with the American Admiral Towers, which resulted in the 'Towers Scheme' under which British naval pilots and observers were trained by the United States Navy, ending the log jam that had arisen while training was still in the hands of the hard-pressed RAF, with its own training needs to consider. The Towers Scheme pre-dated America's entry into the Second World War.

The Americans

Like the Japanese, the Americans had a continuous history of naval aviation between the two world wars, with many of the young officers who had been in at the beginning and also conducted long distance flights after the end of the First World War, by this time holding senior rank. Having control of their aircraft as well as ships meant that the United States Navy was able to involve itself in the development of naval aviation. The best naval aircraft at the outbreak of the Second World War were those in the United States Navy. On the other hand, one can argue over the quality of the ships. The two Lexington-class ships offered unrivalled space, despite being battlecruiser conversions, and a good turn of speed. The Yorktown-class was undoubtedly the best pre-war aircraft carrier design, despite the wooden flight decks, since the thin metal decks of HMS *Ark Royal* hardly inspired confidence, but once the British Illustrious-class started to enter service, these were far superior with their high speed and extensive armour.

The credit for the way in which the United States Navy recovered from the body blow of the attack on Pearl Harbor and quickly went on to the attack was down to the drive of two men, Fleet Admiral Ernest King, the Commander-in-Chief of the United States Fleet, and Admiral Chester Nimitz, the Commander-in-Chief of the United States Pacific Fleet. King himself shows just how different not only the Royal and United States Navies were, but also the Japanese as well. A naval flier, King's inter-war posts included commanding the aircraft carrier *Lexington*, the largest in the world at the time, but he also headed the Bureau of Aeronautics and therefore had a strong influence on the evolution of strategy and the specification and selection of naval aircraft.

King has been criticized by many Britons for seeing the defeat of Japan as his overriding priority, but this is not entirely true. At no time did he fail to recognize the importance of finishing the war against Germany first so that full resources could be brought to bear in the war against Japan. His concerns with the war in the Pacific were borne out of geographical necessity, as were those of the British in the war with Germany. Early in the Pacific war, further attacks and an invasion of Hawaii were very real possibilities, and although the islands were not at the time states of the Union, they were home to many Americans. They were also a stepping stone towards the continental United States, in effect too close for comfort for the Americans to lose them. The next step would be either Alaska or the even then populous cities of the West Coast, stretching from Seattle in the north, home to the Boeing factories, to San Diego in the south, the home base for the Pacific Fleet.

It seems that King also enjoyed a good working relationship with the President of the United States, Franklin Roosevelt, although he failed to resist the presidential proposal to convert Cleveland-class light cruisers to Independence-class aircraft carriers. These ships were not the disaster that they might have been, with just one lost to enemy action, although another three were badly damaged in a severe storm, but it was a distraction from the main task, that of providing sufficient large carriers of the Essex-class. Their one advantage was their high speed. Intended to boost the size of the carrier fleet as the Essex-class numbers built up, no less than seven of the larger carriers were commissioned before the Independence-class was completed. Perhaps the Americans also underestimated their own industrial prowess.

King was a strong advocate of the use of the aircraft carrier and seems to have retained little sentimental attachment to the battleship as he was also an advocate of close cooperation with land-based aircraft. While he didn't exactly sideline General Douglas MacArthur, King always ensured that his plans for a step-by-step advance across the Pacific went ahead and managed to squash or delay some of MacArthur's more ambitious plans, helped by the fact that King had control of the essential transports and landing craft. Described as being both gruff and outspoken, King did not hesitate to argue, and the British found him difficult on a number of occasions, especially at the Casablanca Conference in January 1943, as did the President. He has been criticized for not wanting the British to return to the East, but this was not the case as he wanted a more active role for the British Eastern Fleet. His conditions, as British forces returned to the East, that they should be self-sufficient and not depend on US facilities was simply a recognition of the problems that lay ahead. King had dealt with unprecedented logistics and supply problems himself and devised the 'fleet train' supply system which enabled carriers to remain at sea on operations for extended periods, with ships being rotated out of the front line in groups to replenish and refuel. He knew how stretched his own resources were, and felt that any extra strain would endanger the system.

Recognized as the architect of victory in the Pacific, King became a full Fleet Admiral (United States Navy equivalent to Admiral of the Fleet) in 1944, the year that he reached the then retirement age of sixty-four years, and continued in office as the President, on being advised by King of his birthday, replied: 'So what old Top? I might even buy you a present.'

King's achievements also owed much to the work of Admiral Chester Nimitz, Commander-in-Chief of the US Pacific Fleet. No doubt Nimitz would have been replaced by King had he not matched his superior's standards, but Nimitz's own high qualities as a strategist and organizer deserve recognition. A former submariner, Nimitz was a great advocate of amphibious assault, and without his support and drive, neither the technology nor the tactics might have advanced so much so quickly, with benefits not just to the war against Japan, but that against Germany as well. It also seems likely that without his support, the American submarines would have been denied truly reliable and effective torpedoes for very much longer than was the case, after which they went on to mount one of the most successful submarine campaigns of all time. It was Nimitz's submarines that were most effective in cutting off Japan from its hastily-occupied Asian empire and from the oil and raw materials that the conqurered territory provided.

Nimitz gained an increasingly free hand as given the duty to protect Hawaii at all costs, he was responsible for the American carriers at the Battle of the Coral Sea and then for the great victory at Midway. Nimitz had command of the central Pacific, including Guadalcanal, while MacArthur was given the south-west Pacific. At one time, October 1942, left with just one fully operational carrier, Nimitz nevertheless continued to take the fight to the Japanese, developing tactics as the war progressed. He quickly realized that full frontal assaults were too costly, and instead developed a strategy of attacking less well defended islands to the rear of the main Japanese defences and cutting them off.

Unlike his Japanese opposite number, Yamamoto, Nimitz generally conducted his operations from ashore, almost certainly because communications were better and this made it easier for him to maintain an overall picture of events as they unfolded, rather than becoming involved in the detail of individual battles into which he would otherwise have been drawn. He had in any case two trusted subordinates in Halsey and Spruance able to act as battle commanders. Despite his support for amphibious assault, and the fact that at Guadalcanal a third of the ground attack aircraft had been flown by United States Marine Corps pilots, in 1943 Nimitz decided to omit carrier deck training from the syllabus for United States Marine Corps pilots, effectively sidelining them from the initial assault in many of the campaigns of late 1943 and early 1944. This decision can only have been justified by the need to obtain ever larger numbers of pilots, quantity rather than absolute quality, so that ground-based USMC pilots were available in sufficient numbers to support ground forces, but, as always, this depended on sufficient airfields being available close enough to wherever air support might be needed.

As the war ended, Nimitz had his staff working on plans for the invasion and conquest of Japan, so it must have been a relief when Japan eventually sued for surrender. The formal surrender was signed aboard the USS *Missouri*, his flagship, in Tokyo Bay on 2 September 1945.

Nimitz had two subordinates; Halsey with the Third Fleet and Spruance with the Fifth Fleet. As mentioned earlier, the fleet designations changed with the rotation of commander, so that while one was ashore planning the next campaign, the other was at sea conducting operations. Halsey commanded the operations for the western Carolines and the Philippines, and the strikes against the Japanese home islands in July and August 1945. Spruance was responsible for the Gilbert, Marianas, Iwo Jima and Okinawa operations.

Halsey had replaced Vice Admiral Robert Ghormley in command of the South Pacific area, largely because of the mistakes made by Ghormley in the first assault on Guadalcanal. To be fair to Ghormley, who had been head of the War Plans Division during 1938–39, this was the first major assault made by the Allies in the Pacific War, and while he has been criticized for rushing the operation, lessons had to be learned and intelligence was faulty; perhaps this too was inevitable in the circumstances. King himself had made it clear to Ghormley that his task would be difficult and that the necessary resources were not all available. As it was, after the initial assault, the Japanese were able to reinforce the island.

Nicknamed 'Bull' because of his frequent outbursts of temper, Halsey had commanded the two carrier group that had launched the Doolittle raid against Japanese cities and would also have been in command of the operation at Midway had he not been in hospital. Halsey sorted out the mess that had been left at Guadalcanal, and while he was outmanoeuvred by the Japanese at Santa Cruz, he did stop the Japanese Admiral Abe's plans to bombard Henderson Field. In late November 1942, Halsey was promoted to Admiral.

Further successes followed, and Halsey followed Nimitz's preferred approach by taking Kolombangara before attacking the heavily defended island of Bourgainville, on which he mounted a diversionary invasion before launching the main attack.

Halsey, nevertheless, failed to obey his orders as the Battle of Leyte Gulf developed. Instead of guarding the San Bernardino Strait, and the invasion force, when his aircraft sighted Admiral Ozawa's decoy force he steamed off with his sixty-four ships to tackle an enemy force of just seventeen, allowing Kurita to take his task force through the Strait. Worse still, Halsey failed to let his superiors know what he was doing, so that Kurita's arrival came as a nasty surprise, and no doubt this lack of communication was deliberate realizing that he would be ordered back into position. Many argue that this mistake should not be allowed to detract from Halsey's reputation as a brilliant exponent of naval air power, but had Kurita kept his nerve and had his forces been stronger, the retaking of the Philippines could have been even more costly and the advance across the Pacific could have been stalled, at least temporarily. As it was, of the six US ships lost at Leyte, five were due to Kurita's attack. It was only the fact that Kinkaid's Seventh Fleet had also failed to mount effective reconnaissance that saved Halsey from severe censure, but of such mistakes does defeat come. As it is, there is the feeling that Halsey, who eventually became Fleet Admiral, has been treated more kindly than he deserved by both history and the United States Navy.

Nimitz's other commander was Raymond Spruance. Present in command of Task Force 16 at the Battle of Midway, he took command when Fletcher's flagship in Task Force 17, the USS *Yorktown* was disabled and continued to see all four of the enemy carriers destroyed inside a single day, three of them during the morning. After this, Spruance became Chief-of-Staff to Nimitz and was responsible for much of the planning and organization that went into the Pacific campaigns. Spruance took command of the US Fifth Fleet and was responsible for much of the action in the Gilbert Islands and for the successful campaign to seize Kwajalein Atoll in the Marshall Islands. The direct responsibility for development of the fleet train that enabled the United States Navy to get the best use out of its carriers was that of Spruance. Under his command, Mitscher attacked in the Marshall Islands. Nevertheless, as evidence that no one gets everything right every time, after the Battle of the Philippine Sea, Spruance was criticized for not following up the aerial attack to destroy Ozawa's carriers. The criticism was not entirely fair, since although Mitscher wanted to pursue the Japanese, many of the American strike aircraft had been lost as they ran out of fuel on the return to their carriers after the first strike, and Spruance refused Mitscher's request to continue the operation. Later, Spruance was responsible for the assault on Iwo Jima and for attacks on the Japanese islands, but the fact that he never progressed beyond the rank of vice admiral suggests that the criticism over the Philippine Sea affair stuck, unfair in the light of Halsey's actions and subsequent elevation.

The Japanese

Nothing demonstrated more just how Japanese fortunes were deteriorating than the fact that the Americans were able to ambush an aircraft carrying Admiral Isoroku Yamamato, who had been Minister of the Navy and was at the time Commander-in-Chief of the First and Second Fleets, or Combined Fleet. This gave the Japanese the unwanted distraction of having more than one commander for the Imperial Japanese Navy during the war years while the US Navy effectively had just one.

Japanese society differed greatly from those in the west. Orders were expected to be obeyed without question and individual initiative was stifled, and even contributions from experienced officers such as Fuchida and his friend Genda were discouraged or ignored. There was also a preoccupation with the safety of the emperor.

Although not an aviator, unlike his American opposite number, Yamamato was a brilliant strategist and the brains behind the raid on Pearl Harbor. He was also a realist, and there can be little doubt that had not the pro-war, basically Imperial Japanese Army, faction pushed Japan into conflict with the United States, he would have counselled a different approach. From the outset, Yamamato realized that Japan could not win against the vastly superior resources of the United States. The most that could be achieved would be to win a great victory in the first year of war, and possibly fight to a stalemate as the war progressed. Nevertheless, if the war continued, Japan would be bound to lose.

Pearl Harbor was the one chance that Japan had of crippling the United States for the first year of war. A brilliant strategist and a firm believer in using combined air and seapower, Yamamato realized that success would lie in advancing across the Pacific to cut the lines of communication between the United States and Australia, and ultimately also taking Hawaii. Pearl Harbor was the first step in this strategy, a major sea battle between the two navies was seen as the second step.

The attack on Pearl Harbor was a year in the planning, and at the outset Yamamato had expected the attackers to have to fight their way to the target. While surprised at how low Japanese losses were in the raid, once he learned that Nagumo had failed to order attacks by third and fourth waves of aircraft, Yamamato realized that the war had been lost and that Pearl Harbor would remain operational. While his plans for battle with the US Pacific Fleet centred on an assault on the island of Midway, they were also a reflection of a defensive strategy adopted following the Doolittle raid.

The Americans had broken the Japanese codes before the Battle of Midway, and were prepared for the attack. Partly because of this and poor reconnaissance, as well as poor tactical leadership by Nagumo, the result was a major defeat for the Japanese and, most important of all, Japanese ambitions. Even so, the greater experience and, at this stage of the war, better organization of Japanese forces took their toll on US forces in the battle for Guadalcanal.

A coded message giving details of Yamamato's planned tour of the Solomons in April 1943 was intercepted by the Americans, and fighters from Henderson Field on Guadalcanal were able to intercept and shoot down his plane.

For all his brilliance, Yamamato allowed the Japanese carrier fleet to be sent to and fro during the vital first few months of war, supporting operations as far apart as the raids on Ceylon, the diversionary attack on the Aleutians, and to Darwin in Australia's Northern Territory, none of which were of any strategic value. Meanwhile, the losses of aircraft and, even more important experienced aircrew mounted, while the ships suffered battle damage and the strain of continued use. None of this contributed towards the decisive battle that was sought.

Yamamato's successor, Admiral Mineichi Koga, was also attracted by the concept of the all-out naval engagement, known as Operation Z, and after he died when his aircraft disappeared in a tropical storm on 31 March 1944, his Chief of Staff, Admiral Shigura Fukudome attempted to follow carrying a copy of Operation Z, but he was captured by guerrilla forces in the Philippines and the plans fell into Allied hands.

The man who could have influenced the outcome of the war for Japan for the better was Vice Admiral Chuichi Nagumo, commanding the carrier force *Kido Butai*, involved in the raid on Pearl Harbor. Despite expecting heavy losses in ships and aircraft, especially with the latter as they flew to the target, Nagumo did not simply fail to order a third and fourth wave, even though his men were expecting it and were ready, but explicitly ordered that even a third wave should not be sent. The excuse given was that the objectives had been achieved, but it was made clear in debriefing that this could not be guaranteed. Apologists have explained since that Nagumo was concerned since he did not know the position of the American carriers and feared that they might attack his ships, but this does not match his own expectation of losses. In any case, if this was his real explanation for not seeking further action, rather than just an excuse, he should have ordered aerial reconnaissance.

Again, the failure to take advice and the poor organization of reconnaissance before the Battle of Midway contributed to the Japanese defeat, with these early failings compounded by indecision that left aircraft armed and disarmed in something of a panic, and despite having four carriers available, none was in a position to dispatch additional fighters as the American attack developed. At Midway, he was persuaded not to go down with his flagship, and survived to fight again, but repeated failures continued until Saipan, at which, during the last moments, he finally committed suicide while ashore.

XVIII

THE FLEET AT PEACE

The end of the Second World War came in the Pacific just as massive plans were being made for the invasion of Japan and a substantial Allied fleet prepared for this. In many ways, the end of the war with Japanese surrender was something of an anti-climax, but the carriers still had work to do, taking the surrender of the many occupied territories and helping with the repatriation of the many prisoners of war captured by the Japanese. They then had the task of taking captured Japanese home to Japan.

In fact, for the invasion of Japan, the British Pacific Fleet would have had fourteen aircraft carriers and eighteen escort carriers with a total of 600 aircraft. The United States Navy planned to use twenty-six aircraft carriers and light carriers, and no less than sixty-four escort carriers.

The British force would have used all six of their fast armoured carriers and eight of a new class of carrier, the Colossus-class. Desperate for more aircraft carriers, and yet with their naval yards working at full stretch on warship construction, the British had developed an 'Intermediate Aircraft Carrier' to bridge the gap between escort carriers and fleet carriers, later known as a light carrier, or in their terms, light fleet carrier design; this was the Colossus-class. This was meant to be something more powerful than an escort carrier and with a larger aircraft capacity, but the ships were built to merchant standards so that they could be constructed in yards unaccustomed to warships. The new ships were capable of being built in just two years, displaced 18,000 tons full load and could carry up to forty-eight aircraft, and there were ten of them, with another six built later as the Majestic-class, at 20,000 tons full load. These looked like aircraft carriers in the traditional British style, a scaled down *Illustrious* without armour, a lighter AA armament and just a single hangar deck. To provide the maximum space on both the flight and hangar decks, the superstructure and smokestack were 'sponsored' outwards from the hull. Their one big disadvantage was that the maximum speed was just 24 knots, something that was to prove difficult in later life as heavier jet aircraft came to be operated. Two of the ships, *Perseus* and *Pioneer*, were completed as maintenance ships and aircraft transports, unable to operate aircraft and instead of being flown on, aircraft were loaded by being hoisted aboard using sheerlegs.

These ships were intended for the concluding part of the battle for Japan. Nowhere can the sense of anti-climax have been more marked than with these ships, with the first, HMS *Colossus*, joining the British Pacific Fleet in mid-1945, too late to see action against Japan. HMS *Glory* also joined the British Pacific Fleet, but was at least able to take the surrender of Japanese forces in New Guinea in September 1945. In all, four of these ships, *Colossus*, *Glory*, *Vengeance* and *Venerable* were with the BPF's 11th Carrier Squadron and employed in 'mopping up' Japanese forces.

The end of the war found the Royal Navy with seven large, or fleet, aircraft carriers including the elderly HMS *Furious*, as well as the maintenance carrier *Unicorn*, the elderly *Argus*, five light fleet carriers with more under construction, and forty escort carriers. Half of its aircraft and more than three-quarters of its escort carriers had come from the United States. Still more impressive was the United States Navy, with twenty large aircraft carriers and five more under construction and an even larger class nearing completion, eight light carriers and sixty-nine escort carriers, with a total of 41,000 aircraft, including many that were shore-based for maritime-reconnaissance.

Although the veteran British carriers *Furious* and *Argus* had survived the war, while more up-to-date and better ships had been lost, the latter was reduced to a hulk and *Furious* was also in extremely poor condition. In the United States Navy, of the pre-war ships, both the *Enterprise* and *Ranger* had survived. As for the Imperial Japanese Navy, just one carrier, its first, the *Hosho* had survived the war having been used for training duties. The *Hosho* and two other Japanese carriers found damaged in home waters were made seaworthy to act as repatriation transports before finally going to the breakers.

Another wartime survivor was the sole French aircraft carrier, the *Bearn*, converted from an uncompleted Normandie-class battleship, which had started the war as an aircraft transport bringing much-needed American dive-bombers to France, but too little and too late. At the time of the fall of France, she was in the

Caribbean, at Martinique, where she was effectively interned under US orders for the next three years until the Free French could take control of the island. By this time, the ship's low speed and dated design meant that she was of limited use, and could only resume her duties as an aircraft transport, something that continued post-war as the French fought to retain their colonies in French Indo-China. In 1948, she was reduced to training duties and then, little more than a hulk, as a submarine depot ship.

Most of the escort carriers that survived the war were converted into cargo ships, although some of these were also in such poor condition that they were scrapped. Some, such as HMS *Nabob*, launched as the USS *Edisto* but having spent most of her short life as a British Ruler-class vessel, officially returned to the United States Navy although she was unable to leave British waters since she was stuck on a mud bank in the Firth of Forth. While the United States Navy itself saw most of its escort carriers converted into cargo ships, there was a reprieve for some, such as the USS *Suwannee*, *Chenango* and *Santee*, which all became CVHE, or helicopter escort carriers, and enjoyed a reprieve that lasted until the end of the 1960s. HMS *Nairana*, one of the few British-built escort carriers was not converted into a merchant vessel immediately, but served from 1946 until 1948 as the first Dutch aircraft carrier, renamed *Karel Doorman*, after the Dutch admiral lost in the Battle of the Java Sea leading a mixed force of Allied vessels without air cover, needless to say. The French *Marine Nationale*, also returned to carrier operations with a former escort carrier, in this case the former British HMS *Biter*, a US-built ship, which served as the *Dixmude*, but as other ships were acquired later, she was relegated to an aircraft transport and then suffered further demotion when she became an accommodation ship in 1960, not being returned to the United States Navy until 1966 when she was finally scrapped.

The reason for *Dixmude*'s demotion and *Karel Doorman*'s short stay with the Dutch was simply that both navies had acquired light carriers. The Royal Netherlands Navy bought the Colossus-class carrier HMS *Venerable* in 1948, and renamed her *Karel Doorman*. The French initially acquired two Independence-class carriers, with the USS *Langley* being renamed *Lafayette* when she joined the French Navy in 1951, while *Belleau Wood* became simply *Bois Belleau*, when she followed in 1953. French carrier procurement policy at this time seems to have been somewhat inconsistent, or perhaps they took whatever offered the best value, but the two American ships served at the same time as the former British *Colossus*, loaned to France in 1946 and purchased in 1951, renamed *Arromanches*. *Arromanches* served until 1974 having seen action off French Indo-China and at Suez, as indeed did *Lafayette*, with the latter returned to the US in 1960, being scrapped in 1962, while *Bois Belleau*, after a less exciting career, also returned to the US in 1960 to be scrapped in 1962.

The longest service of any Independence-class carrier was that of the USS *Cabot*, which remained with the United States Navy until a lengthy refit between 1965 and 1967 before being loaned to the Spanish Navy, where she became the *Dedalo*, and was operated until the early 1980s.

The British Colossus-class light fleet carriers saw service with a total of seven other navies; France, the Netherlands, Canada, Australia, India, the Argentine and Brazil, and of those that entered service before the end of the war, *Colossus* and *Venerable* have already been mentioned. *Vengeance* was loaned to the Royal Australian Navy for several years, after which she was sold to Brazil as the *Minas Gerais*, and only decommissioned in 2002. *Glory* never had the chance to live up to her name apart from operations during the Korean War, and she was scrapped in 1961. The only other ships commissioned before the formal Japanese surrender in September 1945 were *Pioneer*, which served as a maintenance ship before being scrapped in 1954, and *Ocean*, which had a distinguished career with a number of 'firsts'. HMS *Ocean* was used for the first carrier landing by a jet aircraft, a de Havilland Vampire, on 3 December 1945, and after operations during the Korean War, became one of the first two ships to operate as commando carriers for the Suez landings in 1956.

The British fast armoured carriers had relatively short post-war lives with the exception of the second ship, HMS *Victorious*. *Illustrious* herself spent some time alternating between reserve and acting both as a training carrier and a trials carrier, and in the latter role was the first carrier to operate swept-wing jet aircraft during trials of the ill-starred Supermarine Swift jet fighter. *Formidable* went into reserve post-war, and was eventually scrapped in 1956. *Indomitable* remained in service until 1953, but then she was scrapped. *Implacable* and *Indefatigable* were both used for training duties, with some spells in reserve, until the former was broken up in 1955 and the latter in 1956. The sole survivor was *Victorious*, which underwent a very extended major refit that lasted most of the 1950s. Many claim that the refit, with design changes to incorporate up-to-date ideas, was more costly than building a new carrier, partly due to the cost and difficulty of incorporating an angled flight deck on a deck that was part of the hull rather than the superstructure, but she returned to service in 1958 as one of the world's most advanced carriers, and received further refits in 1960 and 1967. During the second of these a fire broke out, and while the damage was slight, it was decided that she should be scrapped.

Although intended to be a maintenance carrier, HMS *Unicorn* saw operational service at Salerno, on Atlantic convoys and in the Pacific. After three years in reserve, she recommissioned in 1949, operating mainly as an aircraft transport but after the outbreak of the Korean War she moved to the Far East where she continued as a maid of all work, including an occasional troop ship, but did spend some time as a repair ship.

Of the twenty-four ships of the Essex-class, no less than eighteen were completed before the signing of the Japanese surrender, but the inevitable cuts to the fleet and the reduction in carrier construction meant that the last ship was not commissioned until 1950. One feature introduced during refitting, following 'Halsey's Typhoon' in December 1944, that saw two ships in the class suffer extensive damage to the forward ends of the flight decks, which buckled, and may well also have damaged the forward AA position, were so-called 'hurricane bows', with the plating extended up to flight deck level. In this respect at least, they now began to resemble British carriers.

The USS *Essex* herself went into reserve early in 1947, along with most of the early Essex-class carriers, but recommissioned in time for the Korean War, in which she saw action. Later, she was modified to become an anti-submarine carrier, or CVS, and remained in service until 1969, before being scrapped in 1973. The second ship of the class, *Yorktown*, also decommissioned in 1947, but in 1951 and 1952 she was rebuilt, redesignated CVA-10 (attack aircraft carrier), but arrived in Korea too late to see action. She also became an anti-submarine carrier in 1957, and saw service off Vietnam during the following decade. Decommissioned in 1970, she was taken in hand for preservation in 1975. After being decommissioned, *Intrepid* was later redesignated CVA and returned to service in 1956, later becoming an anti-submarine carrier. Following modernization, she saw action off Vietnam, and was decommissioned in 1974, later passing into preservation. *Hornet*, whose flight deck was badly damaged forward during a typhoon in December 1944, re-commissioned in 1953 after a refit, and joined her sisters as a CVS in 1958. She also saw service off Vietnam before de-commissioning in 1970. After having extensive battle damage repaired, *Franklin* was redesignated CVA in 1952 and CVS in 1953, before becoming an aircraft transport, but never saw service before being scrapped in 1966. *Ticonderoga*'s period in reserve was interrupted by a short commission before a major refit in 1952-54, recommissioning as a CVA and later saw action off Vietnam, her aircraft being involved in the *Maddox* incident. In 1970, she returned to service after a refit as a CVS, but decommissioned in 1973 and was scrapped in 1974. *Randolph* suffered Kamikaze damage which was quickly repaired, and post-war spent a short spell as a training carrier before going into reserve. After a refit, redesignated CVA she returned to service in 1956, later becoming CVS and decommissioned for the last time in 1969 before being sold for scrap in 1973. *Lexington* underwent a major refit before returning to service in 1955, redesignated CVA but this later changed to CVS in 1962, when she became a training carrier. She later became an aircraft transport. *Bunker Hill* was repaired after serious wartime damage, but too late for action, and was redesig-nated as an aircraft transport while in reserve. Removed from the Navy List in 1966, she was used for experimental work before being scrapped in 1973. After modernization, *Wasp* was re-designated CVS and took part in the 1962 blockade of Cuba, decommissioning in 1972 and broken up in 1973.

The first US carrier to be fitted with steam catapults, the USS *Hancock* returned to service in 1954, redesignated CVA, becoming CVS later and seeing service off Vietnam. She was de-commissioned in 1976. Another Essex-class to achieve a first was *Bennington*, with the first mirror deck landing on an American carrier in 1955; she had also suffered flight deck damage in the December 1944 typhoon. Like her sisters, she was redesignated twice, as CVA and then as CVS, before passing into reserve.

Bon Homme Richard saw action off Korea without first being refitted, and after a refit later saw action off Vietnam, before passing into reserve in 1971. *Shangri-La* arrived just in time for action against Japan, and later was involved in support for the atomic bomb tests at Bikini Atoll. She was also redesignated CVA and then CVS, and despite the latter designation saw action off Vietnam, before passing into reserve in 1971. *Antietam* and *Lake Champlain* were commissioned before the end of the war, but arrived too late to see action.

Apart from *Cabot*, *Belleau Wood* and *Lafayette*, which went to European navies, and *Princeton*, the only one of the class to be lost in action, the Independence-class light carriers had a less eventful post-war than the Essex-class ships. The carriers loaned to the French and Spanish navies were scrapped on returning home. This was because their small size, and narrow beam, made it difficult to upgrade them for heavier and faster aircraft. Indeed, even the Essex-class was gradually relegated to the less demanding role of ASW carriers, a role that became more important given the tremendous size of the Cold War Soviet submarine fleet.

Independence herself suffered the ignominy of being sunk as a target in 1951 after a spell as a weapons trials ship. *Cowpens* and *Monterey* were amongst the ships badly damaged in the December 1944 typhoon, and while the former was quickly repaired, she was never recommissioned despite being redesignated as an aircraft transport, and was scrapped in 1961. *Monterey* did in fact have a post-war career with the United States Navy, surviving as a training carrier until 1955, before going into reserve as an aircraft transport until being scrapped in 1970. Only one Independence-class carrier saw post-war combat, *Bataan*, which went into reserve in 1947, but recommissioned in mid-1950 for two operational tours off Korea before returning to reserve as an aircraft transport, and finally scrapped in 1960. By contrast, after going into reserve in 1947, despite being redesignated as an aircraft transport, *San Jacinto* never returned to service and was scrapped in 1970.

That so many Essex and Independence-class ships were kept in reserve for so long was a reflection of the trauma of the United States suddenly being pitched into a global war, and one in which the prevailing strategy depended on aircraft carriers and submarines, with everything else subordinated to their support. The Cold War Soviet Navy, at its peak, had ten times the number of submarines available to the German *Kriegsmarine* in 1939, and they were larger, faster and with longer ranges. The United States Navy was determined not to be put on the defensive ever again.

CHRONOLOGY

1939

3 September, the United Kingdom and France declare war on Germany after an ultimatum to withdraw German forces from Poland expires.

17 September, HMS *Courageous* torpedoed and sunk by *U-29*.

26 September, Blackburn Skua fighter/dive-bomber from HMS *Ark Royal* shot down a Dornier Do18 flying boat, the first German aircraft to be shot down by a British fighter in the Second World War.

1940

9 April, Germany invades Norway and Denmark.

10 April, land-based naval dive-bombers fly from the Royal Naval Air Station at Hatston in Orkney to sink the light cruiser *Koenigsberg* at Bergen, the first operational warship to be sunk by aircraft.

Mid-April, British and French troops land in Norway. HMS *Furious* covers the landings and afterwards acts as an aircraft transport; *Ark Royal* joins her. HMS *Glorious* recalled from Mediterranean.

8 June, HMS *Glorious* shelled and sunk by the German battle-cruisers *Scharnhorst* and *Gneisenau*, during the withdrawal from Norway.

13 June, fifteen aircraft from HMS *Ark Royal* attack *Scharnhorst* at Trondheim, but the only bomb to hit the ship fails to explode. Eight aircraft lost.

3 July, aircraft from *Ark Royal* attack French fleet at Mers El-Kebir (Oran).

5 July, Fairey Swordfish from *Eagle* sink an Italian destroyer and a freighter at Tobruk.

8 July, *Hermes* is part of a British task force attacking the Vichy French fleet at Dakar. The French battleship *Richelieu* is damaged.

9 July, Battle of Punto Stilo, *Eagle* sends her aircraft in an unsuccessful attempt to slow down the Italian fleet. Near misses from Italian bombers damage the carrier's fuel system.

20 July, *Eagle*'s Swordfish sink two Italian destroyers and a freighter at Tobruk.

16 September, Swordfish from *Illustrious* sink two Italian destroyers at Benghazi.

23–25 September, further action by the Royal Navy against Vichy French ships at Dakar includes *Ark Royal*.

11–12 November, twenty-one Swordfish from *Illustrious*, including some aircraft from the crippled *Eagle*, attack the Italian fleet at Taranto. For the loss of just two aircraft, three battleships are disabled, a number of minor warships damaged and a seaplane base and oil storage depot also damaged.

27 November, Battle of Cape Teulada, sees Force H escorting three fast freighters eastwards from Gibraltar, with *Ark Royal* sending her Swordfish against Italian battleships trying to intercept the convoy, and although no damage is caused, the Italians break off the action.

17 December, *Illustrious* sends her aircraft to attack airfields on Rhodes.

1941

10 January, Convoy Operation Excess sees *Illustrious* crippled by 500lb and 1,000lb bombs, forcing her to put into Malta for repairs.

16 January, *Illustrious* provokes an intensified blitz during her stay in Malta for emergency repairs, reaching a peak on this day.

9 February, Force H with *Ark Royal* attacks Genoa and Leghorn, with the carrier's aircraft bombing Leghorn and sowing mines off La Spezia.

28 March, Battle of Cape Matapan. Aircraft from *Formidable* and from Crete attack the Italian fleet at sea, hitting the battleship *Vittorio Veneto* and stopping her, and slowing down the cruiser *Pola*, later sunk by destroyers.

21 April, Mediterranean Fleet bombards Tripoli inflicting serious damage,with aircraft from *Formidable* making attack before bombardment.

20–31 May, German forces invade Crete and Mediterranean Fleet helps resistance and then handles evacuation, during which *Formidable* is seriously damaged.

24–25 May, Fairey Swordfish from *Victorious* attack the German battleship *Bismarck*.

26 May, Fairey Swordfish from *Ark Royal* mount a twilight attack on *Bismarck*, damaging her rudder and sending her out of control.

22 and 25 July, aircraft from *Victorious* attack Kirkenes while those from *Furious* attack Petsamo, losing fifteen aircraft for little benefit.

13 November, *U-81* torpedoes *Ark Royal*, which sinks off Gibraltar the following day.

7 December, Aircraft from the Japanese carriers *Akagi*, *Kaga*, *Shokaku*, *Zuikaku*, *Hiryu* and *Soryu* send 353 aircraft in two waves to attack the US Pacific Fleet in its forward base at Pearl Harbor in Hawaii, with five battleships sinking, capsizing or blowing up, as well as a number of smaller vessels.

14–23 December, running convoy battle off Portugal as U-boats attack HG76, but aircraft from the escort carrier *Audacity* help the escorts account for five U-boats before *Audacity* herself is sunk.

22 December, successful second attempt by Japanese forces to

land on Wake Island is covered by the carriers *Hiryu* and *Soryu*.

1942

23 January, Japanese forces land in the Bismarck Archipelago, covered by the aircraft carriers *Akagi, Kaga, Shokaku* and *Zuikaku*.

1 February, two US task forces centred on the aircraft carriers *Enterprise* and *Yorktown* attack Japanese bases in the Marshall Islands, although damage caused is slight.

13 February, Japanese landings on Sumatra are covered by the carrier *Ryujo*.

19 February, Japanese forces mount heavy air attack on Darwin, using aircraft from *Akagi, Kaga, Hiryu* and *Soryu*, sinking eleven freighters and a destroyer.

28 February, Japanese forces land in western Java covered by *Akagi, Shokaku, Zuikaku, Hiryu* and *Soryu*.

6 March, an attempt to attack convoy PQ12 by the battleship *Tirpitz* and her escorts fails in bad weather, but an attack on the German ships by aircraft from HMS *Victorious* is fended off by intense AA fire.

5–9 April, *Akagi, Shokaku, Zuikaku, Hiryu* and *Soryu* send aircraft against Ceylon, finding the carriers HMS *Indomitable* and *Formidable* are away, but on the last day manage to sink *Hermes*.

18 April, USS *Hornet*, escorted by *Enterprise*, sends sixteen USAAF North American B-25 Mitchell bombers to attack Japanese cities, including Tokyo.

3–5 May, Battle of the Coral Sea with the *Shokaku* and *Zuikaku* sending 125 aircraft against USS *Yorktown* and *Lexington*, with 141 aircraft, while the light carrier *Shoho* covers landings at Port Moresby. In the battle, *Lexington* is lost and *Yorktown* damaged, while *Shoho* is lost and *Shokaku* is badly damaged and out of action for some time. Nevertheless, the Americans stop the invasion of Port Moresby.

5–8 May, British forces land at Diego Suarez on Madagascar, covered by HMS *Illustrious* and *Indomitable*.

3–7 June, Battle of Midway occurs as Japanese attempt to seize the island with its airfield. Japanese ships are *Akai*, *Kaga*, *Hiryu* and *Soryu* with a total of 270 aircraft, while the USN has *Enterprise*, *Hornet* and *Yorktown*. Poor reconnaissance and decision making by the Japanese see all of their carriers sunk, while the Americans lose *Yorktown*.

7 August, *Saratoga*, *Enterprise* and *Wasp* cover initial US landings on Guadalcanal.

10–15 August, Convoy Operation Pedestal mounted in a desperate attempt to lift the siege of Malta, accompanied by aircraft carriers *Eagle*, *Furious*, *Indomitable* and *Victorious*, but *U-73* sinks *Eagle* while *Indomitable* and *Victorious* are badly damaged.

23–25 August, and *Ryujo* with 131 planes provide cover for Japanese transports heading for Guadalcanal, while the USN has 176 planes aboard *Enterprise* and *Saratoga*. *Ryujo* is sunk on 24th. Japanese lose many aircraft.

12–18 September, Convoy PQ18 is the first Arctic convoy to have an escort carrier, HMS *Avenger*, and her aircraft help in the sinking of three U-boats and in shooting down forty *Luftwaffe* aircraft.

15 September, USS *Wasp* torpedoed and sunk by Japanese submarine *I-19* off Guadalcanal.

26–27 October, Battle of the Santa Cruz Islands. Japanese believe that Henderson Field on Guadalcanal has been recaptured and send *Shokaku*, *Zuikaku*, *Zuiho* and *Junyo* with 212 aircraft against *Enterprise* and *Hornet* with 171 aircraft. Japanese suffer further heavy losses in aircraft with *Zuiho* and *Shokaku* badly damaged, but USN losses *Hornet*.

8 November, Operation Torch, the Allied landings in North Africa, are covered by the USS *Ranger*, HMS *Victorious*, *Formidable*, *Furious* and *Argus* and a British escort carrier.

15 November, aircraft from *Enterprise* sink cruiser *Kinugasa*.

1943

18 April, Admiral Yamamoto is shot down by US aircraft after his movements have been discovered.

9–13 May, the double convoy HX237/SC129 escorted by the CVE HMS *Biter* is attacked by a U-boat wolf pack, but only five merchantmen are lost for five U-boats.

10 July, Allied landings on Sicily, Operation Husky, covered by 580 warships, including *Indomitable* and *Formidable*.

9 September, Allied landings at Salerno, Operation Avalanche, covered by *Illustrious* and *Formidable*, and an American light carrier, with the maintenance carrier *Unicorn* operating in the combat role with air cover for ground forces provided by the escort carriers *Attacker*, *Battler*, *Hunter* and *Stalker*.

5 November, US carriers send ninety-seven aircraft to attack Rabaul from *Saratoga* and *Princeton*. Six Japanese cruisers badly damaged for the loss of ten US aircraft.

11 November, repeat raid on Rabaul with 185 aircraft from *Essex*, *Bunker Hill* and *Independence*, sinking a destroyer and damaging a cruiser, while a Japanese counter-attack is beaten off.

19 November, start of US air attacks preceding landings on the Gilbert Islands, covered by 700 aircraft from *Yorktown*, *Saratoga*, *Lexington*, *Enterprise*, *Bunker Hill*, *Princeton*, *Monterey*, *Independence*, *Cowpens* and *Belleau Wood*. *Independence* is damaged by a torpedo dropped by a Japanese bomber on 20th.

24 November, CVE *Liscombe Bay* is sunk by a torpedo from *I-175* in the Gilbert Islands.

4 December, aircraft from two out of the four US carrier groups attack Kwajalein Atoll, with the new *Lexington* damaged by an air-dropped torpedo.

1944

29 January – 6 February, US Task Force 58 mounts extensive attacks on the Marshall Islands, with 730 aircraft from *Yorktown, Saratoga, Intrepid, Essex, Enterprise, Bunker Hill, Princeton, Monterey, Langley, Cowpens, Cabot* and *Belleau Wood*.

17–18 February, assault on Truk begins, using the carriers *Yorktown, Intrepid, Essex, Enterprise, Bunker Hill, Monterey, Cowpens, Cabot* and *Belleau Wood*.

3 April, bombers from HMS *Victorious* and *Furious*, plus four escort carriers, attack *Tirpitz* in a Norwegian Fjord, and put her out of action for three months.

19 April, aircraft from HMS *Illustrious* and USS *Saratoga* attack Sabang on Sumatra.

22 April, US landings on Hollandia supported by eight escort carriers,while the main carrier force attacks bases on Palau Islands.

11–17 June, further attacks on Marianas by US carrier aircraft. Landings on 15 June covered by eight escort carriers.

19–20 June, Battle of the Philippine Sea, or 'Marianas Turkey Shoot', sees *Yorktown, Wasp, Lexington, Hornet, Essex, Enterprise, Bunker Hill, San Jacinto, Princeton, Monterey, Langley, Cowpens, Cabot, Bataan* and *Belleau Wood* pitched against *Taiho, Shokaku, Zuikaku, Junyo, Hiyo, Zuiho, Ryuho, Chitose* and *Chiyoda*, with both *Taiho* and *Shokaku* falling victim to the US submarines *Albacore* and *Cavalla* respectively, while US aircraft sink *Hiyo* and two tankers, and damage *Zuikaku* and *Chiyoda*, while the Japanese also lose 450 aircraft.

25 July, *Victorious* and *Illustrious* send aircraft to attack Sabang.

4–5 August, Mitscher's carrier groups attack Bonin Island and destroy a Japanese convoy.

15 August, Allied landings in the south of France, Operation Dragoon, is supported by nine escort carriers to provide air cover for the ground forces.

24 August, *Victorious* and *Indomitable* attack Padang and Sabang on Sumatra.

31–2 September, US carrier group attacks Bonin Islands.

7–10 September, TF38 attacks southern Philippines.

21–24 September, Manilla Harbour is attacked sinking three destroyers and upwards of twenty merchantmen, while Japanese shipping offshore is also attacked.

10–16 October, Battle of Formosa, Halsey sends 340 aircraft to attack Okinawa, and heavy air battles follow over the next few days against the strong Japanese 2nd Air Fleet.

17–19 October, *Victorious*, *Indomitable* and *Illustrious* send their aircraft to attack the Nicobar Islands in the Indian Ocean.

23–26 October, Battle of Leyte Gulf, divided into four stages. Japanese carriers *Zuikaku*, *Zuiho*, *Chitose* and *Chiyoda* face large US carrier force, but hope to bring their major surface units to action. The US Third Fleet has *Wasp*, *Lexington*, *Intrepid*, *Hornet*, *Hancock*, *Franklin*, *Essex*, *Enterprise*, *San Jacinto*, *Princeton*, *Monterey*, *Langley*, *Independence*, *Cowpens*, *Cabot* and *Belleau Wood*, while the Seventh Fleet covering the landings has eighteen escort carriers. In the ensuing battle, *Princeton* is hit by a bomb and eventually blows up, later, *Gambier Bay* and *St Lo* are sunk and six other CVEs damaged, but the Japanese lose all four carriers. This battle also saw 10,000 Japanese killed against 1,500 Americans.

October–November, First massed Kamikaze attacks. Aircraft carriers *Essex*, *Franklin*, *Hancock*, *Intrepid*, *Lexington*, *Belleau Wood* and *Cabot* hit.

27 November, US submarine *Archerfish* sinks new carrier *Shinano*, the largest built outside the United States.

18 December, 'Halsey's Typhoon' strikes Third Fleet, with three light carriers and two Essex-class carriers badly damaged, while 146 aircraft are washed overboard or damaged beyond repair.

19 December, US submarine *Redfish* sinks new Japanese carrier *Unryu*.

1945

4 January, *Illustrious*, *Indefatigable*, *Indomitable* and *Victorious* send aircraft to strike at the oil refineries in north-eastern Sumatra.

9 January, US landings on Luzon supported by Halsey's Third Fleet. Kamikaze missions sink several ships including the CVE *Ommaney Bay* and damage several more.

10–21 January, Operations in South China Sea also face Kamikaze attacks, with *Ticonderoga* and *Langley* damaged.

24 & 29 January, *Illustrious*, *Indefatigable*, *Indomitable* and *Victorious* send aircraft to strike at the oil refinery at Palembang in Sumatra.

16–17 February, Fifth Fleet sends fast carrier force of sixteen carriers for the first full scale assault on the Japanese home islands, destroying 500 aircraft for the loss of eighty-eight US aircraft.

19 February, US landings on Iwo Jima, to give US bombers attacking Japan from the Marianas fighter protection. Long-range support is provided by Task Force 58, with sixteen carriers, while the landing force has cover by eleven CVEs.

21 February, Kamikaze attacks off Iwo Jima, sink CVE *Bismarck Sea* while *Saratoga* is hit six times, but saved.

18–19 March, 1,200 carrier borne aircraft strike at Japan aiming for naval bases and airfields around the Inland Sea, operating from *Bennington*, *Bunker Hill*, *Enterprise*, *Essex*, *Franklin*, *Hancock*, *Hornet*, *Intrepid*, *Wasp* and *Yorktown* and the light carriers *Bataan*, *Belleau Wood*, *Cabot*, *Independence*, *Langley* and *San Jacinto*. In Japanese counter-attacks, *Enterprise*, *Intrepid*, *Wasp*, *Yorktown* and *Franklin* are damaged, with the last-named suffering 1,000 casualties.

1 April, US landings on Okinawa, with the Fifth Fleet's strong carrier force and the landing fleet's eighteen escort carriers, plus aircraft transports, supported by the British Pacific Fleet with the carriers *Illustrious*, *Indefatigable*, *Indomitable* and *Victorious* with 220 aircraft.

7 April, USN aircraft attack and sink the giant battleship *Yamato*. A prolonged Kamikaze offensive with some 2,000 aircraft lasting six weeks begins, eventually sinking twenty-six US ships of destroyer size and below, while amongst the 164 ships damaged are the carriers *Bunker Hill*, *Enterprise* and *Intrepid*, while the British carriers *Formidable*, *Indefatigable* and *Victorious* are also hit.

9–14 August, even after the atomic bombs have been dropped on Hiroshima on 6 August and Nagasaki on 9th, Japanese resistance continues, so further attacks on Japanese bases are made, ending on 14th.

BIBLIOGRAPHY

Brooke, Geoffrey, *Alarm Starboard: A Remarkable True Story of the War at Sea*, Patrick Stephens, Cambridge

Chesnau, Roger, *Aircraft Carriers of the World, 1914 to the Present*, Arms & Armour Press, London, 1992

Clarke, John D., *Gallantry Awards & Medals of the World*, Patrick Stephens, Yeovil, 1993

Cunningham, Admiral of the Fleet Sir Andrew, *A Sailor's Odyssey*, Hutchinson, London, 1951

Gelb, Norman, *Desperate Venture*, Hodder & Stoughton, London, 1992

Gould, Robert W., *British Campaign Medals: Waterloo to the Falklands*, Arms & Armour, London, 1984

Hanson, Norman, *Carrier Pilot*, Patrick Stephens, Cambridge, 1979

Hickey, Des and Smith, Gus, *Operation Avalanche: Salerno Landings 1943*, Heinemann, London

Hobbs, Commander David, *Aircraft Carriers of the Royal & Commonwealth Navies*, Greenhill Books, 1996

Johnson, Brian, *Fly Navy*, David & Charles, Newton Abbot and London, 1981

Kennedy, Ludovic, *Menace: The Life and Death of the Tirpitz*, Sidgwick & Jackson, London, 1979

Kilbracken, Lord, *Bring Back My Stringbag: A Stringbag Pilot at War*, Pan Books, London, 1980

Masters, A. O. 'Cappy', *Memoirs of a Reluctant Batsman*, Janus, London

Nichols, Commander John B., USN (Ret) and Pack, S. W. C., *Cunningham the Commander*, Batsford, London, 1974

Poolman, Kenneth, *Escort Carrier: HMS Vindex at War*, Secker & Warburg, London, 1983

Roskill, Captain, S. W., *The Navy at War, 1939-45*, HMSO, London, 1960

—*The War at Sea, 1939-45, Vols I-III*, HMSO, London, 1976

Sturtevant, Ray, and Balance, Theo, *The Squadrons of the Fleet Air Arm*, Air Britain, Tonbridge, 1994

Thompson, Julian, *Imperial War Museum Book of the War at Sea, 1939-45: The Royal Navy in the Second World War* , IWM, London, 1996

Vian, Admiral Sir Philip, *Action This Day,* Muller, London, 1960

Winton, John, *Air Power at Sea, 1939-45* , Sidgwick & Jackson, London, 1976

—*Carrier Glorious* , Leo Cooper, London, 1986

—*The Forgotten Fleet* , Michael Joseph, London, 1960

Woodman, Richard, *Artic Convoys,* John Murray, London, 1974

Woods, Gerard A., *Wings at Sea: A Fleet Air Arm Observer's War, 1940-45* , Conway Maritime, London, 1985

Wragg, David, *Swordfish –The Attack on the Italian Fleet at Taranto* , Weidenfeld & Nicolson, London, 2003

—*The Fleet Air Arm Handbook 1939-1945* , Sutton, Stroud, 2001 and 2003

—*Carrier Combat* , Sutton, Stroud, 1997

—*Wings Over The Sea: A History of Naval Aviation* , David & Charles, Newton Abbot and London, 1979

INDEX

242

244

246

247

249